LOGICAL
SELF-DEFENSE

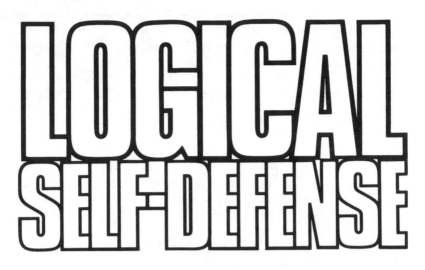

SECOND EDITION

RALPH H. JOHNSON
Professor of Philosophy
University of Windsor

J. ANTHONY BLAIR
Associate Professor of Philosophy
University of Windsor

McGraw-Hill Ryerson Limited

Toronto Montréal New York St. Louis San Francisco Auckland
Bogotá Guatemala Hamburg Johannesburg Lisbon London
Madrid Mexico New Delhi Panama Paris San Juan São Paulo
Singapore Sydney Tokyo

LOGICAL SELF-DEFENSE, Second Edition

Copyright © McGraw-Hill Ryerson Limited, 1983, 1977. All rights reserved. No part of this publication may be reproduced, stored in a retrieval system, or transmitted, in any form or by any means, electronic, mechanical, photocopying, recording, or otherwise, without prior written permission of McGraw-Hill Ryerson Limited.

3 4 5 6 7 8 9 0 WC 2 1 0 9 8 7 6 5 4

ISBN: 0-07-548588-5

Printed and bound in Canada

Care has been taken to trace ownership of copyright material contained in this text. The publishers will gladly take any information that will enable them to rectify any reference or credit in subsequent editions.

Canadian Cataloguing in Publication Data

Johnson, Ralph H. (Ralph Henry), date
    Logical self-defense

Includes bibliographical references and index.

ISBN 0-07-548588-5

1. Fallacies (Logic). 2. Reasoning.   I. Blair, J. Anthony, date
II. Title.

BC175.J63   1983   165   C83-094097-9

Credits

The authors thank the following copyright holders for granting permission to use their material. For permission to use excerpts from columns or articles we thank the following newspapers and magazines: *The Windsor Star; The Globe and Mail,* Toronto; the St. John's *Evening Telegram; The Detroit News; Maclean's; Canadian Tribune; Saturday Review.* For permission to use excerpts from their newspaper columns we thank Mr. Dalton Camp; Mr. Charles Lynch; Mr. John Laycock; Mr. John Coleman (from *The Windsor Star,* Feb. 23, 1982. Mr. Coleman writes on provincial affairs for *The Windsor Star.*) and Ann Landers, Field Newspaper Syndicate, and *The Windsor Star.* For permission to use excerpts from a letter to *The Windsor Star* we thank Professor Lawrence LaFave. We also wish to thank John Jaunzems, St. Lawrence University. We acknowledge permission to print excerpts from the following books: an excerpt from *Ludwig Wittgenstein: A Memoir* by Norman Malcolm, reprinted with permission of Oxford University Press, Oxford; an excerpt from *The October Crisis* by Gerard Pelletier, reprinted by permission of The Canadian Publisher, McClelland & Stewart Limited, Toronto; an excerpt from *Consumer, Beware!* by Ellen Roseman, used by permission of New Press, Don Mills, Ontario; an excerpt from *I Can Sell You Anything* by Carl P. Wrighter, copyright by Ballantine Books, a Division of Random House, Inc., New York; an excerpt from *Confessions of an Advertising Man* by David Ogilvy, reprinted with permission of Atheneum Publishers, New York.

TABLE OF CONTENTS

To Maggie and June
and to Jay and Mary and Sean and Matthew

ACKNOWLEDGEMENTS

Second Edition

First, we wish to express our thanks to our students of the last five years in Applied Logic, many of whom have made useful suggestions and criticisms. Particular thanks to Sheila Dillon, John Mill, Leo Raffin, Donna Sutherland and Pat West at the University of Windsor. Students from other universities have been good enough to forward their own comments: at the University of Guelph; Alex Campbell, Tham Yok Foon, Gordon Graffman, Cameron Nott, Kim Parent, and Donald Stewart. Jay Blair, at Queen's University, read and wrote a critique of an early draft of the new Chapter 8. Thanks should also be expressed to our many teaching assistants at the University of Windsor who have helped in the rethinking of this text, among them: Brian MacPherson, Bill Hutchinson, and Kate Parr.

Second, many instructors have sent along suggestions and ideas which were helpful to us; they include Victor Rodych (York University), and a teaching assistant (The University of Toronto) who challenged some of our interpretations as sexist. Among our colleagues at the University of Windsor's Department of Philosophy, we have benefited from our discussions with Professor Robert C. Pinto, Professor Jerome V. Brown, and Professor Harry A. Nielsen.

Third, we would like to express our thanks to the following philosophers and informal logicians whose ideas (whether in conversation or in writing) have helped immensely: Dr. Trudy Govier, Professor David Hitchcock (McMaster University), Professor Richard Paul (Sonoma State University), Professor Perry Weddle (Sacramento State University), Professor Jack Meiland (University of Michigan), Professor Douglas Walton (University of

Winnipeg), Professor Robert Binkley (University of Western Ontario), Dr. Dennis Hudecki (York University), Professor Baylor Johnson (St. Lawrence University). In addition, we have doubtless been influenced (in ways we may not readily perceive) by the many new texts on the market and the numerous excellent articles we have had the good fortune to read as editors of the *Informal Logic Newsletter*.

Henry Klaise, our sponsoring editor at McGraw-Hill Ryerson during the preparation of the second edition, has been unfailingly cheerful, supportive and helpful. We thank Mrs. Mary-Lou Byng for excellent typing under pressure of time, and Mrs. Joan Reid, for additional first-rate typing. We are extremely grateful to June Blair for proof reading. We would like to thank our assistant editor, Steve Soloman, for his able assistance and patience.

Finally, last, and once again; to our families who once again have had to put up with extended periods when we were closeted and unavailable but without whose love and support this project would not have been completed.

. . . what is the use of studying philosophy if all that it does for you is to enable you to talk with some plausibility about some abstruse questions of logic, etc., and it does not improve your thinking about the important questions of everyday life . . .

—Ludwig Wittgenstein (from Norman Malcolm), *Ludwig Wittgenstein, A Memoir* (Oxford University Press, 1958; Oxford Paperbacks, 1962), p. 39.

INTRODUCTION

The need. Much has been written about the consumer in our society but little has been done to extend that viewpoint to the area of social, political and economic persuasion. As citizens we are constantly being offered persuasive rhetoric from a multitude of directions. Pick up any newspaper or magazine, turn on the radio or TV, or check the mail that comes to your door. The teachers' union, the school board, the city council, irate taxpayers, all are trying to gain your support for higher salaries, lower salaries; a strike, back-to-work legislation; city core redevelopment, rezoning for a suburban shopping mall. Walkathons want you to walk, bikeathons want you to bike, telethons want you to phone in a pledge. A political party wants you to canvass, your Member of Parliament wants you to return a questionnaire, a pollster wants your opinion. Last night's editorial thundered that pornography is demeaning to women and dehumanizes men; a man's buddies want him to go along to a porno movie. Mothers write letters to the editor favouring abortion on demand, mothers write letters to the editor urging that abortion be outlawed; women wonder what they should do if they become pregnant. You are urged to get out and jog; you're terrorized to quit smoking. Should downtown be saved? Is a home of your own an obsolete dream? Are greedy unions the cause of inflation? Or greedy executives? Or neither? Groups and individuals incessantly vie for your adherence to their way of seeing things, for your acceptance of their view of what is true, important or worth doing.

The list of topics will vary, but the point is that you are a consumer of beliefs and values, no less than of products. That raises the question: *how good are your buying habits?* It's an important question, once you realize, as most do, that some arguments are damaged goods — and that buying a bad argument may do you more harm than buying a bad car.

Assuming that your buying habits stand in need of improvement, and that you are willing to work to develop better ones — assuming, too, that you are not so naive as to think that you will waltz through the rhetoric and persuasive appeals without being influenced by them — what are your options? What resources exist to meet this need? How can you equip yourself to distinguish between good and bad arguments?

The resources. Traditionally, logic has been conceived of as that discipline which studies argumentation with a view to differentiating good from bad. And the very least that a consumer of arguments ought to expect from a logic course would be an improved capacity to separate good arguments from bad ones. Unfortunately, in our view, until very recently most logic textbooks and courses had very little interest in this enterprise. They emphasized formal logic, and formal logic (whether deductive or inductive) was not particularly concerned with arguments in natural languages. What formal logic did teach was the ability to work within formal systems, with little thought about the applicability of such systems. Slowly some logicians began to question this approach, and one result was the recovery of the informal logic tradition. In the first edition of this text, we lamented the lack of textbooks in informal logic. Five years later, we are happy to report a flood of good new informal logic texts. The hegemony of formal logic appears to have been broken. Those who wish to improve their capacity to appraise the logic of everyday argumentation are no longer forced to study from texts which presume that propositional logic will get the job done. Most colleges and universities now teach courses (under a variety of names: critical thinking, reasoning skills, informal logic, logic) which take dead aim at that argument in tonight's newspaper with a view to improving the student's repertoire of critical skills.

Our approach to informal logic. The *locus* of action in this text is real arguments in natural language. The *purpose* is to equip the student to provide enlightened logical criticism of such arguments. The *approach* is through fallacy theory: i.e., by identifying recurrent logical flaws that afflict arguments. There are other approaches to the same end, but we believe that for most students — for whom a logic course is a one-night stand — the benefits of the fallacy approach outweigh the dangers. Long after the course is over, they will retain an awareness of these species of illogic. Although our inventory of fallacies is by some standards incomplete, we have included the ones that we think are most commonly committed.

Our treatment of fallacies differs from that found in other texts in several noteworthy ways. First, our objective is to use the concept of fallacy as a device for learning the skill of analysing and appraising real-life arguments. All other features of our approach devolve from this premise. Second, we emphasize not just tagging fallacies, but also, and more important, understanding what is wrong with each fallacious move and seeing how to argue soundly that it is mistaken. Third, virtually all of the examples we use come from actual arguments in newspapers, magazines, and books, and are quoted as they originally appeared. Fourth, we downplay disputes about labels. Other texts use different names for many of the same fallacies, contain fallacy categories that overlap with some of ours, and subdivide fallacies that we assemble under a single rubric. Since the labels and categories are merely tools, once you learn to pick your way through arguments and detect the flaws, it's scarcely necessary to use the labels. The purpose of logical self-defense is to expose flaws clearly and offer sound criticism. Fifth, our list may appear to some to be incomplete, our organization untraditional. We aimed to employ the organization and thought that will be most helpful to the learner who wants practical skills rather than theoretical elegance. Sixth, we have tried to make our treatment of each fallacy as precise and rigorous as possible by giving a list of the conditions specifying its occurrence. This process should help to screen out cases of apparent fallacy, but its full use guides the construction of arguments showing that the given fallacy has been committed.

The real star of this text, we believe, is the roster of real-life examples, both in the body of the text and in the exercises. We've tried to maintain a healthy diet of Canadian examples, while adding for U.S. readers new ones about American issues drawn from American sources. In either case, we have tried to provide sufficient backgrounding to make the examples sufficiently clear for readers from either country. This second edition includes many new specimens of reasoning taken from recent debates and controversies. The reason is evident. Unless you hone your skills on these and similar specimens, you are unlikely to find much improvement in your practical ability to handle arguments. The best move that any student or teacher can make is to compile (and update) a file of examples on which to practice. We have provided our analysis of each example we've selected. You may well disagree with our interpretations, and we welcome corrections or improvements, providing they are supported by well-reasoned arguments.

A word to the instructor: we do not conceive this second edition of *Logical Self-Defense* as a complete logic text. Those who wish to include a unit on formal logic can readily supplement this text with handouts of their own (as we do), or select any of the good formal logic texts to be used with this one.

New features in Second Edition. We would like here to point out some of the other new features of this second edition. Chapters 1 and 2 introduce the basic concepts of argument and fallacy, as before, but they have been expanded and improved. Now we introduce the concept of argument in Chapter 1 by contrasting it with opinion. Next, we confront the practical questions: "How do I know when there's an argument? How can I recognize an argument?" and "How, once it's discovered, is an argument best set out for analysis and evaluation? Our treatments here are detailed, incorporating in revised form material that had been scattered throughout the text in the first edition, and adding much that is new. The instructor is free to follow our order of presentation in full, to follow it while skipping certain subsections, or to return to such meticulous attention to detail later in the course, once the students have worked with some fallacies.

Chapter 2 introduces, as before, the three basic fallacies of relevance, sufficiency and acceptability. Our presentations of all three are considerably revised and improved over the first edition's treatment. In addition, we have gathered into Chapter 2 the fallacies that were previously located somewhat out of place in the chapter on extended arguments. Since *begging the question* and *inconsistency* are such fundamental failures in argument, and since they in fact are species of *problematic premise,* we have included them (along with *improper charge of inconsistency*) under the latter heading. Our descriptions of and conditions for these fallacies have been changed for the better.

Chapters 3 to 7 remain, essentially, a roster of widely committed fallacies. In addition to numerous minor revisions of fallacy descriptions and conditions, the following major changes have been made: our treatment of *two wrongs* has been revised; *common practice* and *past practice* have been combined in *improper appeal to practice;* and *questionable classification* and *loaded term* have been joined in a revised account of *loaded term.* The exercises at the end of each chapter have been thoroughly updated.

Chapter 8 is an entirely new chapter on how to construct arguments. We have added this because we have found that the defensive skills stressed elsewhere in the text do not necessarily transfer to offense; that is, learning how to critique arguments does not automatically teach one how to construct arguments. This belief is based upon our experience in teaching. The payoff to be anticipated seems to us threefold. Once called on to construct arguments of their own (which are then open to criticism by others), students come to appreciate that constructing a good argument is not easy, that perfection is not to be readily achieved. This realization makes them more sober critics of the arguments of others. Second, since it is our conjecture that a great many fallacies occur at least partially because of poor habits of argumentation (though there are other causes as well), it seems to us that by helping students learn to construct good arguments we may expect to thereby lessen the incidence of fallacy in the long run. Third, since offense and defense are not readily separated in reasoning, we see teaching students how to build their own arguments as part of the task of preparing them well to enter the world of rational deliberation. Chapter 8 then is an introduction into the dialectical process from the point of view of the agent or performer, rather than that of the critic.

Chapter 9 is a revision of the old chapter on extended arguments, and here the student is back in the role of critic, this time of longer arguments. The changes in our approach to evaluating extended arguments (which we still conceive to be the heart and soul of the enterprise, the point of it all) result from our realization that the original method was both too cumbersome and also incomplete. It was too cumbersome because it required the lengthy process of standardization. In the new approach, we suggest a modification of tree diagramming for "macrostructure" and resort to standardizing only when required to do so, usually at the level of "microstructure." The older method was also incomplete; it did not call for judgements of the relative importance of various criticisms, nor did it require the student to offer an overall assessment of the argument, based on its perceived weaknesses and strengths. In revising this chapter, we have incorporated two important principles of logical criticism. The Principle of Discrimination requires the critic to get to the heart of the logical problems, to avoid nit- picking and dwelling on marginalia — a danger often associated with fallacy-theoretic approaches to criticism. Our thinking here has benefited from discussions with both Professor Michael Scriven (University of Western Australia) and Professor Robert Binkley (University of Western Ontario). The second principle we now invoke is that of Logical Neutrality; the critic must not attempt to pass on substantive criticisms as logical ones. Here we have learned much from the thinking of Professor Robert Fogelin (Dartmouth College).

For the original inspiration to write this text, we still salute Professor Howard Kahane (University of Maryland - Baltimore County), whose *Logic and Contemporary Rhetoric* persuaded us that logic could be both lively and useful. Our debt to his inspiration is great. In some instances, we have simply adapted or modified his approach, mainly by trying to give a more systematic analysis of the fallacies. For calling our attention to the method of tree diagramming, we are grateful to Professor Scriven, whose text, *Reasoning* (McGraw-Hill, 1976) has the same general aim as ours, but takes a different route.

This text remains, no less than its predecessor, a working text with much room for improvement. That it is not the ideal text we are only too well aware. But we hope it will be useful, to student and teacher alike. We certainly hope the many changes made in this second edition will be viewed as improvements. As before, we welcome critical comments and suggestions for improvements from any of our readers. You can write to us in care of the Philosophy Department, University of Windsor, Windsor, Ontario, Canada N9B 3P4.

CHAPTER ONE

IDENTIFYING ARGUMENTS

Opinions and Arguments

In these days of an inflated dollar and a depressed market, one commodity in abundant supply is opinion. People have opinions on almost every conceivable topic, from the state of the economy and what it will take to get it going again, to the best way of preventing nuclear war, to relations between Canada and the United States, to the artistic merits of rock music. To boot, there are also opinions about opinions; e.g., "Everyone is entitled to their opinion." What is an opinion? Can one assess opinions? What is the relationship between opinion and argument? What is an argument? These are some of the questions we shall deal with in this section. Although our eventual aim is to deal with the fundamentals of argument analysis and construction from the logical point of view, opinions are often the breeding ground of arguments, so it seems natural enough to begin our story there.

What is an **opinion**? We aren't after an iron-clad definition at this point. A rough characterization will suffice. Let's work from an example. Suppose that you and a friend have just seen the movie, *E.T.* As you're leaving the theatre, you ask your friend: "Well what do you think? What's your opinion?" What you are asking for is your friend's reaction to the movie, her first thoughts about it. Perhaps your friend says, "I thought it was terrific; I loved it." That is her opinion. She may or she may not go on to give the reasons why she liked it. If she does, then she has begun to move in the direction of presenting an argument. The point to notice about an opinion is that it is not always presented with reasons or grounds. Frequently, when people have different opinions on a topic, they will begin to sort out their thinking. They

1

may engage in an argument, find themselves hotly contesting each other's views. In this way, the expression of opinion functions as a natural starting point for the construction of arguments, in the logical sense. An argument in the logical sense is more than just a heated dispute between two people who disagree about something, but the contrast between argument and opinion is instructive, so let us say a few more words about the realm of opinion.

Opinions play a variety of roles in our lives, as for example when we are standing in line waiting to get into the movie and we just chat about this and that; sometimes the expression of opinion is mainly a matter of a role, of filling space, as when a newspaper columnist (who must write a column regularly) expresses a viewpoint in order to evoke reaction from readers. Sometimes your opinion is solicited or asked for; sometimes you venture it without being asked, as when you say to a friend, "I know you didn't ask my opinion about this, but . . ." Sometimes opinions are just spontaneously expressed, often in the heat of the moment, so that they amount to little more than verbal spleen. On the other hand, sometimes an opinion carries with it a considered quality, as when you ask your doctor's opinion about how to deal with that lower back pain that's been troubling you for months.

What's an opinion worth? Well, that is partly a matter of its function, and partly a matter of whose opinion it is. If a local columnist is successful in getting people to think about a particular topic by expressing an opinion (even stridently), then the purpose is achieved. Your doctor's opinion on the state of your health is of more value to you, generally speaking, than that of an idle acquaintance.

What is interesting to logicians is that sort of an opinion which acts as a launching pad for an argument, for as we have said already, the expression of an opinion is often the first step on the road to argument. (Unfortunately, for many the expression of an opinion is also the last step.) It is the first step when, in addition to offering a view, the person then goes on to offer *reasons for* that opinion. Then we can evaluate the opinion by looking at the reasons given for it. This sort of opinion, we might say, sketches a possible route leading from a point of departure (the grounds or reasons) to a destination (the conclusion). It has motion; it is headed somewhere; it is the prelude to argument. We want then to be able to demarcate this difference between the kind of opinion which serves as a starter for argument and the one which does not. Let's look at a couple of examples to bring this contrast home.

In October, 1980, the *Los Angeles Times* ran a story about a trial in which the judge, U.S. District Court Judge Andrew Hauk, was quoted as having used the word 'faggots' to refer to homosexuals. This story prompted several readers to write letters to the editor. Here is what C.F. wrote:

1   So Judge Hauk referred to gays as faggots.

        It seems the crooks, weirdos and rapists are all looking for acceptance from those of us who follow the straight and narrow, and frankly I'm sick of it.

If someone is caught in the act of committing a crime, shoot him — with a gun, not a Taser!

Well, C.F. has expressed his opinion. His reaction is intense, but not very well thought through. He seems to wish to defend the judge's use of the term 'faggot' but we aren't sure just why. The tone here is certainly strident but it leaves little room for interplay or evaluation. As far as argumentation is concerned, this expression of opinion is a *non-starter*.

Contrast that opinion with this one, from M.B.:

2   Judges should be fair and honest to handle all proceedings in a just and unbiased way. If Judge Hauk has such prejudices against homosexuals, how many of what other prejudices does he have? How could people of the United States expect Hauk and judges like him to be fair and give out sentences or unbiased opinions when obviously he has prejudices against certain people?

M.B.'s *opinion* is that Hauk is biased (an opinion based on the judge's reference to homosexuals), but M.B. goes on from this opinion to express another view, in the form of wondering whether the judge can be fair. This expression of opinion has both structure and motion; it is headed in a direction, towards a goal, and it is not hard to see what it is: that the judge in question should not be allowed to act as a judge any longer. This opinion is one that we can evaluate *logically,* unlike the first one, which has no clear *structure* or *direction.* And there is another important difference: perhaps both C.F. and M.B. seek to persuade us, but M.B.'s approach is more *rational:* M.B. gives us reasons, whereas C.F. gives us rhetoric.

From M.B.'s opinion (though not from C.F.'s) it is possible to extract an **argument.** By an argument, we mean a collection of claims (or statements) whose purpose is to lay out a route which leads from the acceptance of some claims (called the **premises**) to the acceptance of some other target claim (called the **conclusion**). Because M.B.'s opinion is much closer to this definition than C.F.'s, we want to distinguish between the two. C.F.'s is "pure opinion" whereas M.B.'s is "proto-argumentative."

Opinions which are proto-argumentative differ from arguments proper more in terms of their structure than in terms of their purpose. In an argument, a certain structure is evident (claim plus support for it) which is not always evident in the expression of opinions. Yet both attempt to *persuade rationally,* by dispensing *reasons.* This is an important trait, because, as you well realize, there are other methods of persuasion, other tactics that people use to attempt to induce belief. There is the appeal to *power:* "Believe it because I say so"; the appeal to *fear:* "Believe it, because if you don't . . .";

psychological stroking: "You seem like a bright person; how can you then not believe that . . ." and others. Such methods of inducing belief may at times be legitimate. A four-year-old child is generally not going to be persuaded rationally to keep from running into the streets, so one may have to resort to some combination of power and fear to keep the child out of the roadways. However, as we become mature and capable of reasoning things out for ourselves, we are quite capable both of persuading others rationally and being so persuaded ourselves. Arguments have a prominent role in this enterprise.

From a logical point of view, then, an argument is discourse (whether written or spoken) with a certain structure (support and claim) and function (rational persuasion). It is worth making the point that these notions of structure and function are not absolutely fixed. That is, an argument may have missing parts, and in fact there is a spectrum or range of argumentative expression from relatively incomplete forms all the way up to those which are complete. Most of the arguments we shall be dealing with fall somewhere in the middle of the spectrum, so that one of the tasks that is necessary in argument evaluation is to get hold of the argument. (More about that in the next section.) Also argument can have other purposes than persuading others. One can use arguments in order to inquire into a matter. (More on this topic in Chapter 8.)

In the early going, we will be dealing with arguments which are not completely expressed. We shall be concentrating on what we call "snippets"; i.e., segments of longer passages. This focus will allow the reader to develop his or her logical skills and sensibility.

To conclude this section, we need to complete the spectrum. We began by talking about opinions as, in some instances, the preliminary stages of argument. But arguments themselves function as preliminary to what we might call "the case." People usually argue about controversial matters. On any controversial matter, there are going to be those who advance arguments which arrive at different conclusions. An argument for capital punishment which does not take into consideration and deal with arguments for the opposed point of view moves in one dimension, when what is needed is a multidimensional argument that seeks to rebut arguments for the opposite viewpoint. This multidimensional argument is what we shall call "a case" and in Chapters 8 and 9 we have more to say about this species. In the meantime, we will be for the most part considering arguments which move in one dimension only.

Extracting the Argument

We must now turn our attention to the first step in the logical appraisal of arguments: arriving at a clear understanding of what the argument is, prior to evaluating it. That may sound straightforward enough, but in fact it is not.

When people talk or write they don't always clearly signal whether they intend to be arguing. Even when they do mean to argue, they don't always set out their premises and conclusions clearly and explicitly. As critics of argument, we usually have to decide these two things — (1) whether there is any argument, and if so, (2) what its constituent parts are — in one complex judgement. (This task is like trying to decide whether an advertisement has a hidden, subliminal message in that deciding whether there is a message, and what the message is, if there is one, cannot be separated.) To simplify our exposition, we shall artificially separate these two intertwined tasks. First, we'll list some indicators of the presence of argument, compare argument with a couple of look-alikes, and offer some advice. Then, in the section following, we'll focus on the problem of extracting the argument and displaying its structure.

Is There an Argument?

The first question to address to any piece of discourse which you suspect contains an argument is: Is there an argument here? In answering this question, there are two points to be considered.

The Writer's Intention

A piece of writing or speech — *discourse* is the generic term we will use — is presumably issued with an end in view. Hence the basic cue in deciding whether an argument is present is the intention of the writer. Was it her purpose to present an argument? Was she trying to persuade her audience to accept a particular claim by backing it up with reasons? Sometimes the writer is helpful enough to make her intent clear. She might say: "Now here are my arguments for this position . . ." or "I have just given my reasons for taking that view." In such cases, the only remaining question is what exactly the argument is: what are the premises and the conclusion? Sorry to say, explicit statements of intent are rare, so we have to turn to clues, to textual evidence.

Textual Indicators

Perhaps the most reliable textual clues are certain words which very often signal the presence of an argument. There are two sorts: **premise indicators** and **conclusion indicators**.

Conclusion Indicators

These words almost invariably come just before the *conclusion* of an argument. The most common conclusion indicator of all is "therefore." Not everyone who cries "therefore" enters the domain of argument, but most do. Other words which signal the presence of a conclusion by preceding it are: "hence" (used as a conjunction), "it follows that" (almost invariably a conclusion indicator), "consequently" (sometimes indicates a conclusion and therefore an argument, but also sometimes goes with explanations), "accordingly" (when used as a conjunction), and "so" (when used as a conjunction).

Premise Indicators

These words are followed immediately by a *premise:* "since" (the conjunction, not the adverb, strongly suggests argument), "for" (the conjunction, not the preposition, sometimes indicates argument, sometimes explanation), "because" (tricky: as often as not marks an explanation, but found frequently in arguments too), "given that" and "granted that" (sometimes occur in arguments, sometimes they just mark conditions), some reference to "reasons" (marks either an argument or an explanation, but not which of the two).

Keep an alert eye for these grammatical indicators. Together with other evidence they can be decisive, but alone they are like the rules of spelling: full of exceptions. Also, too often just when you need a verbal indication that an argument might be intended, your writer lets you down and provides nary a one.

Context

Besides using verbal indicators, look to the *context* to help divine the writer's intentions. There's the context in the sense of the habitat of the discourse — where you found it. In certain places arguments are to be expected: courts of law, legislatures, articles in learned journals, to name but three. In other locations they would be surprise finds, e.g., in lyric poetry, *Penthouse Forum,* news reports (though sometimes we get reports of arguments on the news, the report itself isn't supposed to argue), comedians' routines, or prime time TV commercials (as we'll contend in Chapter 11). And then there are contexts that are hospitable to arguments, yet not guarantees of their appearance. Here we'd put letters to the editor, editorials, "opinion" columns, political speeches, college lectures.

"Context" can also be taken to mean what situation is the occasion for the discourse. If your local newspaper has been reporting a battle at city hall over contracting out garbage collection to a non-union company and laying off the city's unionized sanitation department, then you can bet on finding arguments in the interchanges at meetings and in the letters and opinion and editorial columns of the paper. In general, where there is a *dispute* with two or more sides in contention, expect the people involved to be intending to give reasons why their particular view should prevail (e.g. all the "hot" issues: nuclear disarmament, capital punishment, gun control, abortion, affirmative action, the management of the economy, federal-provincial power distribution, native land claims, provincial autonomy and language rights in Canada). The same holds when someone takes a public position that runs counter to the conventional wisdom, even if there isn't a public dispute (yet). (Example: an article in *Rolling Stone* in which the author claims Bruce Springsteen is highly overrated.)

Logical Structure

There is a fourth resource (besides the writer's avowed intention, verbal cues and contextual evidence) available for deciding whether a piece of discourse is intended as argumentative: its internal logical structure. Can its statements readily be put together to form an argument? Do some of them lend support to others?

The point is this: if you can reconstruct from the discourse an argument that the author might have intended to put forward, then you have *some* (only some) evidence that the author intended to argue in that discourse. You have to be careful here. The "argument" so reconstructed might be a logically bad one (we go into the standards of good argument in Chapter 2), and you don't want to attribute to someone a bad argument unless you have no choice.

The Principle of Charity

Logic has its ethical dimension. An argument is an extension of a person, and just as there are ethical obligations which must be acknowledged in our dealings with people, so there are ethical obligations to be acknowledged in dealing with their arguments. The basic obligation that we have is simply put: we must treat a person's arguments (his or her discourse) as fairly as we can. That is the general idea encapsulated in The Principle of Charity, which we will invoke time and again. In trying to decide whether a particular piece of discourse contains an argument or not, we are under the obligation to treat it fairly, which means to provide the most favourable logical interpretation of that discourse consistent with the evidence. If, for example, we can take a particular passage two ways: either as containing an argument (though one which we believe to be stupid), or as not containing an argument but rather something else (an attempt at humour), then charity suggests the second alternative.

Any discourse you will encounter will approximate one of the following five models. (1) The discourse yields a logically good argument, and nothing in the context points against that interpretation. Judgement: treat it as an argument. (2) The discourse yields an argument that, in the context, there is good reason to think the author intended, but it is not a logically good argument. In that case you have to decide between two unpalatable options: either (a) the author did not intend to argue, in which case he cannot be made out to have argued badly, but the cost is that it is hard to make sense out of what he *was* intending to do; or (b) the author intended to argue, in which case there is a reasonable interpretation of the function of his discourse, but the cost is that he has to be taken to have argued badly.

Judgement: sometimes one way, sometimes the other, depending on the specifics of the discourse and the context. (3) The discourse yields an argument, but the way it has to be reconstructed it is a logically bad argument, and there is an alternative interpretation of the discourse based on the context. Judgement: call it *not* an argument but instead . . . whatever it seems to be: a joke, a piece of sarcasm or irony, simply an opinion, or whatever. (4) The discourse might be construed to yield a partial argument, or moves in the direction of argument, and the context is favourable to reading the discourse as argumentative, yet what is stated is so tentative or so unformed that to reconstruct an argument out of it would require in effect creating an argument oneself based on the hints the author gives. Judgement: call it "opinion," not yet argument. (5) The discourse is non-argumentative.

A Word of Warning

This is a text about arguments, and as you read it and work your way through the exercises you may find yourself inclined to see arguments under every rock and behind every tree. Perspective is important. Lots and lots of discourse is not argumentative. People complain, crack jokes, express outrage, pontificate, praise, register observations, make snide comments, make requests, ridicule, stand on their dignity, etc. The list goes on and on, and none of this is argument. Also, as we've said earlier, we are following the policy of withholding the title "argument" from expressions of opinion — those incompletely-thought-out, tentative, often mushy-minded assertions which, although they may make some gestures towards reasons supporting their claims, never do indicate clear lines of reasoning. Critical judgement means discrimination in applying the honourific term, "argument," and the critical apparatus that goes with it.

Examples

Here are two examples, together with as much background as we have available about them, to illustrate some of the above points.

Background: All we know about this passage is that it was a letter written to Emily Wilkens, a columnist with the Newark, New Jersey *Star-Ledger*, and printed there:

3   Dear Emily:

I wish you'd write something about people who are unfeeling about pets. I've had visitors talk disparagingly about my cat — and within her earshot. These same people would be highly indignant if I made a similar remark about one of their children. I can't understand such a lack of feeling.

Irate C.O.

Background: Here is a passage that is famous in philosophy, from Chapter 1 of John Stuart Mill's book, *Utilitarianism* (1863), a book that has had an enormous influence on philosophical thinking about ethics. In Chapter 1 Mill is "preparing the ground," as he says, for the theory that he presents and defends in the rest of the work. This passage comes from a paragraph in which he is pointing out that he will present a proof of his theory, but only a "proof" in a special sense of that term:

4   It is evident that this cannot be proof in the ordinary and popular meaning of the term. Questions of ultimate ends are not amenable to direct proof. Whatever can be proved to be good must be so by being shown to be a means to something admitted to be good without proof. The medical art is proved to be good by its conducing to health; but how is it possible to prove that health is good? The art of music is good, for the reason, among others, that it produces pleasure; but what proof is it possible to give that pleasure is good?

Before reading any further, decide for yourself which, if either, of these pieces of discourse should be construed as containing an argument. Then put down your reasons for coming to the judgement you do in each case. Only after you have done that, turn to our verdicts on these passages, below.

We think "Irate C.O." is expressing his indignation at how people can be unfeeling about pets, and also he is making a request of Emily Wilkens, the columnist to whom he is writing. We don't think there is any point to trying to tease an argument out of this letter. "Irate" finds an inconsistency between what people will do and what they expect others to do (they'll criticize your cat and hurt your feelings, but be upset if you criticize their children and hurt their feelings). He expresses puzzlement, or perhaps dismay, over this phenomenon. If you try to make "Irate" out to be arguing, you have to attribute to him a silly argument from analogy: cats, like children, have feelings, and just as you shouldn't insult a child so you shouldn't insult a cat. So here is a type (4) situation. You have a choice between reconstructing the discourse to yield a logically bad argument, and interpreting it as not functioning to express an argument at all but doing something else, which in the context is entirely reasonable, namely expressing feelings and making a request. The Principle of Charity indicates the second option.

The passage from John Stuart Mill's *Utilitarianism* does contain an argument. The context is not a decisive indicator, for while one expects arguments in philosophy monographs, they are not necessarily presented in an introductory chapter which gives a sketch of the objectives of the work — which is where this passage of Mill's comes from. However, the content of the passage clearly has the logical structure of an argument, and it is on this ground that we conclude Mill intended to argue here. We would para-phrase the argument as follows:

5   1. In the ordinary and popular meaning of the term "proof," a proof that something is good is constructed by showing it is a means to some end which is good. (e.g., medicine and music are seen to be good because they are means to health and pleasure, respectively, which are seen to be good.)
      2. An "ultimate end" is (by definition) one which is not desired for any further end it may lead to.
      3. Hence, an ultimate end cannot be proved to be good by reference to some further end which it is a means to and which is good.
      4. Therefore, a theory that recommends certain candidates for ultimate ends cannot be proved in the ordinary and popular sense of the term.

Whether this argument will stand up to careful scrutiny or not, it is clearly plausible: its steps appear to follow one another, and its premises seem reasonable. There may be flaws in this argument, but it is not a silly one; attributing it to Mill is not setting him up for obvious logical criticism. Hence we believe it is fair to conclude that Mill intended to put forward an argument here. This is a case of type (1): if the discourse contains a logically plausible argument, then read it that way.

Argument and Explanation

One understandable source of confusion in identifying arguments is their similarity to explanations. An argument and an explanation are quite different nonetheless. They perform different functions. The job of an argument, we've seen, is to present reasons for accepting a claim. An explanation, on the other hand, is used to make a thing intelligible or understandable. Often explanations do this by showing how the thing came about, how it came to be; thus we get explanations that do their work by showing the cause or origin of an event, or at least the factor that made the difference in its coming to be. At other times, explanations work by giving the meaning or significance of a phenomenon or event. Both of these functions of explanations are illustrated in the following passage from the book, *Smoke & Mirrors, The Inside Story of Television News in Canada* (Toronto: McClelland and Stewart, 1980, p. 169) by Peter Trueman of Global TV:

6   This tendency of the news media to leave things as they are, partly because of the broadcasters' and publishers' timidity, and partly because of our own intellectual conservatism, means that we have not really provided an adversary press, . . .

Trueman offers a causal explanation of why broadcasters and publishers tend to accept what they are handed without questioning; namely, these people are afraid to question what they are given, or they don't see it as questionable since it coincides with their own views. He also proposes an explanation of the significance of the tendency not to question; namely, it means that the press does not play an adversary role vis-à-vis the sources whose material it accepts (a role which the press often claims for itself).

Notice that in the passage we quoted Trueman did not try to show that it is true that the press tends to accept things as they are. This marks a way of distinguishing argument from explanation in practice. Ask: does the writer try to establish the claim? to show that it is true? to persuade us to accept it? Does Trueman (here) try to prove it is true that the press doesn't question the material it is given? If the answer is "yes," you are looking at an argument; if "no," then it is not an argument. And you can ask: does the writer take this claim for granted, accept its truth, treat it as given or as already established, and then go on to consider or offer an account of why it is? If the answer here is "yes," then you have an explanation.

What can make the choice tricky (if you go by the words used alone and don't look beneath for the function of the discourse) is that certain key words, like "because" and "reason," are used with *both* arguments and explanations. Notice that Trueman used "because" to introduce his explanations of the media's tendency to accept things as they are. Similarly, "reason" can be doing either of two jobs. "The reason for their conservatism is . . ." may mean (1) "The explanation of their conservatism is . . . ," or it may mean (2) "The justification of their conservatism is. . ." (where "justification" implies the position should be accepted). It is a must to look to the wider context when these words are in use.

One more thing. An explanation can be part of an argument. Explain why the accused could have no motive for committing the crime and you have contributed to the argument showing innocence. Also an argument can be part of an explanation. John Stuart Mill used the argument showing that questions of ultimate ends cannot be proved in the ordinary sense to explain why he would be offering a proof of a different sort for his theory. Still, the two functions — arguing and explaining — are conceptually distinct and it will be your task to sort the two out and identify only arguments as arguments.

Reading With Understanding

Everything we have been saying presupposes that you have first read the passage carefully. Deciding whether an argument is present in a piece of discourse requires being able to recognize exactly what was said and what was not said, and being careful not to read in things that were not asserted. This is easier said than done. To show what we mean, we ask you to read the following quotation from the German philosopher, Friedrich Nietzsche.

Please read it carefully, and a couple of times.

7   Gradually it has become clear to me what every great philosophy so far has been; namely the personal confession of its author and a kind of involuntary and unconscious memoir; . . . . In the philosopher, there is nothing whatever that is impersonal; and above all, his morality bears decided and decisive witness to *who he is*.

(Beyond Good and Evil)

Without looking back at this short passage, answer the following questions about it:

(a) Nietzsche holds here that all philosophy is a personal confession of its author. True_____ False_____
(b) Nietzsche believes that you can discern much about a philosopher from the morality he advocates. True_____ False_____
(c) Nietzsche asserts that it is impossible for philosophy to be impersonal. True_____ False_____
(d) Nietzsche holds that morality is subjective. True_____ False_____

Now, review your answers. (a) Does Nietzsche say, in the passage, that all philosophy is a personal confession? No. He says that every *great* philosophy *so far* has been a personal confession. Perhaps Nietzsche thinks minor philosophy is not such a confession; perhaps he holds that in the future this feature of past great philosophy will change. He takes care to qualify his statement; when you read, you need to watch for and be sensitive to such qualifications. The correct answer to (a) is "False."

(b) Does Nietzsche believe that you can discern much about a philosopher from the morality he advocates? Yes, for he says that "his morality bears decided and decisive witness to *who he is*." So (b) is a simple rewording of what Nietzsche says and hence it is fair to ascribe this belief to him.

(c) Does Nietzsche assert that it is impossible for philosophy to be impersonal? No. He does not *assert* this, though what he does assert may imply it. He only asserts that there is nothing impersonal in the philosopher. He might well agree with the further proposition, and he may take himself to be implying the further proposition, that it is impossible for philosophy to be impersonal. Be he does not *say* it. If you say, "It'll rain tonight," do you *say*, "The grass will get wet tonight"? What you say implies this (in the normal course of events), but you may not have been thinking about the grass at all. A writer asserts what he writes; he does not assert the implications of what he writes. When you read, keep distinct what is asserted and what is implied by what's asserted. (If you do that, you will avoid the risk of mistaking what an assertion implies, and then attributing that implication — *your* reading — to the writer when it is not at all what he meant *or* implied.) So the correct answer to (c) is "False."

(d) Does Nietzsche hold that morality is subjective? Maybe, but he doesn't say it in the passage we quoted. What he *says* is that *the philosopher's* morality "bears witness" to "who he is." We aren't sure just what Nietzsche had in mind by these phrases; we would have to read the surrounding material from which this quotation has been taken to try to arrive at an interpretation. Hence, we are not ready to agree that what Nietzsche says here is equivalent to, or implies that morality is subjective. So the correct answer to (d) is *neither* "True" nor "False," but instead: "It cannot be determined." If you answered either "True" or "False," then the moral of the story should be clear. You must be careful not to read into a person's views something that is not there.

What we have said in the preceding pages is the bare minimum of advice for deciding when an argument is present. We now turn to the second half of this division: how to extract the argument from the discourse and display it for evaluation.

Reconstructing Arguments

Our procedure in this section will be to present advice or guidelines for extracting and setting out the argument that's in a piece of discourse. Then we turn to an example that illustrates many of these points and work through it.

Conclusion

We are supposing we have already established that there is an argument present. That judgement requires that we can attribute some view or claim to the writer which she is defending. This is her *conclusion*. Sometimes the claim is not explicitly stated. We have to draw inferences from what she wrote and from the context of her discourse to attribute this claim to her. In that case we call it a *missing conclusion* since it is missing from the fully expressed discourse. The Principle of Charity requires that in attributing a missing conclusion to an author we formulate the most plausible claim consistent with the rest of the discourse and its context.

Premises

To have an argument and not just a statement of opinion we have to have reasons put forward to support the position — that is, *premises*. Write these out and try to organize them in relation to one another. Do two or more of the premises work as a unit to support the conclusion? Do some premises function as reasons for the position quite independently of the others?

Often the premises of an argument turn out themselves to fit together as internal arguments within the whole body of support offered for the *main* conclusion. That is, one set of premises supports a statement (which is therefore a conclusion within the argument), and that statement as a premise, together with others, in turn supports the *main* conclusion. Look back at Mill's argument, where he concludes that an ultimate end cannot be proved good by reference to some further end. He then uses this conclusion as a basis — that is, as a premise — for the further conclusion that any proof of his theory (about ultimate ends) cannot be a proof in the ordinary sense of that word. Sorting out the premises of an argument, then, will involve looking for internal arguments as well as for premises directly supporting the main conclusion.

Missing Premises

Just as the arguer's claim — the main conclusion — may not be explicitly stated in the discourse, so too you may find that premises have been left out of the explicit statement of the argument. We call these *missing premises.* For example, if we argue: "This is a textbook, so don't expect any jokes," we have left unstated the obvious missing premise: "Textbooks don't (usually) contain jokes." We might have argued thus: "Textbooks don't contain jokes, so don't expect any when you read this book," omitting the missing premise: "This book is a textbook." You can see that a missing premise is a statement which is not expressed in the written or spoken argument, but which must be added to an explicit statement in the discourse to make the set relevant as support for the conclusion. The Principle of Charity applies to the formulation of missing premises, just as it does to the formulation of missing conclusions. Your objective is to supply the author's argument with the most plausible statement (consistent with the rest of the discourse) needed to make a stated premise (or group of premises) relevant to the conclusion.

In practice a missing premise can work as a relevance-tie in either of two ways. It can be a member of a set consisting of a generalization plus a particular statement. In this case one of the pair is asserted explicitly in the discourse, and the other is left unexpressed but understood. Our examples about jokes in this text illustrated this kind of missing premise:

8   1. Textbooks don't usually contain jokes. (Generalization)
     2. This is a textbook. (Particular statement)
     3. So don't expect jokes in this book.

If you have 1. and 3., or 2. and 3., in the discourse, you can readily supply what's missing: 2. in the first case, 1. in the second case.

The missing premise can, alternatively, be a generalization which follows from a stated particular premise and in its turn supports the conclusion. We can best explain by using an example. Consider this argument:

9   The government-funded efforts to save the Whooping Crane from extinction are paying off. Therefore, government funding should be continued for programs to preserve endangered species.

You can sense the relevance of the premise, yet one might wonder how the success of a particular present project relates to the desirability of funding future projects in general. If you read the stated premise as working logically to support directly a generalization which applies to past, present and future projects of the same general type, and the generalization as then directly supporting the conclusion, you can see how the stated premise can be relevant to a conclusion about other projects in the future. Here is how we would set it up:

10   1. The government-funded efforts to save the Whooping Crane from extinction are paying off.

MP   2. Government funding can be effective in helping to preserve endangered species.

        3. Government funding should be continued for programs to preserve endangered species.

The "missing premise" in such cases is, of course, both a missing conclusion of an internal argument and also a missing premise in the argument leading directly to the main conclusion (or leading to some further internal conclusion which itself is a premise . . . leading directly to the main conclusion).

Tree Diagrams

It is convenient to have in hand a technique for sketching the logical structure of an argument so you can see it at a glance. "Tree diagramming" is the most efficient device we have encountered (so-called because the diagram of a complex argument looks like the outline of the branches and trunk of a deciduous tree). Here is how it works. (1) Either write out each statement in the argument and assign a number to it, or write a number beside each statement of the argument in the newspaper, magazine, or your photocopy. Then make a diagram, using the numbers to represent the statements they refer to, and drawing arrows *from* the numbers representing premises *to* the ones representing conclusions. Use arrowheads so there is no ambiguity about which way the premise-conclusion relationship goes. The standard convention is to put the premises at the top and the conclusions below them. (2) In order to distinguish both missing premises and conclusions from explicitly stated premises and conclusions, assign letters to the former and numbers to the latter. (3) Where two or more premises work together as a set to support a conclusion, indicate that by placing a "+" sign between adjacent premises. (4) Where there is an internal argument, there will be an arrow pointing to a number (or letter), and an arrow from that number (or letter) pointing to another one. This shows that the middle statement is both a conclusion (of the internal argument) and a premise. (5) When totally separate lines of support back up a conclusion, show this by keeping the premises and their arrows apart.

Now for some illustrations.

11 1. Textbooks don't usually contain jokes.
2. Don't expect jokes in this book.
[a. This is a textbook. (missing premise)]

Tree diagram:

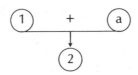

12 1. The government-funded efforts to save the Whooping Crane from extinction are paying off.
2. Government funding should be continued for programs to preserve endangered species.
[a. Government funding can be effective in helping to preserve endangered species.]

Tree diagram:

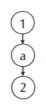

13 1. Capital punishment deters people from committing murder in many cases.
2. People who murder have forfeited their lives.
3. Capital punishment is much cheaper to society than long-term imprisonment.
4. Capital punishment ought to be the punishment for murder.

Tree diagram:

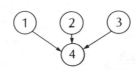

You can see that if an argument is even a little bit complicated, its tree diagram will likely incorporate more than one of these patterns. In Chapter 9 we will be introducing some modifications to these conventions for diagramming longer arguments.

For purposes of clarity and in order to save space, we shall adopt a combination of the tree diagram with printing out an ordered listing of premises, in this text. You may find this useful too. For example, here is how we would now print the Whooping Crane example:

14   1. The government-funded efforts to save the Whooping Crane from extinction are paying off.

        a. Government funding can be effective in helping to preserve endangered species.

      2. Government funding should be continued for programs to preserve endangered species.

We indent premises of internal arguments, and line up only the premises leading directly to the conclusion over the conclusion itself. You will recognize elaborations of this basic scheme or standardization in later examples.

Extraneous Material

Much discourse, we have insisted, is not argumentative. Even argumentative discourse, though, is seldom taken up with nothing besides the argument — the premises and conclusions. Typically, there will also be: an introduction, connecting phrases or sentences, side observations not intended as premises or conclusions, other material that relates the argument to the issue being discussed, and the ongoing discourse which itself is not an argument but which contains one. An argument may be expressed as just two or three sentences in a long paragraph the rest of which is not argumentative, or just one paragraph in a letter to the editor made up of several paragraphs altogether. Identifying the premises and conclusions in the argument, numbering them and perhaps diagramming their logical structure — all this entails that you have discriminated between what belongs to the argument and what, in the discourse, is extraneous to the argument. In making these judgements, you will have to rely on your sense of logical flow, the rhythms that bind premise and conclusion together. The judicious use of tree diagrams can also aid you in rejecting various possibilities, and in detecting missing premises and conclusions. Once the outline of the argument's structure is clear, it becomes an easier task to recognize the peripheral material.

Sometimes it will be necessary to rewrite certain parts of the argument in simpler, more straightforward language. When you do this, you must be careful not to distort or change the meaning of the original material. Your rephrasings must be equivalent in meaning to the original, or your evaluation of the argument will be thrown off. For instance, you should restate rhetorical questions in the form of assertions. To illustrate, consider this excerpt from a column in *The Windsor Star* (March, 1982) in which the writer defends police officers against public criticism:

15   Police officers are damned if they do and they are damned if they don't. How often do we hear comments from the public when they see traffic violations or hear of unsolved crimes to the effect that there is never a police officer around when one needs one? But when the officer is doing his job these same people complain the loudest.

Numbering the statements and restating the rhetorical questions, we get:

16   1. Police officers are damned if they do and damned if they don't.
2. We often hear people complain when they see traffic violations or hear of unsolved crimes that the police are not there when they are needed.
3. The same people complain the loudest when the police are doing their jobs.

Tree diagram:

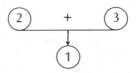

Surface and Depth Analysis

Though it would make the job of the logician easier if people presented their arguments in straightforward assertions, still the rhetorical flourishes and turns of phrase that lace most pieces of discourse add spice. But these same devices often present a challenge to proper interpretation, to figuring out just what was meant. When someone is not expressing herself in straightforward literal terms, you need to decide what is meant. There are times when the flourishes and vagueness so impede that task that we have no recourse but to charge the writer with fallacy (more on that in Chapter 5). But much of the time, it will be possible to get beneath the surface meaning (the metaphor, the roundabout way) to its deeper meaning.

Look back at the last example. Both (1) and (3) fall short of declaring their meaning, and so some interpretation is needed. When the writer says that "Police officers are damned if they do and damned if they don't," what is the likely meaning? In this context, we would say that the writer means (1*): "Police officers are criticized when they succeed in enforcing the law, and they are also criticized when they fail to enforce the law." (3) is a bit trickier to handle. Although the writer says that people complain when the police are doing their job, we don't want to saddle her with the silly assertion that people who want the police to arrest speeders complain whenever they do that. For that is manifestly not what she means. How then to put it? Isn't she probably thinking this: Some people squawk when they get a ticket, even though they also believe that other people should be ticketed. That is the sort of inconsistency that the writer appears to have in mind. So we would rephrase (3) as (3*): "The same people complain the loudest when the police ticket them for a violation of the law."

Our advice: without distorting the discourse and its context, and taking care to make your interpretation clearer and at least as plausible as the original, be prepared to look beneath the surface, explicit meaning of a part of discourse and find the deeper meaning that is probably intended. Once again the Principle of Charity is at work: assume that the person you are interpreting is taking the most sensible position, making the most plausible assertions, consistent with the rest of the discourse and its context.

Postpone Evaluation

Perhaps the most tempting error lurking in the interpretation of arguments is judging the argument before you have extracted it clearly. You can't turn off that critical radar, and it keeps beeping when you sense a logical error in the argument you are interpreting. The effect, too often, is that you are distracted from giving the argument a fair shake. You don't interpret it accurately or fairly. So the rule has to be: withhold judgement of the argument until you have set it out as fully, accurately, and fairly as you can. A corollary of this rule is: when you think you have spotted an error, double-check; ask yourself, "Am I sure that I have understood the discourse correctly here? Is this really what the person is arguing?"

As seems so often the case, there is a complicating factor. We have seen that in order to decide what the argument *is*, we frequently must make a judgement about what *would be* a *plausible* argument, given the surrounding discourse and its context. We have to evaluate, in other words, in order to interpret. How, then, can the rule to postpone evaluation be right? The answer lies in a necessary and defensible distinction between evaluating for the purpose of interpretation, and evaluation of the resulting argument. When interpreting you must work within the limits of what the person said and what, given all the relevant factors, you have good reason to believe he intended or meant. You cannot change those things to make a logically better argument. Your interpretive goal is to give a fair reconstruction of the argument, and that means opting for a more plausible over a less plausible formulation, when everything else is equal. When criticizing the resultant reconstructed argument, however, you are under no such constraints. Here all the standards of good logic, which we shall be introducing in Chapter 2, must be brought to bear. The present point is that all of these standards must be held in abeyance from their full critical application until the argument has been extracted from the discourse and reconstructed as accurately, completely and fairly as possible.

An Example

Now let us put all this advice to work on an example. We begin with some relevant background information about this passage.

At this writing there is no state in the United States in which the wearing of seat belts in automobiles or trucks for regular city and highway driving is legally mandated, though in Michigan, Minnesota, Rhode Island and Tennessee, children under four years of age must be placed in restraining devices when they are in cars. In four of the ten Canadian provinces, on the other hand, you are legally required to wear a seat belt at all times when in a moving car, truck or van (these provinces are British Columbia, Ontario, Quebec and Saskatchewan). The state of Michigan is one in which, as we write, moves are afoot to institute compulsory seat belt use. As you can imagine, the issue is being hotly debated. Canadians will remember many of the arguments. The *Detroit Free Press* supported a seat belt bill in the state legislature with an editorial in late May, 1982. In early June it published several letters to the editor which reacted to its editorial and to the support for the seat belt bill in general. Here is one:

17   They are starting about seat belts again, but if the law is passed, I will be the first to demand a cell in jail. I will not wear a seat belt.

Eleven years ago, I was thrown into the windshield when my van went into a seven-foot ditch filled with five feet of water. Quick thinking by a farmer, who dived into the water and got me out, saved my life. Had I been wearing a seat belt, there is no way he could have undone it and rescued me. I have suffered daily and spent more time in the hospital than out, but I'm still alive.

The seat belt law is one of the reasons I miss the beautiful country drives through Canada.

L.R.J.
River Rouge, Michigan

Is L.R.J. offering an argument here? If so, what is it?

If you think there is an argument here, we agree with you, but can we justify our judgement? Here is how we would try. First, notice that the context is a natural one for argument. The letters to the editor column of the daily newspaper is where people present and defend their opinions about controversial issues of the day. Second, the particular occasion for L.R.J.'s letter is a controversy — the controversy over whether seat belt use should be made compulsory in Michigan. Controversies are natural incubators for arguments; people are trying to convince others which side to take in the dispute. These two factors create a strong presumption in favour of interpreting L.R.J. as arguing. There are no verbal indicator-words that we can see, so the next move is to see if L.R.J.'s letter can be reconstructed in a way that makes sense as an argument.

On the surface it might seem that L.R.J. is simply announcing his own intentions, and explaining them to the *Free Press* readers. He is never going to wear a seat belt — he'd go to jail first — because he was in an accident that would have killed him had he been wearing a seat belt. But this interpretation is implausible. Why should anyone write a letter to the paper to announce private intentions? We cannot see any sensible point to doing so. On the other hand, there is good reason to go on record with a position on a particular piece of legislation. Such public expression of our opinions is one means that we use to shape laws and policies. Going beneath the surface of the mere grammatical form of L.R.J.'s letter, we take him to be writing to oppose making seat belt use compulsory in Michigan. His position might be put thus:

     a.   Seat belt use should not be made mandatory in Michigan.

or possibly:

     a¹.   The bill before the Michigan legislature that would make seat belt use compulsory should be defeated.

It is true that L.R.J. makes no explicit reference to Michigan or the Michigan bill, but he refers to the debate: "They are starting about seat belts again," and he is writing in Michigan to a (Detroit) Michigan newspaper, so we presume he is taking a position on the issue there, although he clearly has a more general position too, for he states categorically that he will not wear a seat belt, and presumably that means anywhere (he stays out of Canada, where seat belt use is required).

We've said that L.R.J. is taking a position, and not just announcing his private intentions, but that doesn't yet show that he is arguing for his position; he might be only expressing an opinion and letting it go at that, as people often do. In fact, though, we can construe his letter as containing an argument for his position as soon as we take into account the middle paragraph, where he recounts the accident he was in eleven years ago. Once again we have to go beneath the surface (which is a personal anecdote) to the underlying point: L.R.J. is arguing that there can be accidents in which the wearing of a seat belt can contribute directly to the death of the occupant of the vehicle. L.R.J.'s personal experience would have no bearing on the issue — it would be irrelevant — unless it is taken as evidence for this general claim about a danger of wearing seat belts. So we see L.R.J.'s argument shaping up (roughly) as follows:

18

    1. I was in an accident in which I would have died had I been wearing a seat belt.
    b. Wearing a seat belt can cause death in an accident.
    c. It can be dangerous to wear a seat belt.
    a¹. The Michigan bill to make wearing a seat belt compulsory should be defeated.

What we are claiming is that L.R.J.'s personal story can be seen to make sense as part of an argument for his position if it is taken to be intended as evidence for a more general claim, which can in turn be hooked up as a relevant reason for accepting his position. We don't know if L.R.J. would agree with exactly the way we have filled in the connections. Had he made his view explicit, he might have reasoned as we have reconstructed his argument above. Or, he might have gone from 1 straight to c. Or, he might have gone from 1 to b, then straight to a^1. The reason we added c is that we can see it warranted as support for a^1 by a further general assumption, namely, that the state should not make the use of potentially dangerous devices compulsory. Whatever general premise or premises we take to connect L.R.J.'s personal experiences with his conclusion, some such further premise that warrants this connection has got to be taken for granted as part of the argument. If L.R.J. just says: "It can be dangerous to wear a seat belt," you can respond: "So what? What's that got to do with the Michigan bill?"; and to your question L.R.J.'s obvious reply will be: "Plenty! The state shouldn't legislate things that are dangerous." Or, if L.R.J. wants to argue directly from b ("Wearing a seat belt can cause death in an accident") to his opposition to the Michigan bill, you can again insist: "What has the fact that wearing a seat belt can be responsible for a person's death in an accident got to do with rejecting the Michigan bill?" And he needs to provide some such warrant for the connection as this: "The state shouldn't legislate the use of devices which can contribute to a person's death."

What we are doing here is reconstructing how L.R.J. might have intended his argument to run. We can make sense of what L.R.J. has written in his letter to the *Detroit Free Press* as an argument, although doing so requires filling in some missing premises. To anyone who complains that we are taking liberties with L.R.J.'s letter, we reply that the alternative is worse. Either L.R.J. intended to be arguing (in which case we *have* to reconstruct his argument and fill in some missing premises so the argument will be plausible and its premise connect up with the conclusion) or else he took the trouble to write a letter to the paper just to tell a personal anecdote and announce to the world his private plans. We think the former interpretation is the more credible — even though the argument we have to attribute to L.R.J. turns out not to be the most cogent one in the world.

We have answered our initial questions about L.R.J.'s letter (is he arguing and, if so, what's the argument?) both at the same time. That was unavoidable: the only way to make a solid case that an argument is intended (in the absence of explicit notice to that effect from the writer or speaker) is to extract a candidate and show how it is plausible. So you end up at one and the same time with two answers: "Yes, there is an argument here" and "Here it is. . . ." To finish the job we should put down in completed form alternative interpretations of L.R.J.'s argument:

19
         1. I was in an accident in which I would have died had I been wearing a seat belt.
        b. Wearing a seat belt can cause death in an accident.
   c. It can be dangerous to wear a seat belt.
   d. The state should not legislate the use of dangerous devices.
   a¹. The Michigan bill to make it compulsory to wear a seat belt should be defeated.

Or:

20
         1. I was in an accident in which I would have died had I been wearing a seat belt.
   b. Wearing a seat belt can cause death in an accident.
   c. The state should not legislate the use of devices that can contribute to death in accidents.
   a¹. The Michigan bill to make it compulsory to wear a seat belt should be defeated.

Summary

In this chapter we have covered a lot of ground. We began with a distinction between opinion and argument — a distinction useful in setting apart those pieces of argumentative discourse that are developed fully enough to be worthy of the effort of careful critical appraisal (namely what we reserve the label "arguments" for), from the rather larger set of under-developed, ill-formed stabs at or gestures towards fully-expressed arguments, and for whose members we reserve the label "opinion."

In the second part of the chapter we turned to the practical problem of extracting arguments from the surrounding discourse in which they're located — indeed, sometimes "buried" or "hidden" might be a more accurate word. The first task here is to discover whether there is in fact an argument present. Our view is that the author's intentions are the crucial determinant, and we pointed out how this can be inferred from the language used (verbal indicators), the fair expectations encouraged by the setting and occasion of the discourse (context), and by the internal logical relations that seem to apply between statements within the discourse (logical relations). We sounded a warning note to you to resist the natural temptation when you are on the hunt for them to interpret everything you read or hear as an argument. We then worked through a couple of examples, to show concretely how the previous points apply, and ended up with two final pieces of advice: keep the distinction between argument and explanation in mind, and read (and listen) with considerable care.

We saw that the second task involved in extracting arguments, once you have determined that an argument is truly present, is to reconstruct the argument, setting it out separately from its surrounding discourse and making its logical structure explicit. We listed, at this point, a set of guidelines. First, identify and write out the conclusion, making it explicit if it is unstated in the discourse. Then list the premises, and try to get clear the pattern of their logical relationships — which ones support which. In the process you will often need to identify missing premises, and we listed some advice for that task. We introduced the convention of making a tree diagram to display the argument's logical structure. In following these steps it is necessary to distinguish extraneous material from what belongs genuinely to the argument, and you will often find yourself having to dig beneath the surface of the writer's prose to bring out its deeper intended meaning. Throughout there is a temptation to mix up your critical evaluation of the argument with your interpretation of its intended meaning. This critique of the argument must be postponed until you have it fairly represented — and we shall be turning to argument crticism next, in Chapter 2 and in detail in Chapters 3-7. We ended our discussion of the guidelines for reconstructing arguments by working with them through an example.

If you have mastered the material so far presented, you already have a solid beginning in the skills of logical self-defense. It is more likely that you will find it useful to turn back to the material presented in Chapter 1 from time to time as you proceed with the rest of the text.

EXERCISES

Directions

The purpose of this exercise is to test your ability to recognize arguments, distinguish them from nonarguments (i.e., mere expressions of opinion, explanations, descriptions etc.), and to extract arguments from their wider surroundings and identify their structure.

If in your judgement the passage is an argument, then use a tree diagram (as in the text) to show its structure.

If it is not an argument, then say what it is and defend your judgement.

1. *Background:* In May of 1982, rock star Rod Stewart, who had been living in the United States for several years, decided to return to England. According to a news report, Stewart said he and his wife decided to move back after a neighbour, a close friend, was held up at gun-point outside her Hollywood home. Stewart said:

   It was a terrible experience for her, and after being robbed myself not long ago, I have the feeling that violence in America is getting worse. It will be a lot worse this summer. The main trouble is unemployment. I don't want the kids brought up in that sort of environment.

2. *Background:* Same as above, with the additional fact that Stewart is here commenting on the fact that one of his cars was stolen:

> They never caught the guys. They never catch anyone over there. It's a bad scene and getting worse.

3. *Background:* In May of 1982, there were many stories in the news about rock records which allegedly contained satanic messages which could be heard if the record or tape were played backwards. One individual testified before the California State Legislatures Committee on Consumer Protection:

> The rock artists add the backward messages because the Church of Satan and their followers have a pact, that if you perform certain things in your particular line of work, in return Satan will give you certain factors back.

4. *Background:* An excerpt from a column by Sydney Harris:

> No one can satisfactorily define "spirit," because to define it is to limit it, and to limit it is to deny its essence.

5. *Background:* Here is an excerpt from an article in *Mass Line,* a newspaper published by the Communist Party of Canada:

> Over five hundred copies of *Mass Line* were sold in one area of Toronto alone in two days, which goes to show that broad masses of people are not anti-communists, and, in fact, are eager to read communist literature and apply it in practice.

6. *Background:* From the novel, *Daniel Martin,* by John Fowles:

> The difference between the craftsman and the true artist is precisely that between knowing what one can do and not knowing, which is why one occupation is safe and the other incipiently dangerous.

7. *Background:* Charles Champlin is the Art Editor of the *Los Angeles Times.* In the wake of the attempted assassination of Ronald Reagan in March 1981 by John Hinckley, Champlin wrote a commentary titled "The Media and Televised Violence":

> An agenda's worth of questions present themselves — again — in the reverberating wake of a tragedy that could have been darker and more apocalyptic than it was, and whose full consequences will be some time revealing themselves.

One of them is whether the media stand as accessories after the fact. Have the reiterated messages from thousands of films and thousands of episodes of television that only violence ultimately solves problems seeped so deeply into the national subconscious that we no longer even question it?

There is no certain answer, no way to be sure, but it might possibly redeem the present tragedy in some minor degree if John Hinckley, the alleged assassin, could be studied with the subtlest, soul-probing techniques of psychiatry.

8. *Background:* An excerpt from that same article:

> What is worrying for the responsible people within the media and in the society is that the fictions can be cleansed of exploitive, glorified violence, the message underlined that neither crime nor violence pays. But there is less — almost nothing — that television can do, or films or the print media, to avoid giving lethal publicity-seekers the publicity they seek. News is news, and conspiracies of silence are potentially more dangerous to society than openness, however painful openness is.

9. *Background:* In an article "Warming Up the Melting Pot," (*Maclean's*, 1982), Terence Macartney-Filgate took the position that there were major flaws in the Canadian psyche — the refusal to confront forthrightly the existence of racism, particularly with reference to newly-arrived immigrants. S.G. responded (May 31, 1982):

> I very strongly believe that immigrants to any country should begin a process of assimilating as quickly as possible into the cultural mosaic. Canada has become a haven for ungrateful, squawking minorities who trumpet their differences as a badge of honor and scream discrimination at any remark or gesture that offends their sensitive minds. As Canada exists today, the problem will grow worse in the future.

10. *Background:* On June 5, 1982, *The Windsor Star* ran an article about a case of vandalism at a synagogue in Windsor. (This occurred during the time of the Israeli invasion of Lebanon.) The headline of that article was: "Arab-Israel conflict hits city synagogue." E.B. wrote on June 24:

> I consider your headline of June 5 as unnecessarily inflammatory. It presupposes that either the Arabs or the Israelis were responsible for the defacement of the Shaar Hashomayim Synagogue. At the time of the reporting of this incident, there was no proof that this was the work of either of these two peoples. What the defacement shows is a case of vandalism for which anyone may be responsible.

11. *Background:* A letter to *Time* (April 1981) commenting on an earlier article about autotransfusion:

> You reported on the recycling of a patient's blood that has been lost in the course of an operation (March 16). Autotransfusion is also used in another way. A patient undergoing elective surgery is asked to contribute blood two weeks before and another batch one week before the operation . . . . The two units of blood are then stored and are used, if needed, by the patient.

12. *Background:* An excerpt from a column about the probabilities of a nuclear disaster which appeared in *Discover* (March, 1981):

> Some of the men who had just created the atomic bomb began publishing a newsletter in 1945. Two years later, when it became the *Bulletin of the Atomic Scientists,* they chose as a cover symbol a doomsday clock, and placed its hands at eight minutes before midnight.

13. *Background:* A letter to the consumer advocate column in the *Vancouver Sun* (April, 1981):

> I have a question for your column. I recently started buying [a certain brand of] frozen cauliflower and broccoli mix. The outside of the package shows small chunks of cauliflower and broccoli flowerets. But inside the package were very large pieces of cauliflower and only stems and mashed pieces of broccoli. I have bought two packages now and they have both been the same. Has anyone else had this problem?

14. *Background:* A response to a story in the *Toronto Star* about the reasons why the voyage of the space shuttle *Columbia* was delayed (April, 1981):

> Your headline "Shuttle scuttled," while a nice example of poetic alliteration, is technically incorrect.
> Both Webster's and the Oxford dictionaries state "scuttle" as to "sink intentionally."
> The German fleet was scuttled at Scapa Flow after World War I. And similarly the Graf Spee at Montevideo in World War II — surely not a similar fate to the Columbia.

15. *Background:* Below is an excerpt from J.L. Mackie's book, *Ethics: Inventing Right and Wrong* (New York: Penguin Books, 1978), p. 195:

As the world is, wars and revolutions cannot be ruled to be morally completely out of the question. The death penalty, I believe, can. The prearranged killing of someone at a stated time is a special outrage against the humane feelings which are a central part of morality, and this is not outweighed by any extra deterrent effect; in fact the use of the death penalty is likely to increase criminal violence.

16. *Background:* A brief excerpt from an article about the city of Seattle in *Architectural Digest* (June, 1981):

    Perhaps more than any other city, the name of Seattle evokes images of natural grandeur, of great mountain ranges on the horizon, of a pervasive sense of water and — always present — the green northwestern wilderness stretching into vast blue distances.

17. *Background:* A letter to the *Montreal Gazette,* (May 1981):

    If the Canadian Egg Marketing Agency (CEMA) is determined to reduce the number of chickens, why don't they contact the external affairs department and arrange to do some good?
    Instead of using tax dollars to buy and then kill these birds, simply buy them and then have them exported to areas of the world where there is a desperate need for food . . . .

CHAPTER TWO

EVALUATING ARGUMENTS

Arguments Good and Bad

Once you have identified and extracted an argument, you are ready to evaluate it, to ask the question: "Is this a logically good argument or a bad one?" To answer this question, you need to have two things: (1) a general grasp of the criteria which enter into the logical evaluation of arguments and (2) practice in evaluating arguments.

Let's go back to what we have said about argument: an argument is an attempt to trace a rational route from a starting point (premise or premises) to a destination (conclusion). "If you begin here," the argument says, "then if you want to be consistent, you must wind up here." We speak metaphorically: an argument is good if the route that it proposes to trace from the premises to the conclusion is a solid one, like a good map with directions which gets you where you want to go. On the other hand, an argument is bad when the route it sketches is filled with detours, deadends, and roadblocks. Later we will call these, less analogically, *fallacies*.

Before going into the criteria which make an argument good, we have a little more to say about good and bad arguments. These are usually matters of degree. Rarely is an argument so good that it cannot profit from criticism and seldom is an argument so bad that it cannot be improved by criticism. So most arguments that have defects are capable of being revised to remedy those defects. If you think a particular argument is airtight, that might be because you have not thought deeply enough about the issues, or don't know enough about the positions it competes with. If, on the other hand, you think a particular argument is worthless, that might be because you've saddled yourself with blinders and won't let yourself consider the possibility that such a line of argument might have merit. Most arguments, in fact, occupy the middle part of the spectrum. The purpose of argument analysis should be to enable you to see the plusses and minusses in an argument *as they really are,* and thereby help you guard against premature acceptance or rejection of the argument.

It is important to avoid utopian expectations about what is required of an argument. Arguments by their nature come into being against a background of controversy, of diverse opinion and differing points of view. Moreover the topics they address usually are difficult ones to resolve: how to prevent nuclear arms proliferation, how to end the vicious cycle of inflation, how to control the rise in crime, etc. The heterogeneity of beliefs and values underlying these issues makes it unrealistic to expect any argument to establish its conclusion as the final word and shut down all alternatives. That just won't happen. So to require of a good argument that it prove its conclusion beyond any possible doubt or criticism is excessive. Proof in the strict sense may be desirable in geometry and algebra, but in the realm of everyday arguing about contentious issues it is mistaken to expect it, let alone hope for it. An argument may be good even without *proving* its conclusion true.

At the other extreme, there is another mistaken attitude about evaluating arguments which needs to be defused. Many people evaluate arguments by one "standard" only: does it support my view or not? That is not a logical standard of evaluation but rather a purely idiosyncratic one. Logical evaluation requires sensitivity to the different positions on the table, and to points of evidence. It requires that you be able to put yourself into the posture of an intelligent and thinking bystander and ask: "Quite apart from whether I am predisposed to accept or reject the conclusion, does this argument display the features of a good argument or not?"

Enough preliminary talk. It's time for you to put your intuitions to work on some examples. For each of the four examples that follow, we ask you to read the argument carefully and make sure that you have grasped it correctly. Then decide whether the argument is a good one or not, and write out your own reasons for the verdict. Only after defending your judgement should you proceed to compare your views with others.

Example 1:

21   Dear Ann Landers:
        My 16-year-old cousin sent for your booklet called "Teenage Sex and Ten Ways to Cool it." She sent her 50 cents and the self-addressed envelope like it said at the foot of your column. When the booklet arrived, she read it right away and phoned me to say that it was very good and gave her a lot to think about. Well, Ann Landers, three months later she was pregnant and got married very fast. Her mother almost had a heart attack. What I want to know is why do you recommend booklets if they don't do any good?

        Highly Disappointed

Example 2: In October, 1981, the Windsor (Ontario) City Council requested the Windsor Police Commission to review the policy of the Windsor Police Department regarding high-speed chases. This request followed several incidents in which citizens were injured during high-speed chases. Responding to that request, Judge Joseph McMahon of the Police Commission stated (quoted in *The Windsor Star*):

22   The Windsor Police Commission should act independently of the City Council, and the police force must be removed from political influence and control. If the individual officer were ever to feel that the discharge of his or her duties were subject to the control of individual members of the Council, then indeed the people of this city would be the eventual losers.

Example 3: This is an excerpt from Josiah Thompson's book, *Six Seconds in Dallas* (New York: Bernard Geis, 1967) about the assassination of U.S. President John F. Kennedy. In a section where Thompson is discussing the question, "Where did the first bullet go?" he writes (p. 39):

23   The testimony of Secret Service Agent Roy Kellerman adds weight to the theory that the first bullet only lodged in the President's back. Seated in the right front seat of the presidential limousine, Kellerman heard Kennedy yell, "My God! I'm hit" just after the first shot . . . . Since the projectile that caused the throat wound ripped his windpipe in passing, it seems unlikely that the President could have spoken after receiving the throat wound

Example 4: The March, 1982 issue of *Harper's* published an article by David Owen titled, "The Secret Lives of Dentists" in which Owen discussed in great detail the hazards of being a dentist and the pressures they face, both financial and psychological. He stated, "The divorce rate in the profession has risen 12 percent in the last decade, and drug abuse, alcoholism, and suicide have also been on the rise." Many dentists took exception. One, whose letter was quoted in the May, 1982 issue of *Harper's* (p. 5), stated:

24   If someone had read David Owen's article "The Secret Lives of Dentists" to me, I would have sworn it had been published in the *National Enquirer.* This childish bunch of half truths and snide innuendo is a low blow to a hardworking and dedicated profession . . . . I do not know a single case of a dentist who took his own life. An alcoholic dentist doesn't stay in business very long.

Before reading further, make your own judgements about each of the four arguments.
Now compare yours with ours.

Example 1. This is not a good argument. Intuitively you might have said that *Highly Disappointed* is *jumping to a conclusion.* He reasons from one case in which the booklet apparently failed to prevent someone from becoming pregnant to the (implied) conclusion that the booklet is not effective in general. If *Highly* were reasoning more carefully (less in the throes of his disappointment) he would have seen that more evidence is needed to reach that general conclusion, such as how others who have read the booklet have been affected. The booklet's failure to convince *one* person would not show that it does no good at all. (Note: One can also raise the question of whether this case presents any evidence at all for the general thesis. *Highly's* cousin may have read and then rejected the advice in the booklet. Moreover, there is some difficulty in deciding upon the criteria by which one should judge the effectiveness of such a booklet.)

Example 2. This is not a good argument. From the context, we infer that the judge was opposed to acceding to the request of the Windsor City Council. So the conclusion of the argument would be: "The Windsor Police Commission should not review the policy on high-speed chases as requested by the City Council." One of the reasons the judge gives for his implicit conclusion is this: "If the individual officer were to feel that the discharge of his or her duties were subject to the control of individual members of the council, then the people of the city would be the eventual losers." As a reason for rejecting the request, this is totally *irrelevant.* The request was not from individual council members to individual police officers, but rather from one official body (the Council) to another (the Police Commission). Certainly what the judge said was true enough; but by itself it just doesn't have a bearing on the conclusion he was implicitly urging.

Example 3. This is a good argument. If the first bullet had pierced Kennedy's throat (as some allege), then Kellerman could not have heard what he said he heard. Hence his testimony adds weight to the theory that the first bullet only lodged in the president's back. The conclusion is presented in a qualified way ("adds weight") and Thompson later acknowledges contrary evidence (no one else heard what Kellerman heard the President say). But if the facts are as recorded here, they provide pretty good evidence that the first bullet did not pierce Kennedy's throat but lodged in his back.

Example 4. This is not a good argument. This dentist means to argue that Owen has his facts wrong. The dentist adduces two premises: (1) He does not know of a single dentist who took his own life; (2) An alcoholic dentist won't stay in business very long. Of course we can grant that (1) is true and yet it doesn't follow that Owen's claim about the rate of suicide is wrong, for this dentist's colleagues may not be representative of the profession. And (2) certainly needs to be defended with some reasoning and evidence, for it is not obviously true. Some alcoholics, including doctors, lawyers and business executives, manage to keep at work for years. Owen hasn't shown that dentists are different in this respect. It may be that Owen got his facts wrong (indeed, the dentist would have a more effective line of objection here had he challenged Owen to produce some evidence for his claims), but the dentist's argument does not succeed in showing that.

Our brief exercise contained three bad arguments and one good one. In this text, we will be spending more time on bad arguments, why they are bad and how they might be improved, than on good ones. We are quite aware of the dangers of such an emphasis. Not only will the tone often be critical (finding faults with arguments) but the impression may be created that most arguments are flawed. The standard rap against the fallacy-theory approach to argument analysis is that it produces jaundiced students, determined in advance to flog any old weakness in an argument but blind to potential strengths.

A spirited defense of fallacy theory against such accusations, which have merit, is not appropriate here. Instead, we make the following observations.

First, it is undeniably useful to be able to play a solid game of defense. All that can be objected to is over-use of the defensive tools fallacy-theory provides. But this is a problem for the teaching and learning of almost any new skills: the beginner initially wants to apply them, and at first lacks the finesse to do so with discrimination. The same danger applies to any new technique of logical criticism.

Second, the ability to spot bad reasoning in others' arguments can profitably be turned inward. Indeed, there is slender profit in picking out weaknesses in the reasoning of others if one is unable to spot these same shortcomings in one's own arguments. By using knowledge of fallacies to be self-critical as well as critical of others' logic, you can double your gain and avoid one-sidedness.

Third, in the exercises that accompany each chapter we shall sprinkle in what we think are good arguments along with the bad ones — to keep you on your toes and guard against the overly negative mindset. And there'll be a few other surprises along the way.

Fourth, while in the early going it will be enough to do a good job of picking out this or that fallacy, in the long run you are going to be given the responsibility of showing good judgement and discrimination in your criticisms. Are the flaws really serious ones or not? You will have to decide, and defend your judgements.

It is now time to say what these standards are. The flaws we will be discussing are called **fallacies.** By fallacy we mean a violation of one of the criteria which govern good arguments. Our evaluation of each of the examples referred implicitly to these criteria. We said that Example 1 was a bad argument because *Highly Disappointed did not provide enough evidence.* Example 2 illustrated a different flaw: the premise used by Judge McMahon was *unrelated* to his conclusion. Finally, Example 4 was a bad argument because we could not *accept* the dentist's premises. Looking back over the italicized words, the key words in our assessments, you will see readily that there are three different criteria that an argument must satisfy in order to be a good argument.

First, the premises must be *relevant* to the conclusion. Second, the premises must provide *sufficient* support for the conclusion. Third, the premises must be *acceptable*. We shall have more to say about each of these criteria in the next section. The point that needs to be underscored here is that this RSA triangle

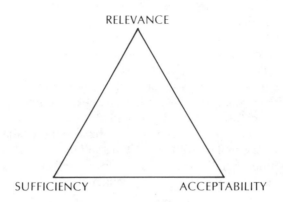

RELEVANCE

SUFFICIENCY   ACCEPTABILITY

defines a logically good argument; and that any argument which fails to satisfy one (or more) of these requirements is a fallacious argument.

We must point out that other logical traditions take a different view on what is required for an argument to be a good one. Thus, traditionally, logicians have distinguished between two types of argument (or two types of inference found in arguments): an inductive argument (or inference), whose characteristic feature is that the premises render the conclusion probable, and a deductive argument (or inference), whose characteristic feature is that the conclusion follows necessarily from the premises. Inductive arguments are typically found in the empirical sciences. Most prominently, they are featured in polling and opinion research. Deductive arguments are characteristic of mathematics. If one accepts this dichotomy (which the authors of this text are not happy with), then one does not speak of good arguments across the board, but rather of good deductive arguments and of good inductive arguments, and what goodness is in each type.

To conclude this section, we shall offer a few more observations about the fallacy approach to argument analysis, which is what you'll be learning in this text.

First, the fallacies we shall discuss are logical miscues which occur with some regularity in arguments in everyday discourse. Our coverage is narrower than that of some texts, but includes those fallacies which we believe show up with most frequency. A standard rap against the fallacy approach is that there can be no complete inventory of fallacies because there is not a complete list of the ways people go wrong in their reasoning. That may be true, but we believe that a list of errors needn't be complete to be useful.

Second, the fallacies all have names or labels selected with a view to describing their central features. Some are quite vivid (straw man, red herring), others less so (questionable cause). What we want to impress on you at the outset is that the objective in learning fallacy-theory is NOT to enable you to throw these terms around in casual conversation in order to impress people with your logical savvy. The fact is that it is never enough just to sprinkle your conversation with claims such as "That's a red herring!" Indeed, most of the people you talk with will probably not be conversant with fallacy-theory, so when you go public you will have to switch gears. You will have to be able to make your points about arguments without resorting to the labels used in this text. The fallacy approach is a way of introducing you to certain sorts of logical mistakes. The function of the names is mainly that of mnemonic devices: to enable you to recall or beckon from memory the varieties of mistakes.

Third, our treatment of each fallacy centres around **the boxed conditions.** These conditions serve a dual function. Not only do they define the fallacy, but the conditions are also meant to guide you in your effort to show that the fallacy in question has been committed in a specific argument. For one cannot score logical points by simply *claiming* that an argument is fallacious. You must establish that it is. To explain this crucial point, we resort to an analogy. The three criteria we have mentioned may be said to be the "laws of logic," like the laws of society; compare individual arguments then to the actions of individual citizens; and think of your role of a logical critic as like that of the prosecutor in a court of law. The prosecutor must show that there is enough evidence to convict a citizen of having violated a specific and named law or statute. (The prosecutor would be laughed out of court were he to say, "He's guilty of something or other, but I can't say what.") Nor can the prosecutor get by with simple assertions (though he must assert). He cannot just state, "The defendant smuggled people across the border" without being ready to produce evidence (eyewitnesses, sworn statements, etc). Similarly, you must be able to show that a given argument is guilty of a specified violation. To do this, you need to show that each of the fallacy conditions is satisfied in the case at hand. If you were to assert no more than some such unsubstantiated charge as, "This premise is irrelevant to that conclusion," without arguing for your claim, your case should be waived out of court — for lack of evidence.

Fourth, and this hearkens back to a point made at the beginning of this chapter, the charge of fallacy is nothing more than an initial critical probing of the argument. It is an attempt to locate a potential weakness, not the bold (and sometimes arrogant) assertion that because of this flaw the argument goes by the board. Even if the charge of fallacy is justified in a given instance, that does not mean the argument cannot be repaired over the flaw. Nor does it follow that the conclusion of the argument is false. It's possible to argue poorly or inadequately on behalf of a true statement (as conclusion) just as it is possible to argue well on behalf of a false (or unacceptable) belief. So when you criticize an argument as fallacious, remember that all you have shown is that there is a potential obstacle on the route traced by the arguer from premises to conclusion.

Lastly, the three fallacies to be discussed next are the three most basic types of fallacies. They stand to the fallacies to be discussed in Chapters 3-7 as genus to species, as general form to particular instance. *Irrelevant reason,* for example, the first one we will examine, assumes a more particular form in each of the fallacies of *straw man, ad hominem, guilt by association* and *red herring,* which are the subjects of Chapter 3. On occasion you will encounter in an argument a logical mistake that as far as you know has not been more narrowly classified. Still, you will recognize it as a fallacy of relevance, sufficiency, or acceptability and so you can for convenience assign to it the appropriate generic fallacy label. Wherever possible, though, you should try to make your criticism of an argument as specific as you can, so that the precise nature of any flaw in it is made explicit (and the exact manner in which repairs are needed is, by implication, set forth). This means that where you can you should supply the specific fallacy label that fits the particular mistake in question. The three basic fallacies, coming up, serve then both as general principles of organization, and as back-ups to fill in any gaps between specific labels belonging within each genus.

Three Basic Fallacies

Irrelevant Reason

The first fallacy in our catalogue is **irrelevant reason.** (You may find it referred to by its Latin name, *"non sequitur,"* meaning, "it does not follow." Example 2 in the last section is an instance of this fallacy. The judge's premise was *irrelevant* to the conclusion he was urging. Look at two more examples.

In the '70s, Grace MacInnis (at that time the federal Member of Parliament for Vancouver-Kingsway, British Columbia) charged in the House of Commons that the federal Department of Health and Welfare had been cooperating with the Kellogg Company in permitting the sale of a cereal (*Kellogg's Corn Flakes*) which, she alleged, contained "little or no nutritional value." Seeking to rebut that charge, Minister of Health Marc Lalonde stated:

25   As for the nutritional value of corn flakes, the milk you have with your corn flakes has great nutritional value.

In the context of this declaration, we are justified in attributing to Lalonde the implicit conclusion that *"Kellogg's Corn Flakes* do have significant nutritional value." Of course, it is possible that Lalonde had a much stronger conclusion in mind: he might have been thinking that *Kellogg's*

Corn Flakes have great nutritional value. But in setting forth his argument, we are required by the Principle of Charity to attribute to him the weakest (or minimal) statement that brings him into dialectical conflict with MacInnis's view. That is because, in interpreting an incomplete argument, we are obliged to not overcommit the arguer (as supplying the stronger implied conclusion would have done). Thus, we reconstruct Lalonde's argument as follows:

26   1. The milk that one has with *Kellogg's Corn Flakes* has great nutritional value.
        a. *Kellogg's Corn Flakes* have significant nutritional value.

It is not terribly difficult to see that the premise here furnishes no support for the conclusion. The nutrient properties of milk have no bearing on the nutrient properties of *Corn Flakes,* even if the two usually are consumed together. To determine the nutrient values of any food, one needs to measure the values of the food itself (protein, carbohydrate, fat) — not those of its companions.

One way of seeing the irrelevancy here is by constructing a **counter-example**: i.e., formulating an argument that employs the same reasoning, though with a different subject matter, and in which the illogic of the argument is graphic. Thus, if we were to accept Lalonde's reasoning here, we would also have to believe that (here comes the counter-example) salt possesses great nutritional value because the steak you sprinkle it on has great nutritional value; or that water has great nutritional value because the powder you mix it with to produce milk has great nutritional value. In sum, Lalonde's premise is irrelevant to his conclusion, so the argument commits the fallacy of *irrelevant reason.* (This criticism, keep in mind, is open to a response; it remains possible that Lalonde — or someone who shares his view — can reject the criticism by showing how the premise affirmed, in conjunction with some as yet unmentioned assumptions, would generate the conclusion.)

Here is a second example. In the early '70s, a doll was being sold in stores in Ontario which was found to have the unsavoury feature of allowing a small but pointed spike to protrude if the head of the doll were removed. Tests showed that this feat was manageable by infants. When parents discovered this danger, they complained to the Department of Consumer and Corporate Affairs. Informed of these complaints, a spokesman for the company which manufactured the doll stated:

27   All of the legislation in Canada isn't going to protect a child from the normal hazards of life.

Once again, we have to identify the implied conclusion: "It would be inappropriate to draft legislation seeking to prevent the manufacture and sales of dolls such as . . . ." But the premise here is relevant to the conclusion only if we assume that the dolls in question fall under the category "normal hazards of life." Admittedly, that category is rather broad and hard to define precisely; but one would classify as normal hazards things like busy urban streets, rusty nails left in planks, icy sidewalks, roving dogs, etc. Certainly the bounds of that category would have to be stretched to include within it a plaything such as a doll which, by its very nature, is not supposed to be dangerous in any way. So although the spokesman's claim was true, the argument is not a good one because the premise is *irrelevant*.

We can set down the defining conditions of this fallacy now:[1]

IRRELEVANT REASON

1. *M* has put forth *Q*, *R*, *S*, . . . as premises for *T*.
2. In conjunction with *R*, *S*, . . . , *Q* is irrelevant to *T*.

It is one thing to suspect an argument of being guilty of *irrelevant reason*, another thing to justify the charge of irrelevance. The conditions are meant to guide you in the latter task. That is, you must show that these conditions are satisfied in the argument under consideration. For instance, returning to the first example we gave: Lalonde (*M*) put forth "The milk you have with *Kellogg's Corn Flakes* has great nutritional value" (*Q*) as a premise for the conclusion that *Kellogg's Corn Flakes* have significant nutritional value (*T*). (There are no other premises offered, no *R*, *S*, . . .) In so specifying, we show that Condition 1 is satisfied. Now for Condition 2. We begin with the appropriate assertion: *Q* is irrelevant to *T*. But we cannot stop here. We must defend this claim, and we do so by replaying the line of reasoning set forth a few paragraphs back, just below example 26: "The nutrient properties of milk . . . companions." It is never enough merely to assert that the premise in question is irrelevant to tip the scales of logic in one's favour; one must produce justification of one's assertion. Otherwise the situation remains a stand-off: your undefended claim that the premise is irrelevant *vs.* the arguer's implicit (and likewise undefended) claim that the premise is relevant.

How can one establish irrelevance? To that thorny problem, we turn next.

The notion of **relevance** is difficult to analyse. To mention synonyms, such as "germane to," "has a bearing on," is merely to transfer the problem

---

[1] *Variables and Abbreviations:* Throughout the text we will use the letters of the alphabet as variables according to the following conventions, *M*, *N*, *O* will stand for the names of persons; *Q*, *R*, *S*, *T*, *W* will stand for assertions, statements, claims; *X*, *Y*, *Z* will stand for events, actions, or situations. We shall reserve *P* as the abbreviation of "premise" and *C* as the abbreviation of "conclusion."

to the new terms. The difficulty of the task cannot be minimized. Formal logicians, for example, have been trying for two decades to capture the notion, but thus far have not enjoyed great success.[2] In courts of law, questions of relevance are decided by the judge (on the basis of his or her experience of law), but a judge's decisions are notoriously subject to appeal to, and often reversal by, higher courts. The point seems to be that relevance is always a judgement call, and there is no reason to think that any algorithmic procedure will come along to change that. The following observations about relevance may be useful.

First, relevance (unlike truth) does not inhere in each individual premise but rather in an individual premise taken together with certain other items of evidence or information. The point can perhaps best be seen by imagining the sort of artificial case that makes for dramatic TV fare. The prosecutor asks: "Is the defendant left-handed?" The defense lawyer objects: "But that is irrelevant." The prosecutor presses on: "But, Your Honour, we shall establish that the murderer had to have been left-handed, so if the defendant is left-handed, that is relevant to the question of whether he could have been the murderer." Here the connection becomes clear; the relevance becomes obvious with the addition of the new information. Sometimes, a charge of irrelevance may be prompted by the arguer's failure to complete his reasoning. When that missing piece is provided, the logical focus then changes from the question of the relevance of the original premise to the question of the acceptability of the newly added, relevance-supplying premise. But sometimes irrelevance occurs because the position has not been thought through carefully enough, and no additional premise with any plausibility at all can be found to supply relevance.

Second, it is sometimes useful in testing for irrelevance to use the method of assigning *truth-values* to the suspected premise and conclusion. "Truth-value" is simply a generic way of referring to the truth or falsity (whichever it is) of a statement. The method of assigning truth values is an exercise of logical imagination in which you say to yourself: "Let me suppose that Q is true; does the truth of Q dictate a truth value for T (the conclusion)?" That is, if Q *were* true (just supposing), would that give some basis for judging that T is true, or that T is false?" If, in both cases, the answer is "*No*," then you have reason to assert that Q is irrelevant to T.

Let's try this strategy on the case of the corn flakes examples. Here Q = *The milk you have with your corn flakes has great nutritional value,* and T = *Corn flakes have significant nutritional value.* Suppose Q is true; does that increase the likelihood of T's being true? No, for corn flakes and milk are two different and distinct food substances, each with its independent nutrient properties. Milk doesn't react chemically with corn flakes to

[2] The effort was spearheaded by two logicians: Alan Ross Anderson and Nuel D. Belnap. For further details, the reader may consult: "Entailment" in *Logic and Philosophy,* ed. Gary Iseminger (New York: Appleton-Century-Crofts, 1968), pp. 76-108.

create or increase nutritional properties of corn flakes. Does Q's truth increase the likelihood of T's falsehood? Not at all, for milk does not decrease or remove whatever nutritional value corn flakes might have. Now suppose Q were false; what difference would that make to T's truth-value? If milk were not very nutritional, that would neither make corn flakes have nutritional value (and so make T true), nor would it detract from any nutritional value corn flakes may have (and so make T false). The truth and falsehood of Q and T, then, are totally independent; hence Q is irrelevant to T.

We conclude our treatment of irrelevant reason with an example which illustrates not only this flaw, but the other two basic fallacies as well. The background of the passage is the ongoing debate in Canada and the United States about doctors' salaries. This particular excerpt comes from a spirited defense of doctors and their incomes in a column, "Stiff Medicine for Doctor Bashers," by Dr. Nicholas Rety, a urologist in Vernon, British Columbia (*Maclean's*, August, 1981). In this passage, Rety takes a stab at those who think the salaries are too high:

28   Robert Evans, a University of British Columbia economics professor, sneers indignantly that doctors earn three times the average income of the general public. He gets wide coverage in the West Coast media, yet he ignores the fact that theoretically a worker of modest skills earning $12 an hour, with standard overtime benefits, would almost equal the doctor's average of $53,422 by working a doctor's 66 hour week. Much public resentment is stirred up by such critics who, in truth, only *comment* on issues from a professor's chair with tenure (the ultimate in job security) and enjoy a year's sabbatical at public expense every few years.

There are several things going on here that need logical inspection. In the last sentence, Rety attacks Evans personally, bringing in the fact that Evans has both job security and regular sabbaticals at public expense. This seems to be an attempt to discredit Evans's attack, but the fact that Evans has tenure and has regular sabbaticals is irrelevant with respect to his (implicit) claim that doctors' earnings are too high. Evans's own personal employment situation may make him envious of doctors, but it does not *necessarily* influence him to distort the truth in his arguments. So we cannot accept or reject Evans's charges simply on the basis that they come from someone in a comfortable academic position. Hence, a charge of *irrelevant reason* can be charged against Rety's last sentence if it is intended as a reason for rejecting Evans's claims (and we can see no other reason why Rety would have included it). This particular form of irrelevant reason is called *ad hominem*; we shall have more to say about *ad hominem* specifically in Chapter 3.

By the way, perhaps Rety thought Evans was arguing that doctors should not get paid more than professors. If so, then Rety's last sentence can be read as making the point that since doctors don't have working conditions like tenure and regular paid sabbaticals the way professors do, they should get paid more than professors in compensation. If this is what Rety meant, then he wasn't guilty of *irrelevant reason*. However, there is no evidence in Evans's original statements that he meant to criticize doctors' salaries on the grounds that they are higher than professors' salaries. Consequently, on this interpretation of Rety's reply, he would still be guilty of a logical flaw — misrepresenting Evans's position — called *straw man*. More on *straw man* in Chapter 3.

There is yet another logical problem with Rety's argument. Against Evans's implicit claim that doctors are overpaid, Rety argues that they are not overpaid, citing as his grounds a comparison of their hourly rate of income vis-à-vis that of a worker of modest skills. What does he mean by "a worker of modest skills"? Where does the $12/hour figure come from? We need to be sure that his facts are plausible, since his argument that doctors are not overpaid depends heavily on them. The failure to provide sufficient defense of these claims is the fallacy that we term *problematic premise*, and which we shall deal with later.

There is another problem here. Certainly it does seem a relevant standard of comparison to compare hourly rates of pay. But that by itself cannot settle the question of fairness, for two reasons. On the one hand, doctors can to some degree control the number of hours per week they work, are often in a position to work as many hours a week as they want, and normally have enough work to keep them working full time at least five days a week, 52 weeks a year; whereas a great many hourly-rated workers cannot control the number of hours they work, and in many cases must go without work for parts of the year (layoffs during plant re-tooling, slack construction periods, seasonal slow periods). On the other hand, it may be that *both* doctors and the hourly-rated workers making $12/hour are paid too much. Rety needs to argue further that these workers are not overpaid, and also show that the doctors' opportunity to book a 66 hour week is not a relevant difference. Hence more evidence is needed to make his point; without it, the argument commits the fallacy we shall now discuss in detail: *hasty conclusion*.

Hasty Conclusion

Even when the premises of an argument pass the relevance test, they may as we've seen fail to provide sufficient support for the conclusion. The resulting fallacy, often referred to as a "hasty generalization" or "jumping to a conclusion," we call **hasty conclusion**. We just saw an example in Dr. Rety's argument against Professor Evans's critique of doctors' salaries, and earlier we saw another in *Highly Disappointed's* letter to Ann Landers. We shall now bring out some of the specific features of *hasty conclusion* by considering additional examples.

Participaction was a public service program initiated by the Canadian government to encourage Canadians to exercise. One resident of the Toronto suburb of North York found that campaign ineffective, as her letter indicates:

29   After hearing those advertisements from *Participaction* for the last couple of years, I thought that when I joined a large recreation centre in North York, the place would be packed! Hah! How come out of all the people who could visit, there were only eight people there the other night? Seems to me that most Canadians are just too lazy for their own good.[3]

It may be that most Canadians are too lazy, but the evidence cited here (the fact that only eight people were exercising in a particular recreation centre in one area of Toronto on a particular night) doesn't show that to be the case. In the first place, the evidence is *anecdotal* — taken from the personal experience of one individual. On a question of this sort (whether Canadians are lazy about exercising or not), you can see that anecdotal evidence is powerless to decide the question. Suppose the individual had gone on some other night and found the centre a hub of activity: could it be concluded then that most Canadians were trying to become or stay fit? No, for this one instance — just like the one cited — might have been an exception due to unusual circumstances. The writer was assuming that the sample in question was a typical one from which to draw a conclusion; but there are reasons to question the sample. The writer would be on better ground if observations were made over a period of time (different months and days throughout the year) in different centres throughout Canada. In other words, the evidence needs to be gathered *systematically.*

Even then we would have only one *kind* of evidence. After all, not all people who decide to exercise will join or work out at a centre. One of the most popular forms of exercise is jogging, and people don't need to go to a recreation centre to do that. Biking and walking can be done anywhere. In short, to decide whether or not Canadians are lazy about fitness, we would need *more* of the kind of evidence cited here and we would also need to have other *kinds* of evidence: reports from doctors, health agencies, medical research, insurance companies, etc. In promoting this single anecdote to the status of sufficient evidence for her conclusion, while ignoring other forms of evidence, the writer commits the fallacy called *hasty conclusion.*

While on the subject of fitness, we give another example of the fallacy from Sydney Harris, a syndicated U.S. columnist. Here is an excerpt from his article (January 1982), "Jogging is an un-natural activity for human beings":

30   . . . while exercise [such as running] is beneficial for the lungs and heart and the whole circulatory systems, it is debilitating to the legs.

---

[3] Thanks to Claire Smith-Victor for this example.

That is why most physical fitness experts recommend swimming as the ideal all around exercise, not walking or running: because in swimming the legs move easily through the surface and do not pound a hard surface.

While walking may do more good than harm, in terms of total bodily welfare, I cannot believe that jogging is anything but a bonanza for the podiatrists and the orthopedic surgeons. Some medical specialists indeed have already begun to warn the public of the probable perils in jogging as a daily routine.

Harris clearly believes that jogging is not a good method of exercising, on the grounds that it is debilitating to the legs and that specialists have begun to warn the public about the perils of jogging. The problem with his argument is the *evidence that it fails to take into consideration*. This untapped evidence is of two sorts. First, there is no doubt that jogging leads to injuries in many cases, but the questions have to be asked: How many cases? How many in relation to the total number of joggers? Under what conditions do injuries arise — under conditions of intelligent mileage or only conditions of overambitious running schedules? If only a relatively few joggers get injuries, and then only when they try to run too far too soon, and don't rest properly, or run with inferior shoes, then Harris's evidence, while relevant, doesn't add up to a good case for his claim. Second, it may be that there is a risk of injury to all joggers, but that the gains to them in better circulation, increased lung capacity, lower weight, improved self-image and greater energy outweigh the dangers. In that case Harris's evidence would fail to support his claim because it was partial in a difference sense. So we need to know that the risk is widespread, not restricted to a select group, and that the disadvantages outweigh the benefits. Harris fails to provide this further evidence; his conclusion is drawn without taking it into consideration; hence he is guilty of *hasty conclusion*.

Consider one more example before we discuss the conditions of this fallacy. Here is an excerpt from a book, *Off Madison Avenue,* by David Lyon in which Lyon attempts to defend advertising against its critics. At one point, he writes:

31 . . . I think I can show you that, on balance, advertising carries a higher proportion of truth than you are likely to encounter in most of the discussions you hear or the books you read. Consider the detergent commercial that you hate the most. You may, if you wish, question whether it actually does make clothes whiter than white; you may doubt that it gets out more stubborn dirt than any other washday products leave in; you may wonder whether it really leaves your clothes squeaky-clean and ever so manageable. But there is one thing that you may bank on with a considerable degree of confidence. It is a detergent. Doubt, if you wish, that Winston tastes good — but doubt not that Winston is a cigarette.

Lyon's argument borders on the ludicrous. He claims to be showing that advertising carries more truth than most books and discussions. His lone premise for this claim is that products advertised do indeed belong to the product-type which the advertisements assert them to belong to. Certainly the premise is relevant, for it shows that there is some minimal truth in advertising. But to establish the conclusion, he would have to show that there is even less truth in most books and conversations; and that he has not done. Indeed, Lyon ignores (in reaching this conclusion) the contrary evidence right under his nose: that most ads are guilty of puffery, inflated claims which are not literally true; and the ratio suggested by his own argument is 25 percent (one true claim for every three false ones).

Here then are the conditions of the fallacy:

HASTY CONCLUSION

1. *M* presents *Q, R, S, . . .* as sufficient support for a conclusion *T.*
2. *Q, R, S, . . .* taken together are not sufficient support for *T,* because:
   (a) they do not supply sufficiently systematically gathered evidence; and/or
   (b) they do not supply a sufficient sample of the various relevant kinds of evidence; and/or
   (c) they ignore the presence or possibility of contrary evidence.

As in the case of charging *irrelevant reason,* you have two tasks to perform in making a case for hasty conclusion. First, you must properly identify the premises, and from among them note the ones offering evidence to support the conclusion. That's Condition 1. Then you must not only assert but argue for the assertion that the evidence is not sufficient. You may do this in several ways. (1) You may show that what the evidence presented does show is less than what the arguer concluded. Or (2) you may have to indicate what sort of additional evidence is needed to generate the conclusion: (i) whether more evidence of the same sort, or (ii) evidence of a different type. Or (3) you may argue that the arguer has ignored or overlooked evidence that bears on the conclusion. Whatever the case may be, it is never sufficient for you to merely assert that more evidence is needed; you must defend or justify your assertion.

Let's work through one last example showing how the conditions are to be used. Andrew Greeley is another U.S. syndicated columnist. This is an excerpt from a column entitled "The evil of communism is manifest in Poland" (December, 1981):

32   As far as political systems go, communism is the worst thing the world has ever known. . . . Were Cubans better off, all things considered, under Fulgencio Batista than they are under Fidel Castro? Were Nicaraguans better off under Anastasio Somoza than they are going to be under the Leninist regime that is shaping up there? Would Salvadorans be better off under a communist rule than they are? One might ask Polish unionists what their advice would be to the Catholic clergy supporting communist or communist-front movements in Latin America or Asia.

We can extract and structure Greeley's argument as follows:

33   1. Cubans were better off under Batista than under Castro.
       2. Nicaraguans were better off under Somoza than under the Leninist regime shaping up there now.
       3. Salvadorans would not be better off under a communist regime than they are now.
       4. Poland is suffering under a communist regime.
       a. As far as political systems go, communism is the worst thing the world has ever known.

Greeley has drawn his conclusion from a list of examples which he clearly takes as evidence for it. He does so without qualification, so we may take it that he believes these examples suffice to prove that communism is the worst political system the world has ever known. Thus, we contend, Condition 1 of *hasty conclusion* is satisfied here.

Grant, for the sake of argument, that Greeley's premises are true — controversial though they may be. The question is, if they were true, would they provide sufficient support for the conclusion? We think not, for a couple of reasons. There is no mention here of The People's Republic of China, where some immense strides in improving human welfare have been made (though clearly not without human costs and restrictions), or Chile, where progress towards greater freedom and democracy was being made until, as the evidence seems to indicate, the U.S.A. interfered. So there is, first, evidence overlooked by Greeley that some countries have done better under a communist (or at least Marxist) system than other forms of political system. There is also to be considered whether there are certain forms of political system which are not just as bad as, or worse than, communism. Right-wing military dictatorships now in existence, and Nazi and Fascist systems come to mind as examples. So, second, evidence of different sorts needs to be produced in order to justify the claim. For these reasons we conclude that Greeley's evidence is not sufficient; Condition 2 is satisfied: Greeley commits *hasty conclusion*.

People commit *hasty conclusion* because we get a notion in our heads, cast about for a few bits of evidence and settle into our position. We promote intuitions and half-truths to the status of full and incontrovertible truths without bothering to weigh and consider evidence: "Don't confuse me with the facts." We reason from our own personal experience (anecdotal evidence) to draw conclusions which run far in advance of it. We ignore evidence. Sometimes we *suppress* evidence. Or we simply fail to bring all the evidence to bear on the situation.

As critics, though, we need to be reasonable in our demands for sufficient evidence. There is no handy gauge that tells us how much evidence is enough. The onus is on the critic to cite, in each individual case under scrutiny, specific ways the evidence put forward is insufficient. In effect, the evidence advanced in an argument can be fairly challenged as insufficient only when you, the critic, can cite some item of relevant evidence that would make a difference to the verdict and that has not been taken into account in the argument.

Often, too, the argument can be retrieved and made immune from the *hasty conclusion* criticism by a simple qualification added to the conclusion; for example, by changing an "always" to "usually"; or an "in every case" to "in most cases"; or an "entirely" to "partially." And the qualified conclusion may be all the arguer needs to make the point. In such cases the critic needs to be aware of the minimal force of the *hasty conclusion* charged, and the critic can suggest the qualification that would immunize the argument from this criticism.

This advice can be turned around and put to good use when you are the person constructing the argument. You have no business thinking your opinion or claim is sufficiently supported until you have gathered enough evidence to answer all the reasonable challenges you can imagine. You should be careful to qualify your conclusion so that its generality does not go beyond the limits justified by the evidence you have been able to assemble. These two moves — anticipating and trying to meet challenges, and qualifying the conclusion — will nip many a case of *hasty conclusion* in the bud.

Problematic Premise

We have considered so far how the premises, in relation to each other, must be relevant to the conclusion, and how the premises as a set must provide sufficient support for the conclusion. The third standard for a logically good argument calls for us to consider each premise individually from a different point of view — that of its *acceptability*. The fallacy we call **problematic premise** occurs when an undefended premise should not be granted or accepted without support.

The idea of the requirement of acceptable premises stems from the very point of persuasive argument. The purpose of such argument is to get someone who is sceptical of, or downright opposed to, a claim to see that he should grant it. The method is to begin by citing some *other* statements that he would grant (your premises), and then by showing how, having accepted those premises, he must, to be consistent, accept the claim in question (your conclusion). If your interlocutor should not accept your premises, he will have no starting points from which to get to your conclusion, and so he would have to reject your argument. A logically good argument, therefore, must start from premises that the audience is prepared to accept — or ought to accept.

When ought we, as the critical audience of an argument, accept its premises? Two considerations apply here, and they pull in opposite directions. On the one hand, the arguer's job is to persuade us, and so it is up to her to argue in defense of any premise she thinks we might not accept without defense. You might think, then, that the arguer should defend every premise in order to be sure to convince her audience. However, a moment's reflection will enable you to see that this demand is an impossible one. If *every* premise in an argument had to be defended before it would be acceptable, that requirement would engender an unending chain of premises. To defend a premise, you'd have to use other premises, and if these in turn had to be defended, you would have to use still others, and so on. No finite argument could ever have all its premises acceptable; hence every finite argument would be fallacious; consequently the distinction between logically good and bad arguments would collapse. Since there certainly are logically good arguments, it follows that it must be possible to use at least some premises in an argument without having to defend them.

So we come back to our question: how do we tell when a premise ought to be accepted without defense? Since arguments occur primarily when there are controversies, and since, as we've noted, the arguer's goal is to persuade his audience, our rule of thumb shall be that the onus rests with the arguer to defend any premise that is open to doubt, question, or controversy. Another way to put the point is to say that acceptability is a "dialectical" matter. In the back-and-forth interchange of a dialogue on a controversial subject, if one party were trying to persuade others, those others would raise questions precisely at points where they were uncertain about a claim or where they believed a claim to be false. The arguer would have to respond with a defense of that claim, at that point. Persuasive argument is dialectical, so an arguer needs to imagine an audience of people representing the known contending positions on the issue being argued about, to anticipate their questions and objections, and to provide further arguments in reply. (See Chapter 8 for our detailed account of the dialectics of argument.) This explains again why we say that a premise is acceptable without defense only if it is *not* open to doubt, question, or controversy.

A premise is "problematic," we shall say, if it is used without defense but is unacceptable without defense. Anyone who uses a problematic premise in an argument commits the fallacy we call *problematic premise*. Before listing the conditions of this fallacy, we shall flesh out our account of acceptability by discussing some specific types of cases where undefended premises are acceptable and where they are not.

It is reasonable to accept an undefended premise if it is generally known to be true, or at least represents knowledge shared, and known to be shared, by the arguer and his audience. Thus, for example, in the part of the world where western Christianity has historically been the predominant religion, it would be acceptable to use as an undefended premise that Christmas is December 25th; in Canada and the United States you could say, without needing to defend it, that the World Series is held in the fall; and in Canada, but perhaps not in the U.S.A. and probably not elsewhere, you could assert in an argument, without defense, that Canada's first permanent European colonists came from France.

A word of caution at this juncture. People are inclined to think that a premise is obviously true if they happen to agree with it, and doubtful or false otherwise. In the former case they may be inclined to think the premise doesn't need defense, but in the latter case that it does. Unfortunately, unless an individual is extremely logical, well-informed, and judicious in the formulation of his beliefs, the inference from "I agree with it" to "It's true" is unreliable. All of us carry a mixed assortment of beliefs, some true, some false; some rational, some not; some well-founded, some rash; and so on. The question to ask of an undefended premise, therefore, is not, "Do I think it is true?" but rather, "Is it generally known to be true?"

That, however, is not the only question to ask. Its truth alone cannot make an undefended premise acceptable. To see this, imagine the following case. An advertisement in an astrology magazine offers for sale as a sure-fire cancer cure the ground-up root of a plant found only in the remote Tonga Islands of the Pacific. Now someone tries to convince you, a cancer patient, to buy some of this root, using as a premise in his argument the claim made in the advertisement. You have no warrant for accepting this premise. Its credentials are dubious in the extreme. Furthermore, and here's the point, you would be mistaken to accept that claim even if it were true. Suppose that, although the advertisement was the work of a charlatan out to profit from the desperation of cancer patients, it were to turn out, ironically, that researchers years later identified an effective cancer-curing chemical in the root, established its efficacy through clinical tests, and developed a theory to explain how it works. The fact remains that when you encountered the claim made in the advertisement, neither you nor anyone else had any basis for believing it, even though it was true. This shows that the mere truth of a premise does not ensure its acceptability.

Nor is it enough, for it to be acceptable, that a premise is known to be true, if that knowledge is not accessible to the audience of the argument. Imagine an engineer who has developed a new and potentially profitable industrial process. She has tested it thoroughly and knows that it works. When she goes to a bank seeking financing for large-scale production, the bank cannot treat her claims as acceptable evidence even though they are true and she knows they are true. The bank must ask for references to check her credentials as an engineer and perhaps hire independent consultants to check out her claims for the process. The audience of the argument, in other words, has to have its own access to the truth of the premises — where truth is a relevant consideration at all.

This example shows that the known truth of the premises is not enough to make them acceptable: there must be *shared* knowledge, generally accessible knowledge. In fact, even shared knowledge is not necessary in every case to make a premise acceptable. For instance, it may suffice that the premise is *credible*. If a professor of American history, for example, mentions in an argument that Benjamin Franklin never was president of the United States, the professor's authority plus the straightforwardly factual nature of the claim gives his statement enough credibility that it would be unreasonable of you not to accept it — even if your recollection of American history were a bit shaky and you could not recall exactly all of Franklin's public offices. A premise's acceptance may be warranted if it is sufficiently probable or sufficiently accurate for purposes at hand. A meteorologist's prediction of a 50 percent chance of frost may be acceptable as a premise in an argument in defense of covering up your single tomato plant, but not in an argument that an orange-grower should spend thousands of dollars to light fires to try to warm his orange groves. If we, having made the drive many times, argue that it will take you all day to drive to Ottawa from Windsor on the grounds that the cities are 800 km apart and the speed limit is 100 km/h, you would be foolish to reject our premise simply because the distance is rounded off.

In all the examples we have discussed so far, the matter of the premise's truth *could* be established — measured, double-checked, verified. There is an entirely different class of cases, where it is unclear or unlikely or impossible that a premise could be known to be true, just because in those cases it is unclear what would *count* as "known to be true" or else because *nothing* would count as "known to be true."

We have a wide range of cases in mind. Most of the issues that are of public interest and subject to controversy belong here: nuclear arms reduction, nuclear power, unemployment, inflation, health care, tax reduction, national debt, foreign trade, education policy, affirmative action, native land claims . . . the list goes on and on. These matters are subject to dispute partly because the different positions taken entail different values, partly because the relevant facts are often hard to establish or estimate, and partly because the different positions are shaped by different concepts and definitions. For each of these three ingredients of any public policy position — values, data, and concepts — while the goal in some ideal sense may be "knowledge" (though that is arguable), in practical terms the objective is a "reasonable belief," and that is nothing more or less than a belief that is supported by plausible arguments. It follows that in arguments about such subjects any premise which asserts a controversial position will have to be defended: it will be unreasonable to accept any such premise without that defense.

Besides public policy questions we might mention two other sorts of cases where premises in arguments are likely to be controversial, yet their "truth" is not what is at issue. One comprises all those questions where values and norms are involved. Moral questions are a clear case here, but so are questions about values in music, art, literature — aesthetic judgements in general. We are emphatically not claiming that arguments and rational, defended beliefs are out of the question in these areas. Our point is that in arguments about such subjects the main premises will tend to be controversial and hence will require defense. The same goes for the second subset we have in mind — arguments involving the investigation or application of scientific theories. Here "truth" is a desideratum for the starting data, but not for the resulting theories, where the sought-for qualities are such factors as predictive power and comprehensiveness. In much of science and its applications, theory is unsettled and disputes within the scientific community are the order of the day. Different schools contend. Except in the central and established areas of a science where the claims are universally agreed-upon by qualified practitioners, claims of science itself (the modern deity), when used in arguments, require defense.

Yet even when the premises of arguments belong to such areas of controversy, and not to the domain of common knowledge, there remain a few situations where the requirement that premises be defended can be waived and where it would be reasonable for you to accept an undefended premise. We would include, as examples, the following:

1. The premise in question has already been defended elsewhere.
2. The arguer acknowledges that the premise needs defense, and accepts the responsibility for providing that defense if need be.
3. The premise is offered "for the sake of argument" in order to show what follows from it.

As you can see, these are situations where the requirement to defend is suspended, deferred or transferred, not where it is done away with.

We can now state the conditions for the fallacy of *problematic premise:*

PROBLEMATIC PREMISE

1. *M* asserts *Q* as support for *R*.
2. *M* presents no defense for *Q*.
3. In the circumstances in which the argument is presented, there is some specific reason why *Q* should not be accepted without defense.

We emphasize that to make a charge of *problematic premise* stick you need to cite reasons specific to the particular argument in question. We have of necessity been discussing in general terms the sorts of situations where a premise ought to be defended, but for any particular argument, unless you can give a specific reason relating to that subject matter and that argument, your charge will amount to no more than a general accusation which is problematic itself.

We need now to bring these conditions and the discussion leading up to them to bear on some actual examples.

First, the text of an argument:

34   No man can be a total feminist because in order to be a total fem-
          inist, a man would have to know what it feels like to be discrim-
          inated against as a woman, and no man can have that experience.

then our reconstruction of the argument:

35   1. No man can have the experience of what it feels like to be
         discriminated against *as a woman*.
      2. In order to be a total feminist, a man has to know what it feels
         like to be discriminated against *as a woman*.
      3. No man can be a total feminist.

We have quarrels with both premises, a minor one with the first and a more fundamental one with the second. The first premise comes close to the truism that no man can be a woman. Still, there are cases where women have had sex changes and become men, and so as men can report from direct experience what it was like to be discriminated against *as a woman*. Also, any man could masquerade as a woman in order to find out what it feels like to be treated as women are. This would be analogous to what John Howard Griffin did when he put black pigment on his skin and so lived and was identified by others as a black person — as reported in his book, *Black Like Me*. These possibilities represent a minor objection to the first premise, because it remains true that for most men the direct experience of being discriminated against *as a woman* is inaccessible.

As for the second premise, it is not clear that a man (e.g., one who is black, or handicapped or homosexual) cannot have direct experience of what it is like to be discriminated against in respects that are sufficiently similar to what a woman experiences to permit him to be a total feminist, i.e., to sympathize totally with women. Moreover, it is not clear that some men (perhaps not many) who have never been discriminated against them-selves are nevertheless sufficiently sensitive and imaginative to have all the sympathy with women needed to make them total feminists. Our verdict, then, is not that the second premise is false, but that it is pretty controversial.

It may be true, but we have raised enough contrary *possibilities* to show that it needs some support — support that would refute or block the points we have made. This is just what we imply, then, when we find this argument — as it stands — guilty of *problematic premise*.

Our second example comes from a letter to the editor of the *New York Times* (November 4, 1979) written by a Mr. Richard Ahern. Mr. Ahern argued cleverly that since smokers die sooner than non-smokers, and since there are so many smokers, smokers actually save taxpayers vast sums of money in Social Security and Medicaid benefits. In support of his two premises he wrote:

36   Recent news stories told us that:
— Thirty-three percent of all Americans smoke.
— An actuarial study by State Mutual Assurance Company concluded that a healthy, non-smoking 32 year old man can expect
to live 7.3 years longer than a healthy, smoking 32 year old man.

The question we want to raise is whether these premises ought to be ac-
cepted. Notice that if we were seriously to challenge their *truth,* we would have to do a good deal of work. We would have to look up the studies, check their methodology, and possibly repeat them ourselves. The appraisal of this part of Mr. Ahern's argument does not require the effort, for there is no particular reason to question his claim that this data was reported or that the data is reliable. Furthermore, even if the figures are significantly high, the conclusions Mr. Ahern drew from them — that there are large numbers of smokers in America and that they die earlier than non-smokers, and further that the numbers are such that the earlier demise of the smokers saves significant amounts in Social Security and Medicaid benefits — these con-
clusions would still be warranted. So while we might challenge the strict ac-
curacy of Mr. Ahern's figures, we have no basis for a charge of *problematic premise* here. (Mr. Ahern's argument, as it stands, does commit *hasty conclusion.* We will leave it to you to figure out how, if you haven't done so already.)

A final example, this one from an article in *Today,* the weekend supple-
ment widely distributed in Canada, written by Prof. George Grant and titled, "The Case Against Abortion":

37   In 1978, more than 62,000 women had their children killed before
they could be born. An increase in these numbers takes place every
year, so that by the end of 1981, we may nearly have reached the
100,000 level. The percentages are similar in Western Europe. They
are greater in the Soviet Union. Obviously, one cannot be against
abortion when the woman's life is at stake, but that situation is now
exceedingly rare. The present mass fetucide takes place almost

always for convenience. The medical professionals tell us that 95% of abortions are now done to kill healthy offspring of healthy women. How has it happened that this quiet medical slaughter has become part of modern societies everywhere?

Although the last sentence indicates that Grant's argument has broad scope, let us restrict ourselves, in reconstructing it, to its application to Canada. The implicit claim which is the target here seems to be that under present abortion laws, we have a situation of mass fetucide. Here is our diagram of the structure of the argument:

38
1. In 1978, more than 62,000 Canadian women had their children killed before they could be born.
2. An increase in these numbers takes place every year so that by the end of 1981 we may nearly have reached the 100,000 level.
    3. The medical professionals tell us that 95% of abortions are now done to kill healthy offspring of healthy women.
4. The present mass fetucide takes place almost always for convenience.
a Under present abortion laws, there is a situation of mass fetucide (quiet medical slaughter) in Canada.

Grant commits *problematic premise* twice here. (1) requires at least some indication of its source before it can be accepted. Where does Grant get his figures? This is an important point, because it is crucial to his case (how else can he justify the term "mass fetucide") and yet it's not clear to us how he obtained these figures. Hence we would say that there is a reason for not accepting (1) until some defense is offered. (This shows that Condition 3 from the box on problematic premise is satisfied; the diagram makes clear that Conditions 1 and 2 are.) (3) also needs defense. For this is a surprisingly high figure and the judgement "healthy" is a call that could well be controversial, if not ambiguous: is it physical or mental health that is being judged? Who are the medical professionals referred to here? These are some of the problems impeding acceptance of (3) and indicating the need for defense. It, too, is a case of *problematic premise*.

Variants on Problematic Premise

Begging the Question

With three exceptions, we shall be presenting our treatment of a variety of common species of the three basic types of fallacy (irrelevance, insufficiency, unacceptability) in Chapters 3-7. Two exceptions, the fallacies called *begging the question* and *inconsistency*, will be treated here because they are paradigm instances of arguments in which the acceptability requirement is violated. The third, *improper charge of inconsistency*, belongs here because of its connection with *inconsistency*.

Arguments are brought into being by controversy, and by the lack of consensus. Thus the very existence of an argument presupposes the existence of an audience which does not or is not disposed to accept a particular point of view, i.e., the conclusion. Since the purpose of an argument is to lay down a route leading from premises (which the audience already believes or is prepared to accept on reflection) to the conclusion, it is clear that one may not use as a premise of one's argument the conclusion one is seeking to establish. (Such a manoeuvre is the logical equivalent of trying to pull oneself up off the ground by tugging on one's own boot straps.) Yet people often smuggle into their arguments, as premises or support, propositions which are identical to or the equivalent of the conclusion. This is a non-starter. If the conclusion were acceptable, then no argument would be needed in support of it; and if the conclusion is not as it stands acceptable then it cannot be appealed to as a premise. Arguments violating this stricture that the premises must be acceptable independently of the conclusion in this way are said to commit the fallacy of **begging the question** (sometimes still called by its Latin name, *petitio principii* or *petitio*, for short).

The essence of the fallacy is illustrated by the following tale. Two medieval Jews were engaged in a dispute about the spiritual gifts of their respective rabbis. To clinch his case, one of them said, "I'll give you proof positive that my rabbi is the most gifted in the world. Is there another rabbi who dances with the angels every night after he falls asleep?" His friend was skeptical. "How do you know that your rabbi really does dance every night with the angels?" he demanded. "Why," replied the first, "because he told me so himself!" The skeptic insisted, "But can you believe him?" "What?" exclaimed the first angrily, "would a rabbi who dances with the angels each night tell a lie?"

In trying to prove that his rabbi really did dance with the angels, the first chap was called upon to show that his rabbi's word could be trusted. In trying to do that, he used as a premise a proposition ("A rabbi who dances with the angels each night would not tell a lie") which contains as one of its components the conclusion he was trying to establish — that his rabbi danced with the angels. You can see why this form of *begging the question* is also called "arguing in a circle." So the argument offends against the acceptability requirement that the premises may not include the conclusion; that is, each premise must be *different* from the conclusion.

A premise can be the same as the conclusion without having exactly the same wording, as in the example just discussed. As long as the premise expresses the *same proposition* as the conclusion, the effect is the same. Here is the classic textbook example, from the 19th-century treatise, *Elements of Logic* (London, 1862), by Richard Whately:

39   To allow every man unbounded freedom of speech must always be, on the whole, advantageous to the state; for it is highly conducive to the interests of the community that each individual should enjoy a liberty perfectly unlimited of expressing his sentiments.

The flowery phrasing of the argument serves to disguise that it begs the question. If we put the argument into standard form and use some common sense, we can see the flaw.

40   1. It is (a) highly conducive to the interests of the community that (b) each individual should enjoy a liberty perfectly unlimited of expressing personal sentiments.
     2. (b₁) To allow everyone unbounded freedom of speech must always be, on the whole, (a₁) advantageous to the state.

What does it mean for a practice to be (a₁) "advantageous to the state" if not that it is (a) "Highly conducive to the interests of the community"? These two phrases express the very same notion but in different words. And what does it mean to (b₁) "allow everyone unbounded freedom of speech" if not (b) "that each individual should enjoy a liberty perfectly unlimited of expressing sentiments"? "Unbounded freedom of speech" and "a liberty perfectly unlimited of expressing sentiments" are synonymous. The premise says that "each individual should enjoy" such a freedom, while the conclusion states, in effect, that "everyone should be allowed" such a liberty. But these statements are merely semantic variations on the same theme. The premise and the conclusion are one and the same proposition expressed in different words. Thus, the argument *begs the question.*

The first two examples offend against the requirement of acceptability that the premise must not be the same as the conclusion — either in the same words, or in the form of a logically equivalent proposition. The next example shows a violation of the more general stipulation that the acceptance of the premise must not require prior acceptance of the conclusion. The example is from David Ogilvy's *Confessions of an Advertising Man.* Ogilvy was touting his own Rolls-Royce ad, in the last paragraph of which he had written: "People who feel diffident about driving a Rolls-Royce can buy a Bentley." He then went on to argue:

41   Judging from the number of motorists who *picked up* the word "diffident" and bandied it about, I concluded that the advertisement was thoroughly read. (Emphasis ours.)

We've standardized this much of Ogilvy's argument:

42   1. Many motorists picked up the word "diffident" and bandied it about.
      2. The word "diffident" occurred near the end of Ogilvy's 700-word advertisement.
      3. Research shows that readership of advertisements falls off rapidly up to fifty words of copy, but drops very little between 50 and 500 words.
      4. Many motorists thoroughly read Ogilvy's Rolls-Royce advertisement.

Focus on *1*. Is it acceptable? That depends on where Ogilvy thinks the motorists "picked up" the word "diffident," and there's no doubt he thinks they were influenced to use the word by reading his advertisement. That supposition, however, *begs the question*. For if we are to accept *1* — that the motorists picked up "diffident" from Ogilvy's ad — we must already have accepted the argument's conclusion, *C* — that many motorists read the Rolls-Royce ad thoroughly. Since the acceptability of *1* depends on our already having accepted the conclusion, *1* cannot be used to prove that conclusion.

Another form of *begging the question* crops up in arguments against abortion and in arguments against capital punishment. The word "murder" plays a key role in both. Here is what is frequently argued:

43   Abortion is the murder of the (innocent) fetus, so clearly it is wrong (immoral).
      Capital punishment is legalized murder, so it ought to be abolished.

We would agree that if these premises are acceptable, the conclusions are established by the arguments. The problems arise in deciding whether to accept the premises. Is abortion the *murder* of the fetus? Is capital punishment legalized *murder*? Consider what "murder" means. It refers to the killing of a human being, but more than that, to killing which (unlike self-defense) is without moral justification and is therefore wrong. We can accept that abortion and capital punishment are murder only if we already accept that these actions are without moral justification and so wrong. Notice, however, that this is just what the above arguments set out to establish. Their conclusions are that abortion is wrong and that capital punishment is unjustified (and so should be abolished). You can see, then, that we must already accept these conclusions if we are to accept the premises used in these arguments to support them. We are asked, in both cases, to grant in advance the question at issue. Both arguments *beg the question*. The acceptance of a premise must not require prior acceptance of the conclusion of the argument.

The next example introduces a different way *begging the question* can occur. Mickey Spillane's novel, *The Erection Set* was alleged to be pornographic by a Florida political candidate who urged its removal from the shelves of a local library. Spillane's response was very like the following (though it differed in a crucial respect, as we shall see in a moment):

44   For the first thing, I wouldn't write pornography.

Had that been all there was to Spillane's response, we would be asked to grant his conclusion, that *The Erection Set* is not pornographic, on the basis of the premise that Spillane would not write pornography. Can we accept Spillane's premise (as it stands)? Well, we could do so only if *The Erection Set* is not in fact pornographic. Even if nothing Spillane wrote previously had been pornographic, we couldn't accept that he would not write pornography unless his latest book also was not pornographic. But that is exactly what is in dispute; so we would have been asked to accept a premise that would be acceptable only if the conclusion were already true. That argument *begs the question*.

This sort of question-begging has a pattern. *M* makes a charge. *N* replies to the charge by asserting a *more general* claim which, if true, would rebut *M*'s charge; but the claim cannot be accepted until we know on *other* grounds that *M*'s charge is false. Accused of plagiarism, a student defends herself by saying, "I am not a cheater." This may be true, but her premise begs the question and so cannot serve to support her innocence.

We must, to be fair to Mickey Spillane, return to the above example and reproduce his actual first response to the charge that *The Erection Set* is pornographic. What he was quoted as saying was:

45   For the first thing, I wouldn't write pornography because it doesn't sell.

The added clause, "because it doesn't sell" makes all the difference. By including it in his defense, Spillane is seeking to establish his claim that he wouldn't write pornography on evidence that is independent of the contents of *The Erection Set*. He is offering a reason that stands on its own to convince us that he wouldn't write pornography. If he can succeed in doing that, then he will have independently-established evidence that he does not write pornography to use in support of his conclusion (that this particular piece of his writing, *The Erection Set*, is not pornographic). Given his move in the direction of that independent evidence, Spillane did not in fact commit *begging the question*. What may bother you a bit about his response is that it skirts what might seem to be the obvious defensive strategy of an innocent man — appealing directly to the contents of the book. (If he uses indirect arguments when direct ones are available, we think, maybe there is something to the charge.) As it happens, though, the direct route is not as easy as it seems. How do you prove by reference to a book that it is not pornographic without quoting extensively from it, supplying the needed context, and arguing at length? We can see no other way, and Spillane may have rightly reasoned that the accusation was not serious enough to be worth all the effort of a direct defense.

In general, then, one does not *beg the question* if the general claim introduced to rebut a specific charge is argued for on further, independent evidence. So, for example, our friend accused of plagiarizing could avoid *begging the question* by giving lots of evidence that she is not a cheater, evidence that is entirely independent of whether she plagiarized in the case in question. This would not be the strongest kind of case against the charge, but it would not, with that addition, be guilty of *begging the question*.

We can now summarize *begging the question* and present its conditions. Two species are to be found. In one, the premises contain the conclusion, either expressed identically or else stated in a form that is logically equivalent to it. This first version of the fallacy is usually found in longer, compound arguments. The question-begging premise tends to occur in a subordinate argument; the conclusion it begs is one or more steps removed. In the second kind of *begging the question*, the guilty premise is plausible or reasonable only if one already accepts the conclusion. The acceptability of the premise depends on our first accepting the conclusion which it is being used to defend. In brief:

BEGGING THE QUESTION

1. *Q* is offered in an argument as a premise in support of a conclusion *R*.
2. (a) *Q* asserts the same proposition as *R;*
   or (b) in the context of this argument, *Q* is acceptable only if *R* has already been accepted.

We commit *begging the question* in our own arguments, and overlook it in the arguments of others, particularly when we are dealing with issues whose truth strikes us as just self-evident. It is difficult to think of reasons for a claim that seems obvious on the face of it. Hence we end up repeating the claim in different terminology when we try to argue for it, or using premises that *of course* show it to be true (because they presuppose its truth). The message, therefore, should be clear; when dealing with matters close to your heart that seem ever-so-true to you, be on your guard against question-begging reasoning.

When you try to show that this fallacy has occurred, your first move should be to identify the conclusion and the accused premise, and your second move involves finding arguments to show (a) how the two say the same thing, or (b) how in this instance the premise cannot be accepted unless the conclusion is accepted first.

We will add to these remarks about *begging the question* when we get to the fallacies collected under the rubric of *loaded term*, in Chapter 5.

Inconsistency

Without trying to pinpoint the notion exactly, let's talk for a moment about inconsistency. On the one hand, it is debilitating. Psychological experiments have shown that when subjected to inconsistent treatment by researchers, laboratory animals get so frustrated that they become inactive. Nor is it much different with us humans. You yourself must have experienced the frustration of coping with inconsistent demands from parents and teachers. Given the erratic way in which we humans form our beliefs and the sometimes impulsive ways in which we act, it is not surprising that we hold inconsistent beliefs and act in ways that are inconsistent with what we have preached. Another complication is the fact that we sometimes change our minds, whether as the result of careful review of the evidence or the sheer force of a more attractive opinion that comes along and captures our fancy. In short, inconsistency is a frustrating but widespread phenomenon of human life. What we are interested in here is not simply the phenomenon, but specifically the way in which inconsistency betokens a logical failure.

In argumentation consistency plays a crucial role. A good argument lays down a rational route from premises to conclusion: in effect, if you accept the premises then (if you wish to be consistent) you must accept the conclusion. Argumentation, then, assumes that people are sensitive to the requirements of consistency. In short, though we may rightly tolerate some inconsistency in other areas, in argument we cannot do so without defeating the point of the enterprise.

Let us express the concept of inconsistency with more precision. Two *statements* are inconsistent when from the truth of one of them the falsehood of the other follows. For example, consider:

46   (1) Aldo is unfailingly truthful.
          (2) Aldo lied to Louise about his age.

You can see that if (2) is true, then (1) must be false, so (1) and (2) are inconsistent.

We speak of a *person* being inconsistent when he asserts or believes two propositions which cannot both be true at once. Thus if Roger held, in 1982, that Downhill Skiing World Cup winner Steve Podborski was then the best downhill skier in the world, and at the same time believed that Harti Weirather was as good a downhill skier as Podborski, Roger was inconsistent. We also speak of a person being inconsistent if he asserts one thing yet acts in a manner that would not be justified if his assertion were true. A high school advisor wrote to Ann Landers (August 1976) with this comment:

47   A question frequently asked by students is this: "My mom gets bombed every night, double-bombed on weekends, fills the house with smoke, then raises hell when I smoke and gets crazy if I have a drink. Does she have the right to keep me from doing things she says are bad for me when she doesn't practice what she preaches?"

This is a complicated example, but according to part of it the student's mom says that smoking and drinking are bad, yet she smokes and drinks. Her own smoking and drinking would be defensible only if they are not bad. So it looks here as though what she does is justified only if her assertion is false. Mom is inconsistent.

It is *not a fallacy* to assert inconsistent statements or to behave inconsistently with one's pronouncements. The fallacy occurs only when inconsistency of one sort or another undermines an argument. When two premises of an argument are inconsistent, for instance, we are getting conflicting signals from the arguer. She asks us to grant the conclusion on the basis of the premises she offers. However, we cannot tell which of the two inconsistent premises to accept and we can only accept one, at most. Or else a premise presented in the argument is incompatible with something else the arguer says, either on the same occasion or at some other time. Then we face the question: which are we to accept, the premise or the incompatible assertion? We have no way of deciding. The effect of either kind of inconsistency in an argument is to undercut the acceptability of a premise. We cannot then be justified in taking that premise as support for the conclusion. Inconsistency in arguments short-circuits the part of the argument in which it occurs. Vincent Theresa, a former Mafioso, published his reminiscences about the Mob and included the following qualified defense of the brotherhood:

48   Not that mobsters are all bad. There are plenty of good things about them the public might be interested in. For instance, does the public know whether mob guys are patriotic or not. The truth is, most are. *We don't think about undermining the government. We corrupt politicians, but that's only so we can do business.* (Emphasis ours.)

Theresa is trying to persuade us that mob guys are not without redeeming features. The premise is that the Mob is patriotic, and it is defended in turn by Theresa's contention that the Mob has no intention of undermining the government. Theresa then tries to undercut the counter-argument, that the Mafia corrupts politicians, by maintaining that the purpose of such corruption is only to do business (and, presumably, not to undermine the government). The trouble is that, whatever the Mafia's intentions, corrupting politicians does in fact serve to undermine the government. When people find out that politicians are being bought off by the Mafia, they lose confidence in those politicians; and the knowledge that some politicians can be corrupted is bound to undermine one's faith in government. So we are asked to believe that Mob guys are patriotic, and at the same time given evidence that they are not. The result is that the argument goes nowhere. Either the premise that the Mob is patriotic should be accepted, in which case we must reject Theresa's evidence that the Mob corrupts politicians; or else we accept Theresa's evidence, and deny that the Mob is patriotic. We can't do both; we haven't, from the argument and Theresa's comments, any basis for choosing one or the other: we cannot accept the premise.

It is harder to see how inconsistency between assertion and action can undermine an argument. After all, an argument is a piece of discourse, a collection of assertions, while an action is not a statement in any unmetaphorical sense. Still, actions imply statements in that the principle by which any action is justified can be expressed as a statement. This explains why, when the principle of an adjacent action is incompatible with the premise or conclusion of an argument, we find ourselves at a loss which to accept — the premise or conclusion, or the principle. A good example was cited by Professor Trudy Govier in an article in the *Informal Logic Newsletter* (June, 1981):

49   . . . several years ago Ontario and Federal government officials in Canada, having exhorted Canadians to spend winter holiday money at home in Canada, nevertheless abandoned our northern country for winter vacations in Florida and the Caribbean.

We can imagine the following fairly plausible arguments the Canadian officials might have made:

50   1. To help Canada's balance-of-payments position as many Canadian dollars should be kept in the country as possible.
      2. The Canadian economy would benefit from increased spending in our winter tourism and entertainment industries.
      3. Canadians should spend their winter holiday money at home in Canada.

Yet many of these same officials who vacationed in Florida and the Caribbean must have been operating on some such principle as the following:

      PR: It is not imperative that Canadians spend their winter holiday money at home in Canada.

Now our problem as consumers of this argument, given this principle, is that if we accept the principle we clearly must reject the conclusion of the argument (in which case, incidentally, its premises *cannot* be adequate support for it.) On the other hand, if we accept the premises, we are led to accept the argument's conclusions; but then we must reject the principle. The same officials enunciated the argument and acted in conformity with the principle. Which are we to believe; their argument or their actions? The two are inconsistent and we have no way to decide which is acceptable. Hence the argument's premises are undercut and we cannot accept its conclusion in this situation. We shall say, in such cases where conduct conflicts with argument in this way, that the fallacy of **inconsistency** has been committed.

Here are the conditions for the fallacy:

INCONSISTENCY

1. Q is a premise in M's argument for T.
2. (a) Q is inconsistent with some other premise, R, or with some other assertion, S, made by M.

or (b) Q or T is inconsistent with the principle, U, of some action performed or recommended by M.

Here is an example that will test your understanding of these conditions and the fallacy of *inconsistency*. Syndicated columnist Joseph Sobran, in a column that ran in the *Detroit Free Press* (July, 1982), took the liberal press in the U.S. to task for preaching in favour of women's rights and equality for women, while in their practice failing to hire women to top management positions.

51   After the defeat of the Equal Rights Amendment, *Time* ran a cover story about women and equality. The story was written by a man, with the aid of a woman or two. Never mind. It said all the right things. It ringingly affirmed that we are all equal, ...

In the same issue of *Time*, Sobran reported, 24 out of 26 stories were written by men, and only one of the top 24 names on the masthead belonged to a woman (and none of the top 14). Sobran also noted that at *Newsweek*, the top seven jobs are held by men and only three of the top 16 positions are held by women. He found that similar proportions apply to the "great liberal dailies," the *New York Times* (two of the top 16, none of the top eight names on the masthead belong to women) and the *Washington Post* (one female in its top seven, three in its top 17). Sobran went on:

52   Day after day, these publications favor us with articles and columns designed to raise our consciousness on the subject of women's role in society. Why are we so hypnotized by their pompous cant that when an editorial assaults us with it, we don't automatically look down the page to see how the preacher *himself* is behaving?

Our question is this: has Sobran identified instances of the fallacy of *inconsistency*? Note first that unless the articles and columns in question contained *arguments* for equality for women, we cannot speak of a fallacy here, though we could still make the moral judgement of hypocrisy (as Sobran does). Let us assume that some of these press sources do present arguments. Is the fact that an editorial argues for equality for women, while the newspaper or magazine in which it appears is dominated by men at top editorial and management levels, grounds for a charge of *inconsistency?* We believe the answer depends on the hiring practices and policies of the newspaper or magazine in question. Only if it has a policy of hiring women in order to achieve a balance of men and women at all levels of the organization, and is implementing that policy, would the principle of its conduct be consistent with its editorial position. Otherwise, a charge of *inconsistency* would be applicable. Each newspaper and magazine has to be examined on the merits of its own practices, but we are inclined to agree with Sobran that the statistics he cites make a *prima facie* case for inconsistency between preaching and performance, and if the preaching is argument, to suspect that a case for the fallacy of *inconsistency* could be made out.

Improper Charge of Inconsistency

Imagine the following (not-too-likely) state of affairs. The numbers Sobran cited are accurate, but actually *Time, Newsweek, The New York Times* and *The Washington Post* all are at the beginning of five-year plans to balance their male-female ratio in senior editorial and management positions. The women currently in top positions are in fact the leading edge of a development that will result in a 50-50 male-female split by 1988. If that were the case, then Sobran's charge of hypocrisy would not be justified.

Allegations of inconsistency (hypocrisy, double-dealing, two-facedness, insincerity — call them what you will) are serious moral or political charges. If warranted, they often sanction severe condemnation. Hence, when such allegations are unfounded, the indictment is mischievous, or worse. Moreover, charges of inconsistency are among the more common forms of moral and political criticism. Because of the frequency and gravity of accusations of inconsistency, we reserve a fallacy label for unjustified charges: **improper charge of inconsistency.** This will most often be a fallacy of insufficient evidence, though variants that involve arguments with irrelevant or unacceptable premises also can occur.

The following conditions define this fallacy:

IMPROPER CHARGE OF INCONSISTENCY

1. *N* accuses *M* of inconsistency — between assertions, between beliefs and assertions, between beliefs and actions, or between actions.
2. *N's* argument supporting his/her charge fails to provide adequate support for it.

Notice that *improper charge* requires an allegation of inconsistency in some form or another, but not necessarily an allegation of what we just characterized above as the fallacy of *inconsistency*. In other words, arguing inconsistently is only one of many ways of being inconsistent, and we are calling an inadequately defended accusation of *any* form of inconsistency the fallacy of *improper charge*.

Let us turn to some examples.

In the early 1970's *The Windsor Star* excised an entire story from an edition of *Weekend Magazine* and offered the following editorial justification:

53   The removal of a story from the issue of *Weekend Magazine* distributed with Saturday's *Star* was a matter of principle and not of censorship. There was nothing to censor in the story concerned. It was the first of three excerpts from a book written by Bill Trent about the case of Steven Truscott, who was the central figure in a sex crime 12 years ago. Publishing such a story, in the *Star's* opinion, would have been pandering to base tastes.

Do you see any *inconsistency* in the Star's argument? We do. The paper claimed its action was not censorship, but rather the removal of a story avoided "pandering to base tastes." But refusing to print material which "panders to base tastes" *is* censorship, by definition. (The *Star* ought to have said that it considered censorship legitimate in that kind of case. The "principle" referred to in the editorial and used by the *Star* elsewhere to justify cutting out the Truscott article was that convicted criminals should not profit from their notoriety by being paid for their stories.)

Here is an example of an accusation of inconsistency. In October 1975, Canadian Press did a survey of responses to Ontario Attorney-General Roy McMurtry's announced crackdown on hockey violence. (The previous year William McMurtry, a brother of the Attorney-General, had prepared a report for the Ontario government on violence in amateur hockey, recommending that steps be taken to reduce it and citing violence in pro hockey as a contributing factor.) Among those whose views were quoted in the CP story was John F. Bassett, then president of the Toronto Toros. Bassett was quoted as saying:

54   He (McMurtry) was the dirtiest hockey player who ever played, but now that he has the golden robes of office he has become the messiah for his little brother's cause.

Let's assume Bassett's quoted depiction of McMurtry's own hockey play is accurate. The question is, was McMurtry inconsistent because his policy as Attorney-General is incompatible with his own conduct as a player?

Clearly, one can change one's mind and come to disapprove of one's own earlier conduct. And hockey violence is only beginning to be challenged in a large-scale way. Perhaps McMurtry played the game the way it was played in his day (only more so), but later — maybe persuaded by his brother's report — came to disapprove of that style of hockey. So we can imagine a possible line of defense for McMurtry against Bassett.

There's a problem of burden of proof here. On whom rests the onus to produce the evidence? We think it lies with the person who initiates the criticism — in this case, Bassett. He made the accusation of inconsistency and presented evidence for it. However, there is the possible explanation of McMurtry's position that removes the grounds for Bassett's charge. Hence it is up to Bassett to respond to that explanation and either show that his evidence is indeed sufficient to warrant his accusation or else to produce additional evidence to strengthen his case. Since he did not do so in the Canadian Press report of his remarks, we can lay a fallacy charge of *improper charge of inconsistency* against him. The cash value of this charge is not that it refutes Bassett's accusation — for he may have been right, and he may have either been mis-reported or quite ready and able to produce the additional evidence we require. No, its point is rather to serve notice that as things stand, on the basis of the Canadian Press report alone we cannot take Bassett to have proved his case. The fallacy charge then mainly serves here as a red-flag to us, the readers, not to accept without more evidence the claim that McMurtry was inconsistent when he came out as Ontario Attorney-General with a clamp-down on violence in hockey.

Concluding Observations

We've covered three basic fallacies in this chapter, together with three special variations, and we're about to begin an inventory of more. A general point of importance that applies to all fallacies is that the weakness in an argument due to the presence of a fallacy will vary in severity from fallacy to fallacy and instance to instance. *Irrelevant reason* is generally a serious flaw in an argument, for either the premise alone simply does not relate to the conclusion, or relevance can be repaired only by the addition of a further premise the acceptability of which is as dubious as the relevance of the original premise. Check each case on its own merits, for sometimes the irrelevance of a stated premise taken by itself disappears when an obvious and uncontroversial missing premise is made explicit. *Hasty conclusion* in an argument is usually less debilitating than irreparable irrelevance, for it signifies only that although the premises are relevant as they stand, more premises (more evidence) are needed. However, on occasion the problem is not simply that the evidence has not been provided, but that it is not available — it does not exist. In the latter case *hasty conclusion* is fatal to the argument. *Problematic premise* usually signals the least serious flaw in an argument of the three. Its presence generally merely marks the need for additional argumentation — the defense of the premise in question. Again, there will be exceptions, as when the undefended premise turns out to be indefensible.

An argument that *begs the question* is destroyed by that fallacy, or at least the portion of the argument depending on the question-begging premise must be discarded. *Inconsistency* has the same effect; it forces the audience to disregard the opposing premises. Inconsistency can be repaired, however, by instructions from the arguer about which of the incompatible premises to discard. These two fallacies, then, tend to mark extremely serious flaws in an argument. *Improper charge of inconsistency,* depending on the type of case made, may be a fallacy of relevance or of sufficiency or of acceptability, so the harm it does to an argument will vary.

A final point to end this chapter and introduce the next part of the book. Please treat the presence of a fallacy in an argument as a *warning* light, and not as a stop sign. Rare is the argument that is destroyed completely by the presence of a fallacy. Even arguments that beg the question usually contain other, non-question-begging premises. And treat the warning light as an amber flash on your own mental dashboard, not a strobe to beam into the eyes of the arguer whose argument you are assessing. Accusations of "Fallacy!", like personal character attacks, are about the least efficient way to elicit a change in your opponent's reasoning or conclusions. Gentle, patient argument of your own promises much more success.

EXERCISES

Directions

Determine which, if any, of the fallacies discussed in this chapter — *irrelevant reason, hasty conclusion, problematic premise, begging the question, inconsistency, improper charge of inconsistency* — occur in the passages below. Be sure to argue that the *conditions* are satisfied, and do not assume in advance that each of the passages contains a fallacy. Some may be good arguments.

1. *Background:* The following is an excerpt from a book review by J.M. Cameron (*New York Review of Books,* October, 1980) entitled "On the Edge." The book under review is Hayman's book on Nietzsche, and Cameron begins by citing a quote from it:

   This mistake is connected, I suspect, with Hayman's initial agreement with Nietzsche:
      "Nietzsche saw that we can have no objective knowledge about the facts which determine our condition . . . "
   As it stands, this is surely false or without sense. We know many of the facts that determine our condition, even though there are

philosophical techniques for inducing in us perplexities about their analysis.

2. *Background:* Michigan is one of many states which, at present, does not allow capital punishment. Nineteen eighty-two witnessed another round in the debate about whether or not to reinstate the death penalty. One letter opposing the idea came from Willis X. Harris, President of the Michigan Lifers Association (individuals who have been sentenced to life in prison). The following is an excerpt from his letter to the *Detroit Free Press* (March, 1982):

> We have capital punishment in 38 states and their statistics show no significant decrease in capital crimes. The first-degree murderer is least likely to repeat but is more likely to repent. Nationwide, corrections officials report that lifers are the best prisoners and stabilizers in their prisons.

3. *Background:* In his book *The Soviet Approach to International Political Communication,* Paul Herscheneto attributes the following argument to Soviet communicators (p. 305):

> There is a manifest evil in the world. All right thinking people, regardless of party, abhor that evil. The main exponents of the evil are the enemies of the Soviet Union or of the Communist Party. The Soviet Regime, or the party, unflinchingly combats it. Hence, all right thinking people, regardless of party, must count the Soviet Union, or the Communist Party, as an ally, and act accordingly.

4. *Background:* The excerpt below is from "In Defense of Culture, the Unravelling Tie that Binds," by Robert Solomon. It appeared in the *Los Angeles Times* in January, 1981. Solomon is arguing that American cultural identity is threatened and that neither television nor contemporary music is capable of forging the needed cultural ties which would bind Americans together. He writes:

> The same is true of our musical heritage. The Beatles are only a name to most 12 year-olds. Beethoven, by contrast, continues to provide the musical themes we can assume (even if wrongly) that all of us have heard, time and time again. This isn't snobbery, it's continuity.

5. *Background:* From a column by Bob Talbert, a columnist for the *Detroit Free Press:*

> Airlines are funny. They make sure you aren't carrying a weapon of destruction and then sell you all the booze you can drink.

6. *Background:* From a column by James J. Kilpatrick, "Has it been proved that cigarettes cause cancer?," which appeared in the *Detroit Free Press* (March, 1982):

> If cigarettes were carcinogens as surely as cyanides are poison, every person who smokes would come down with cancer. But this is not so. Some heavy smokers live to their 90s and die not of cancer, but of boredom.

7. *Background:* A letter to *The Windsor Star* from E.B. (June, 1982) objected to some of the paper's recent reporting:

> May I draw your attention to a few instances which show either strong bias or gratuitous statements on your part? There are two stories I recall from memory — one dealing with a commemorative service on the second anniversary of the death of Archbishop Romero of El Salvador, and the other on the annual Right to Life demonstration in front of Windsor Western Hospital. In both instances the reporter noted the exact number of people present and then compared this number with the previous year's figures reporting those in attendance at these two events. Both these stories implied that the smaller numbers this year indicated a lessening of interest or importance whereas I know that this is not the case.

8. *Background:* In a column called "Watergate: Who can ever forget it?" (*Detroit Free Press*, June, 1982), William Safire quotes this excerpt from a *Time* article: "Certain effects have found their way into law as a result of Watergate. Congress established the Freedom of Information Act, for example." Safire then writes:

> That act was signed into law by Lyndon Johnson on July 4, 1966 . . . . *Time's* minor historical error illustrates the tendency of journalists to attribute everything good for civil liberty in the past decade to the overthrow of the Nixon gang.

9. *Background:* July 1 is the anniversary of Canadian confederation under the terms of the British North America Act of 1867. The BNA Act refers to Canada as a "Dominion," and the term, "the Dominion of Canada" was used by Canadians and our governments to refer to the country until recently. Over the past dozen years, the word "Dominion" has been phased out by the federal government. For instance, federal departments have been renamed (the "Dominion Bureau of Statistics" became "Statistics Canada," for example). For years, Canadians called the July 1 national holiday, "Dominion Day," but in line with its new

terminology elsewhere the federal government has begun to call it "Canada Day." Against this background you can understand the following letter that appeared in *The Ottawa Journal*:

> In your editorial on Canada's birthday . . . you referred to July 1 as Canada Day. We are all aware that there has never been an act of Parliament to change the name of Canada's birthday from Dominion Day and I am quite sure you are not ignorant of that fact. When you include in your paper, on the editorial page, such a gross inaccuracy, it is difficult for your readers to put much faith in any editorial appearing in your paper.

10. *Background:* In Chapter 11 we shall argue that many advertisements today do not offer arguments to support their claims. Some, however, still do, including the newspaper ad from which we quote this example. The ad was for a brand of so-called "natural" potato chips which were said to contain no additives whatever. The strategy of the ad was to contrast its "no additives" ingredients with the ingredients of a competitor's brand, and making reference to the competitor's ingredients the ad contained the headline, "Is this a 'potato chip' or a chemistry set?". Part of the ad's copy ran as follows:

> The ingredient list on the package of a new so-called "potato chip" reads as follows: Dehydrated potatoes; vegetable shortening; salt; mono- and diglycerides; dextrose; ascorbic acid; sodium phosphates; sodium bisulfite, and BHA added to preserve freshness.
> Now a chemist probably understands this concoction, but where does that leave the rest of us? Are we supposed to eat what we can't even pronounce, much less understand?[4]

11. *Background:* In the early 70s, a commission was established in New York City to investigate allegations of corruption in the police department. One of the witnesses was a police officer who, having once himself been guilty of taking payoffs, turned undercover agent. He was a key witness before the commission, claiming that all plainclothes detectives took regular payoffs and that "there's no way one man can go in a division and remain straight." Following his testimony, the police commissioner told reporters:

> That is an absurd charge. I know for a fact that there are plainclothesmen who are not "on the pad."

---

[4] Thanks to Virginia Kepran for calling this example to our attention.

CHAPTER THREE

FALLACIES OF DIVERSION

Introduction

The four fallacies in this chapter work by diverting attention from the proposition at issue; each accomplishes this diversion in a different way. What is crucial is the *effect*, the tendency to distract or shift the focus of the argument.

Worth noting is the locale of these four fallacies. They typically reside in **adversary** contexts; that is, one person is *attacking* someone else's position, or is *defending* his or her position from someone else's attack. Examples of such contexts are political campaigns, management-labour disputes, public controversy about issues of extreme importance such as capital punishment. In such cases, the arguer runs the risk of wanting too much to defeat the opponent, a desire that can work at cross-purposes to the goal of arriving at the most reasonable position available. This fallacy can happen when the arguer diverts attention from the topic under dispute to territory the arguer thinks provides better ground for victory. So watch for these fallacies, particularly in the adversary context.

Straw Man

You're having an argument with someone. The topic is one you're pretty emotional about. You are aware of several positions that you consider dead wrong. Now your antagonist makes a claim that sounds awfully close to one of those dreadfully mistaken views. In that kind of situation, in the heat of controversy, it is tempting to jump on your opponent for holding that view you're familiar with and (you think) know to be false. You have little patience to be attentive to what may be a fine distinction between what your opponent actually said and the position you are eager to demolish. Or if you think your opponent's stand sounds downright dangerous, or morally loathsome, your emotional antagonism can completely blind you to significant differences between what was said and what it reminds you of. You can find yourself launching into a defense of democracy, free enterprise, or the institution of marriage when your opponent didn't really mean to put any of those in question. Or, finally, if you're devious, you can deliberately misrepresent the views of your opponent, and proceed to make your opponent look silly for saying something you're quite aware he or she didn't say at all.

In any case, when you misrepresent your opponent's position, attribute to that person a point of view with a set-up implausibility that you can easily demolish, then proceed to argue against the set-up version as though it were your opponent's, you commit **straw man**.[1]

Here is an example of the sort of thing we're talking about. The following letter from A.D. to *The Globe and Mail* (June 12, 1982) was occasioned by an article "Disarmament Issue Galvanizes Women" which appeared in the *Globe and Mail* on June 3:

55   From your article, "Disarmament Issue Galvanizes Women," I gather that the Women's Movement, casting around for a badly needed focus, has decided to jump on the nuclear disarmament bandwagon. However, apart from the naivete of this support for a peace movement that Soviet Russia has been praising for some time now, what struck me as ludicrous were the comments of those who believe that only women can solve the world's problems because they claim women have a "different mind set" and believe in negotiation, whereas men believe in war.

These women should be reminded that the toughest, most single-minded rulers in this modern world have been, or are, women — Margaret Thatcher, Golda Meir, Indira Gandhi to mention but three of many. They also need to be told what should be obvious: only the strong stay free, and if we disarm unilaterally (this is the ultimate goal of this highly manipulated peace movement) we shall be taken over by totalitarianism.

There are two distortions here that need to be noted carefully. In the second paragraph, A.D. attributes to the peace movement the aim of unilateral disarmament, which he then goes on to attack briefly. There may of course

---

[1] The term probably originated from the practice of making a straw effigy of someone under severe criticism, then burning it. Cf. Alfred H. Holt, *Phrases and Word Origins* (New York: Dover Publications, 1961), p. 172.

be some individuals or groups who favour this course of action. But most of those active in nuclear disarmament favour mutual disarmament, i.e., simultaneous moves by both the Soviet Union and the United States. Or they wish a "no first strike" position to be reached. A.D.'s description, therefore, is a distortion of the position held by most rather than an accurate statement of it.

In the first paragraph, he attributes to the Women's Movement the notion that "only women can solve the world's problems" which he then goes on to attack. Again, this is a distortion. It may be that a few feminists hold this position, but most do not. What they do wish to see is greater involvement of women in high level talks and discussions.

In both instances here, A.D. misrepresents the position he opposes, and then proceeds to criticize his distorted version of it, leaving the (false) impression that his criticisms undermine the actual position held by the people he identifies. This is the fallacy we call *straw man*.

A lovely run of straw man fallacies appeared in an exchange over capital punishment in *The Windsor Star* a few years ago. First, here is part of the letter to the editor from Prof. Lawrence LaFave against capital punishment that started the debate off. Please read this excerpt carefully:

56   The vast majority of Canadian policemen appear to favour capital punishment, especially when one of their colleagues is murdered in the line of duty. These policemen are entitled to their opinion. However, the public should not take their views on this subject seriously and the mass communications media (with special reference to *The Windsor Star*) should not continue to give so much space to their views.

Reading Comprehension Test

Without glancing back at Example 56, answer the following questions about it:

(a) Prof. LaFave opposes letting police express their opinions. True____ False____

(b) Prof. LaFave thinks the public should disregard the views of police on capital punishment. True____ False____

(c) Prof. LaFave thinks the media should not report the views of police on capital punishment. True____ False____

(d) Prof. LaFave thinks the pro-capital punishment view of police should be suppressed, censored, or ignored. True____ False____

The correct answer is, in each case, False.

(a) The only thing LaFave says that might relate to whether policemen should be allowed to express their pro-capital punishment views is his statement that they are "entitled to their opinion." That might be understood to imply he thinks they should be allowed to express it; he certainly nowhere says they shouldn't be allowed to.

The second statement, (b), is tricky. LaFave does say the public shouldn't take police views on capital punishment seriously, but that's not the same thing as disregarding their views. For instance, you may not take the views of terrorist revolutionaries seriously, yet still think it important not to completely disregard those views. You don't ponder their ideology trying to decide whether to adopt it yourself, but you do make a point of noting it, particularly since it represents a threat to international security.

Third, (c), LaFave didn't encourage the media not to report police views; he merely urged them to reduce the amount of space devoted to reporting the police viewpoint. Finally, (d), he said absolutely nothing at all about suppressing or censoring police opinions, nor did anything he said lead to such a suggestion. What we've said about "disregarding" goes for "ignoring" those opinions, too.

If you answered "True" to any of the questions, you did not read carefully enough. It is an imperative starting point we cannot stress too much that you read or listen to the statement of a position with great care. Unless you do, you won't be evaluating the actual assertions you're looking at. You'll be reviewing some different position — if you criticize it, you'll be committing *straw man* yourself.

The point of this little exercise was not just to reemphasize the importance of careful reading. It was also to prepare you for *The Windsor Star*'s editorial response to Prof. LaFave's letter, The *Star* began by quoting the segment of the letter we've been looking at, and then went on to say:

57   Wrong, Dr. LaFave. The policemen are entitled to their opinion, as your letter says. But policemen — and any other group — are also entitled to express their opinions and have them reported. The media would be failing in their responsibility if they did not give space to the opinions of such groups. And on the subject of capital punishment, a good case can be made for greater attention to the view of police groups, which are close to the situation. Nor should such views be disregarded by the public.

The Star agrees with Dr. LaFave in his opposition to capital punishment, and disagrees with the anti-abolition stand which he feels is the majority view of Canadian police officers. But the Star does not agree that the view should be suppressed, censored, or ignored. Democracy is a process of making choices after the facts are known and the alternatives discussed and the opinions weighed.

We want to charge the *Star* with four counts of *straw man* in this rejoinder. The fallacy can be characterized in general in terms of the following conditions, so we'll need to show that the *Star's* response to LaFave qualifies on each point:

STRAW MAN

1. *M* attributes to *N* the view or position, *Q*.
2. *N*'s position is not *Q*, but a different one, *R*.
3. *M* criticizes *Q* as though it were the view or position actually held by *N*.

We've already covered the first two. By basing our four questions on quotes from the editorial (see Reading Comprehension Test, above), we've shown that the *Star* misrepresented the writer's position. And the *Star* went on to criticize the views it falsely attributed to LaFave. It wrote, "Wrong, Dr. LaFave," referring to the first three claims, and in the second paragraph proceeded to disagree with the fourth. If you'll reread the *Star's* rejoinder, you'll see that it is engaged in supporting claims it takes to be opposed to Dr. LaFave's position. That's one standard way of criticizing a position: show its opposite to be true. Of course, this procedure also reinforces the erroneous impression that LaFave actually did hold the opposite view.

The parade of *straw men* in this exchange did not end there. Prof. LaFave wrote a rejoinder to the *Star* exposing the *straw men* we have noted, adding:

58   The Star suggests I am anti-democratic. By its view of democracy, if an inmate of a feeble-minded institute, innocent of physics, argued he had refuted Einstein's theory of relativity, his statement ought to be granted as much press coverage as the same claim by an eminent physicist. If 10 out of 10 physicians believe a man has measles, while 11 out of 11 street cleaners deduce he does not, then by Star logic he (by a vote of 11 to 10) does not have measles.

The writer's point here is that the *Star* is committed to a view of democracy that would give the incompetent as much voice as the expert and permit majority rule to decide in matters best left to specialists.

We shall turn the tables on LaFave and accuse him of committing *straw man* in the above passage. But before we do, we must take time out for two ancillary observations.

1. Look at our sentence following this last quotation from the writer. In that one sentence we have compressed his views, and given an interpretation of what he's saying or actually committed to. We've tried to cut through his vivid metaphors and express the point that it seems he meant to make.

Slipping your fingers through the murk of rhetoric and withdrawing the kernel of assertion is a skill you'll need to become proficient at to evaluate arguments in ordinary situations. That is, a requisite skill of applied logic is identifying and stating the proposition that's actually being conveyed in a text of heavily rhetorical speech or writing.

2. Notice, too, that LaFave was extrapolating the view of democracy he attributed to the *Star*. He drew an inference from what was said. The position he attributed to the *Star* was one he took to be logically implied by what it stated. Specifically, he took three points: (i) the *Star's* insistence that it should give space to police opinions about capital punishment, (ii) the *Star's* disregarding his own claim (argued elsewhere in his letter) that the police have no special competence to judge the merits of capital punishment, and (iii) the *Star's* lecture on democracy. From them he drew the inference that the *Star* endorsed a view of democracy that would extend majority rule to decide matters of specialized knowledge and give equal media coverage to the views of both laypersons and authorities on subjects calling for expertise.

This move, extrapolation from a stated position, is frequently a means of exploring the merits of the position. To avoid *straw man,* it is essential to stick to inferences logically warranted by the original position.

Now to Professor LaFave: he committed *straw man* himself in this part of his rejoinder because he attacked (by ridicule) an extrapolation not entailed by the *Star's* stated views about democracy. We say it's not entailed because we don't think enough is said in the brief response to be able to pin this theory onto it. The *Star* may hold this view, but neither LaFave nor we can know that from the scant bit that's been said. In ridiculing a theory of democracy that he had no adequate grounds for attributing to the *Star,* LaFave committed the very fallacy which he had rightly accused the newspaper of.

Next consider this example. R.R. wrote the following letter to *The Vancouver Sun* (November 1974):

59   I was shocked to read about the Canadian Bar Association's proposal to make heroin legally available for addicts to prevent them from being the "criminal menace" they are now.

Such an absurd proposal coming from a prestigious body as the CBA must be a sure sign that they feel no other workable solution exists for the handling of the heroin addiction problem. It is frightening to realize that the bar association is willing to condemn a man to a life of addiction on a deadly drug just to keep him from stealing and to keep him out of their legal hair . . .

Ignore the *hasty conclusion* in the second sentence and look at the last sentence. R.R. asserted there an extrapolation from the CBA's proposal. He was assuming that making heroin legally available to addicts would condemn them to lifelong addiction. For that reason he denounced the proposal as "absurd."

R.R.'s objection would be fair enough if indeed a probable consequence of the CBA's suggestion would be guaranteed addiction for present addicts. But why expect that outcome? If heroin became legally available to addicts, most of these addicts would be more easily identified as needing treatment. There would be no reason to expect that rehabilitative programs would cease to function with the legalization of heroin. On the contrary, they might be more successful, since they would not have the added obstacle of dealing with the criminal subculture. For these reasons, we believe that R.R.'s extrapolation is iffy; consequently, his slam against the CBA's proposal is based on a distortion. The conditions for *straw man* are satisfied.

To detect *straw man*, you have to keep abreast of the positions taken by others on matters you're interested in. If you don't know who holds what position, then your defenses are down and you'll find yourself persuaded by implausible criticism. All argumentation in the adversary context must abide by this principle:

> The position under attack must actually be the position held.

If we add the realization that even the best-intentioned critic may alter the position he or she is attacking, we come up with another principle of logical self-defense:

> When *N* and *M* are on the opposite sides of the issue, you should be sceptical of *M*'s characterization of *N*'s views.

Be cautious of arguments with this move: "Now my opponent believes that . . . , but such a view is surely wrong because . . . ." Find out for yourself what the opponent's position is, don't take the critic's word for it. If you follow these two principles you will avoid being diverted by *straw man* rejoinders.

One final example. Early in U.S. President Ronald Reagan's presidency, he forwarded to the Senate the name of Justice William P. Clark to be the deputy secretary of state under Alexander Haig. Many Senate Democrats objected to this nomination on the grounds that Clark did not have sufficient knowledge of world and current affairs, a fact which became clear in his testimony before the Senate, where Clark astounded some by his ignorance of world politics. Herewith a letter from R.B. of Pasadena to the *Los Angeles Times* (February 10, 1981):

60 The criticism of Justice William P. Clark's nomination to be deputy secretary of state . . . emanates from those who worship at the Shrine of Rote Recall — as though life's problems were like a big crossword puzzle instead of analytical.

That a big collection of miscellaneous facts on every subject under the sun available at the tip of the tongue is not sufficient for success has been well illustrated by a recent occupant of the White House.

In claiming that the big collection of miscellaneous facts is not a sufficient condition for success, R.B. is implicitly attributing to those critical of Clark's nomination the position that the possession of such a big collection is a sufficient condition. But that was not their position at all. They were not saying that if Clark had such a collection he would be successful. They were arguing that absence of detailed knowledge of world politics was a significant lack in the man who is to occupy the number two position in the State Department. Nor were they worshipping the Shrine of Rote Recall: their complaint was not that Clark did not have rote recall but that he didn't seem to know these things in the first place. So R.B. here is attacking a *straw man*.

Ad Hominem

When you disagree with something, the logically appropriate response is to aim your critical arrows at that position itself. We have just seen how one diversion from the issue consists instead of attacking a *straw man*. Another common tactic in adversary contexts is to ignore the issue altogether and go for the person who asserted it. An irrelevant attack on the person, instead of the position, is the fallacy called **ad hominem.**

In April 1976, Paul Desrochers launched a scathing attack on the media in a speech before the Montreal Chamber of Commerce. (Desrochers was an advisor to Quebec Premier Robert Bourassa from 1969 to 1974.) In that speech (according to an editorial in *The Windsor Star,* April 1976), Desrochers urged businesses to withdraw advertising from the news media that do not admit errors and falsehoods; claimed that the press was conducting "a systematic campaign . . . aimed at weakening our institutions and the men who run them so as to bring them down more easily"; stated further that the media "are conducting hate campaigns against businessmen and their 'natural allies' politicians, reminiscent of the inquisition of the Middle Ages"; and charged that the press is destroying careers and reputations without reason. As the *Star* itself commented, "Pretty heavy stuff, that."

The *Star* could have attacked Desrochers's position by, for example, claiming that his allegations were vastly overstated or by challenging Desrochers to back them up with specifics. Instead, it chose to attack Desrochers personally and thereby attempted to discredit his position without actually confronting it:

61   We shall temporarily overlook the fact that the 1975 Cliche Commission Inquiry into Labor Violence: said that he was "imprudent"

for having held shares through his family in a Montreal building where the provincial government rented space while he was a Bourassa adviser;

revealed that patronage appointments to senior James Bay hydro project jobs had been done through his office, completely bypassing the Quebec Public Service Board;

discovered that Desrochers attempted to negotiate a 10-year no-strike deal, illegal at that time, with construction union leaders at James Bay, and approached the same leaders at election time . . .

And perhaps it is pure coincidence that he resigned his governmental post just after a story broke about his part in awarding a $25 million television contract to the Olympics, suggesting a substantial bribe, and just prior to the Cliche Commission report.

Note what the *Star* has done. It has attempted to discredit Desrochers's character by suggesting, with its reference to the findings of the Cliche Commission, that he is a shady operator. But the *Star* managed to say nothing about the charges made by Desrochers. It attacked his person rather than his position. Even if Desrochers were guilty of the misdeeds the *Star* imputes to him, would that show his criticisms of the media to be unfounded? Whether the media are guilty of weakening business and political institutions by conducting hate campaigns against businessmen and politicians is one question; whether Paul Desrochers sailed a little close to the winds of illegality or impropriety in his own business dealings is quite another. The *Star's* personal attack on Desrochers is irrelevant to the truth of his allegations, and so the *Star* commits *ad hominem.*

It is instructive to look at this example a bit more closely. Having exposed the *Star's* ad hominem attack, we wonder what may have been behind the editorialist's irrelevant rejoinder to Desrochers's charges. Perhaps the *Star* was reacting with a natural enough defensiveness, and lashing out with a counterattack. More likely, though, the *Star* was trying to make the point that Desrochers's own conduct was precisely the sort of questionable mixture of business and politics that the press was rightly exposing, so Desrochers's criticisms of the press were themselves a defensive counterattack — an attempt to divert attention from his own dubious conduct to a different topic, namely, the conduct of his critics. The trouble is that the *Star* did not *say* any of this; it did not put its personal criticisms of Desrochers into such a context that would give them relevance. In this case, our charge of *ad hominem* initiates a deeper probing of the argumentative interaction and leads to a different, and less harsh, verdict against the *Star's* reasoning.

Most often *ad hominem* occurs when someone attacks the individual who has advanced an argument instead of attacking the argument itself. However, the *ad hominem* is not limited to responses to arguments; it can occur wherever anyone has taken a position, even if that position is without benefit of argumentative support. For instance, we give you the following typical reply. In the April 1982 issue of *Harper's,* James Kenneson had an article called "China Stinks," in which he detailed his year's experience in the province of Zhengzhou. What Kenneson had to say about Zhengzhou was not at all flattering, and it brought this response from C.S. of Dallas (*Harper's,* June 1982):

62　　I regret that *Harper's* was used as a vehicle to spread the stench by James Kenneson, who wrote the article "China Stinks," in the April issue. I can't believe that such a distinguished magazine would want to nauseate its readers with such undigested material. It is obviously the work of a *constipated* and *jaundiced* man who has just spent a year in outlandish and poverty stricken Zhengzhou, where there was no running water, toilet or other amenities of life to which Mr. Kenneson had been so accustomed in Indianapolis. (Emphasis ours.)

Instead of addressing the response to the actual assertions that comprise Kenneson's position, C.S. attacks Kenneson personally (in the words we italicized). If Kenneson's position were inadequate, if his facts were incorrect, his interpretations questionable, then C.S. should be willing to detail these for us instead of launching a personal attack on the author. Such an attack is irrelevant (we don't need to know or determine whether Kenneson was constipated, literally or metaphorically) as far as an assessment of his position goes.

　　"Ad hominem" — from the Latin phrase *argumentum ad hominem,* meaning "argument against the person" — is characterized by the following conditions:

AD HOMINEM

1. *M* responds to *Q*, a position *N* has taken, by attacking *N* rather than by attacking *Q*.
2. The attack on *N* is not relevant to the assessment of *Q*.

The attack on the person can come in a variety of forms: a criticism of his or her personality or character, a derogatory crack about the ethnic or racial background, a condemnation of behaviour ("People in glass houses shouldn't throw stones" is an example of that one), or speculation about motives or special interests. In fact, any response qualifies as "attacking *N*" for purposes of *ad hominem,* if the response steers attention away from the substance of what is under debate and toward the person who proposed it by seeking to discredit that person.

However — and we want to put this "however" in flashing lights — finding a controversy in which someone has been personally criticized is not enough to charge *ad hominem*. In certain situations it is relevant to attack a person as a means of discrediting that person's views. That's why we require Condition 2: to say, in effect, that *ad hominem* cannot be charged when reference to the person can be relevant to an assessment of his or her position.

It's difficult to come up with a rule of thumb for distinguishing legitimate from illegitimate criticisms of the person when the dispute is over a position. You will have to judge each case on its merits.

Try on this next example. First the background: in July 1972, novelist Joan Didion wrote an essay-review of the literature on "The Women's Movement" for the *New York Times Book Review*. In reviewing a sample of 15 books, Ms. Didion argued that the literature was "mired in trivia" and didacticism; that "half truths, repeated, authenticated themselves"; that many women supporting the movement were "converts who want not a revolution but romance." In sum, she concluded, "the Women's Movement is no longer a cause but a symptom." Her article brought in a flood of replies. Here's one:

63   So Joan Didion can afford the luxury of intellectualizing the Women's Movement . . . I can't. My reaction to her article is pure, gusty anger. "Litany of trivia," she writes. "Not revolution but romance!" Miss Didion, may your next review for the *Times* be written while one diaper needs changing, one grilled cheese needs tending, and a lasagna needs to be made for company dinner. Baby, that's how I'm writing this letter . . .

Once again, we need to sift through the rhetoric, and identify the point being made. The writer thought Didion was mistaken in her assessment of the Women's Movement, but instead of arguing her point, she challenged Didion's credentials as a critic of the Movement. Her point seems to have been: Unless you've tried to do something outside the role of homemaker, while at the same time having to look after babies, make meals, and so on, you can't know what it's like, so you're in no position to criticize the Movement. The writer attacked Didion, but did not try to show that her criticisms were wrong. The first condition of *ad hominem* is met, but is the second? Can a person sufficiently understand the Women's Movement and its literature to assess it intelligently without having experienced the confinement and frustrations of the roles of homemaker and mother? Was this slam at Didion's qualifications in fact irrelevant? (Consider analogous questions: Can one understand what it is like to live in poverty without having been poor? Is the experience of poverty necessary for a fair assessment of discussions of poverty?) Since we see arguments in both directions, we reserve judgement about whether Didion's critic committed *ad hominem* until we can follow them up.

Instead of a rule of thumb or a general principle indicating when it is relevant to attack the person, and hence when such a criticism cannot be called *ad hominem,* we can give a partial list of sorts of circumstances.

A. Appeals to authority, or to expert opinion. If I ask you to believe something I say using the argument that an authority or expert on the subject says it's true, you may legitimately question the background or motives of that authority. If I'm asking you to accept the point just because she or he says so, then it's fair to challenge credentials and to be critical of the authority's interests. Suppose I tell you that a certain make of ski is good and cite Kathy Kreiner's endorsement of it as my authority. If you point out that Kreiner is employed by that manufacturer and makes a percentage on gross sales of those skis each year, you don't commit *ad hominem* — even though you are attacking her motives in endorsing the product instead of evaluating the skis on their own merits. For, in the case we're imagining, Kreiner's endorsement of the skis may be judged — indeed, should be judged — in the light of her tie with the manufacturer. She would have an interest in people's buying those skis whether they were good ones or not. On the other hand, she might have chosen to endorse one manufacturer's skis over the other brands because of their superior merits — and this fact should be noted in the argument too.

B. Candidates for positions of public trust. No matter what arguments a candidate puts forward for being qualified for the office sought, it is always legitimate to consider his or her character and background. Not every facet would be fair game for critical appraisal. It wouldn't particularly matter if the leader of a party turned out to have a preference for the Rolling Stones rather than Ravel. If, on the other hand, he or she had a history of coronary attacks, or were suffering from an incurable and interminable disease, these factors would probably outweigh even the best arguments and someone who made them known would not be guilty of *ad hominem.* The reason is clear: in electing an official, we elect the human being, not just the mind that shapes the policies.

C. Cases of credibility. Courtroom proceedings furnish the clearest examples here. Suppose someone has testified in court. If that person is found to be a habitual liar, then this fact damages his or her credibility. The lawyer who points out this personality trait is attacking the person as a means of discrediting the testimony, not as an alternative to confronting it.

It should be clear why *ad hominem* is a fallacy. An argument is an attempt to elicit our consent to the truth of a proposition by appealing to other propositions we accept — not by appealing to force, flattery, or personality. If you disagree with a claim, logic demands that you inspect the reasons put forward to support it. You normally need know nothing about the person who happens to put forward the claim, whether he or she is rich or poor, Indian or WASP or Québecois, votes Liberal, Conservative, or NDP.

Ad hominem is obviously fallacious. Why do people continue to commit it and be persuaded by it? Maybe because there's something satisfying, emotionally, about putting down someone you disagree with. It's irritating to admit that someone you dislike has made a valid point. Also, when you identify with a view, an attack on it seems like an attack on you, so it's natural to counter with a personal challenge of your own. Logical self-defense requires some detachment from your beliefs — the Socratic ideal of pursuing the truth, wherever the path to it may lead.

Guilt by Association

Suppose one of your friends works for a day-care centre and another for a family-planning bureau; because of these friends, your parents conclude that you're "one of those Women's Libbers" and a pro-abortionist. Suppose you express agreement with environmentalists' concerns about pollution from petroleum exploration in the Arctic, so your parents accuse you of being "a damned socialist." What has gone wrong? Certainly people who associate with one another have some common interest, but that doesn't mean all their beliefs are identical. And people and groups can have some beliefs in common without accepting everything the others believe.

These obvious rules can be ignored in the heat of debate. Especially in adversary contexts, you can be tempted to transfer some perceived discredit to an opponent, based on some association that person has with a supposedly discreditable individual or group. The attack is usually (though not always) *ad hominem* in form, since its objective is to refute or discount the opponent's position by focusing on his or her person. But it is an *indirect* strike against the person, made by transferring alleged "guilt" that has accrued to someone else, or to some other group or doctrine, from them to the opponent, using the connection between them as a bridge. The move is the fallacy called **guilt by association**, when the mere association is *not* reason enough to attribute any opprobrium to the opponent.

Some examples should elucidate the fallacy. In 1975 the Liberal federal government proposed a pay raise for Members of Parliament. The federal New Democratic Party opposed it, and soon the debate hit the newspapers. At one point an NDP worker wrote to several newspapers outlining his party's position. The publication of that letter was soon followed by the publication of a reply from a Liberal Party official, from which we take this excerpt:

64   Every NDP member accepted the parliamentary increase in 1970, even when they spoke against it; and Ed Broadbent, the NDP parliamentary leader, has already admitted that he will accept any new increase. It seems to me that the NDP is engaged in a large scale exercise in hypocrisy. This impression is strengthened by the knowledge that the NDP government in British Columbia doubled members' salaries there shortly after taking office.

Are the *federal* NDP Members of Parliament hypocrites because the British Columbia *provincial* NDP government increased salaries for members of the provincial Legislative Assembly in Victoria? The "guilt" alleged here is inconsistency — a respectable line of political criticism if it can be backed up. But the federal NDP cannot be held responsible for the policies of a provincial New Democrat government. The two are independent authorities, dealing with different social, economic, and political exigencies. The Liberal official who wrote the above letter tried to get us to accept that the association in name and general political outlook would carry over to particular political policy. Since it does not, he committed *guilt by association.* (We must be careful not to charge the federal Liberal Party with the fallacy. If we did so, we'd be guilty of it ourselves — tarring the whole party with the brush that can in fairness only be used against one of its overzealous officials.)

When Dr. Bette Stephenson was president of the Canadian Medical Association in 1974-75, she pressed for liberalized abortion laws. Her stance provoked this letter from L.M. to *The Edmonton Journal* (January 1975):

65　　Perhaps it is not Canadian law which ought to be called into question but the arrogant attitude of the president of the Canadian Medical Association. Laws should be designed to afford reasonable protection for all human life. Statutes made and enforced by sensible, civilized societies should not provide for the thoughtless, wholesale slaughter of those considered to be less than human by some. Remember Dachau and Auschwitz.

L.M. associates Dr. Stephenson's position with the Nazi concentration camps where millions of Jews and other "undesirables" were murdered under Hitler's horrifying program of genocide — and invites enormous antagonism to her views. To suggest that association, L.M. had first to create a *straw man,* by describing Dr. Stephenson's proposals for more liberal abortion laws as entailing "the thoughtless and wholesale slaughter of those considered to be less than human by some." With the distortion in hand, L.M. had only a slight jump to make to forge a link with the Nazi extermination camps. But the link is complete fabrication. The CMA president wasn't calling for thoughtless and wholesale slaughter. Furthermore, favouring liberalized abortion laws does not require believing that the fetus is less than human. One might, for example, take the position that the fetus is a human being but that the mother's right to life can, in some circumstances, take precedence over the fetus's. Finally, even if Dr. Stephenson did believe that a fetus is "less than human," that's a far cry from considering it subhuman in the way Hitler and the Nazis viewed so-called non-Aryans. L.M. committed *guilt by association* by alleging a non-existent association. That's a slightly different blunder from the one in the Liberal official's attack on the NDP, where an association did exist, but wasn't strong enough to support the connection based on it.

The following conditions cover the central cases of this fallacy:

GUILT BY ASSOCIATION

1. *M* attacks *N* (or *N*'s position, *Q*) on the basis of some alleged association between *N* (or *Q*) and some other person, group or belief(s).
2. (a) The alleged association does not exist at all;
or (b) the alleged association does not provide relevant or sufficient support for *M*'s criticism.

Guilt by association crops up in a variety of forms. It took a curious turn in the reaction of a political official to a rowdy reception given Queen Elizabeth in Stirling, Scotland, by anti-royalist students (AP, October 1972):

66   Four hundred students chanted obscene songs and hurled insults at the Queen, jostling the royal entourage during a ceremony at the university . . .

The scenes involving the Queen, the worst in Britain of her 20-year reign, were criticized by leading Scots. The Conservative party chairman in Scotland, Sir William McEwan Younger, said: "*The damage done to all Scotland's image across the world is incalculable.*" (Emphasis ours.)

Sir William's fear would have foundation only if we assume that people the world over would commit *guilt by association*. For there is no reason to condemn "all Scotland" just because of the behaviour of a few hundred Scottish students. Did Sir William commit the fallacy, or did he merely assume that *we* would?

Identifying *guilt by association* becomes dicey when it is not clear whether the association does justify the criticism based on it. This problem is well illustrated by a passage in Gérard Pelletier's book, *The October Crisis*, about the kidnappings of the British trade commissioner, James Cross, and the Québec government labour minister, Pierre Laporte, by the terrorist group working for the separation of Québec from Canada, the FLQ (le Front de Libération du Québec) — and the federal, provincial and Montréal civic governments' handling of that crisis — in October 1970.

The crisis began on October 5, when a cell of the FLQ kidnapped Cross from his home in Montréal. In return for his release they demanded the release from jail of several people they claimed were political prisoners — FLQ members who had been convicted of terrorist bombings, among others — and also the dissemination through the media of an FLQ "manifesto." The manifesto was read on TV, and its description of economic conditions in the province of Québec struck a sympathetic chord with many who in no way approved of the FLQ's terrorist tactics. But the prisoners were not released, and on October 11 a second FLQ cell kidnapped the provincial Minister of Labour, Pierre Laporte, a popular and influential Québec politician, from his home in a Montréal suburb. Five days later the federal government invoked the War Measures Act — a law passed to deal with internal crises during wartime, and hitherto invoked only during the Second World War. The government claimed that a state of "apprehended insurrection," one of the conditions which permit applying the Act, existed in Québec. The army was called in to protect federal Members of Parliament in Ottawa, and to police Montréal. Civil liberties were suspended across the country. It was declared retroactively illegal to have belonged to the FLQ. And over four hundred people were arrested and jailed without warrants. On October 17, Laporte's garrotted body was found in the trunk of an abandoned car. Several weeks later the police located the FLQ hideout where Cross was being held. The federal government negotiated his release in return for allowing the kidnappers and their families to leave Canada for sanctuary in Cuba. Laporte's murderers were subsequently caught, tried, convicted and sentenced to long jail terms.

The following passage comes from the section of Pelletier's book titled, "The confusion between the *FLQ* and the Parti Québecois." The Parti Québecois is a Québec provincial political party, led by René Lévesque when Pelletier wrote (and as we write), which had (and has) as its long-term goal the separation of Québec from Canada by legal political means. The FLQ, in contrast, was an underground urban guerrilla group committed to the goal of independence of Québec from Canada by any means, legal or illegal.

Pelletier was generally careful to distinguish the two, but he argued that the Parti Québecois should "purge itself of its undesirable elements," and went on to berate Pierre Bourgault, a leading member of the party:

67   When Mr. Bourgault declares: "We are five million political prisoners," he is clearly saying: "The FLQ is leading the action and it is they who represent us. The political prisoners are being punished for our sake because they tried to free us from slavery." These words are proof of an unconscious indulgence on Mr. Bourgault's part towards the strategy of the FLQ. When Mr. Lévesque says that people are doing their utmost to confuse the PQ with the FLQ, he should begin by cleaning his own house.[2]

---

[2] McClelland and Stewart Limited, Toronto/Montreal, 1971, paperback edition, p. 179.

In extrapolating the way he did from Bourgault's statement, Pelletier left himself open to a charge of *straw man*. Still, he may have just overstated an otherwise valid case. Did the similarity of Bourgault's rhetoric to that of the FLQ, pronounced in the midst of the crisis, warrant the conclusion of "an unconscious indulgence" towards the FLQ strategy? We can imagine arguments on both sides in answer to that question. However, Pelletier goes further and uses his association of Bourgault with the FLQ to criticize in turn the Parti Québécois. Can the entire party be discredited because of the views of one of its members? The answer is not so clear, since Bourgault was a leading figure in the party. In this sort of case, the question whether *guilt by association* has been committed leads to further questions about substantive issues, as it leads, in the case of Pelletier's charge, to a need for a judgement about political responsibility.

Red Herring

You will recall the spiked-doll example we used to illustrate the generic fallacy of *irrelevant reason* in Chapter 2. Consumers were objecting to a doll on the market whose head could be removed by any toddler to reveal a dangerous spike (which had held on the head). They wanted the government to outlaw such products. A spokesman for the toy company manufacturing the doll replied to this proposal by saying, "All the legislation in Canada isn't going to protect a child against the normal hazards of life." We argued then that this reply was irrelevant: the issue was not protecting children against "the normal hazards of life," but protecting them against hazards that could readily be avoided.

Now, in defense of the toy company spokesman one might object that he surely did not believe his reply was relevant. Its irrelevance was so blatant that it would be uncharitable to believe he could have intended it as a reason for not having legislation to protect children against hazards due to cheap and ill-designed construction of toys. If we accept this rejoinder, then we are left with the question: What *was* the point of the spokesman's reply? It seems plausible to interpret it along the following lines. The toy company was under attack for a pretty blatantly dangerous feature of its doll, and faced pressure for legislation which would force it to redesign the doll, as well as possibly withdraw all the spiked dolls already manufactured from the marketplace — both expensive prospects. No sound defense of the doll that would meet public acceptance seemed available. (The public would unlikely be sympathetic with the argument that this was the cheapest way to attach the doll's head, or that complying with the proposed legislation would cost the company money.) In that adversary situation, it may have appeared that the best defense was to take the offensive. Set up a new issue — the sensibleness of trying to protect children against the normal hazards of life — that has some tenuous connection with the old one, and where the company could hold a defensible position. Then, by thus changing the subject, attention would be distracted from the hazards of the spiked doll and the heat would be taken off the company. Such a strategy, while it might not appear ethical to an impartial observer, would at least be clear of the charge of silly irrelevance.

Whether or not we have accurately described the spokesman's intent, his reply certainly could easily have had the effect of changing the subject and so distracting the critics from the original issue. This move, intentional or not, is quite common in arguments in adversary situations. It is called introducing a "red herring," and from this term, which is in widespread use, we take the name for the fallacy it represents. This move *is* logically fallacious for, although the introduction of the **red herring** makes sense as a tactic of defense when under criticism (defense by counter-attack), it remains irrelevant to the original issue in dispute.

The origin of the term "red herring" makes it a good descriptive label for this fallacy. It comes from the sport of foxhunting, in which the hunters on horseback follow a pack of hounds tracking a fox's scent. To divert the hounds from the hunt — either to save a good fox for another day's chase, or to call off young hounds being trained — a red herring (one that's been dried, smoked, and salted) was drawn across the fox's track ahead of the pack. The dogs would be diverted by the fresher, stronger scent. The term's application to this fallacy is evident.

A typical *red herring* was committed by then-Senator Paul Martin, well-known for extolling the virtues of his hometown of Windsor, Ontario. On this occasion, Senator Martin rose to defend Windsor against a slur contained in Arthur Hailey's novel about the U.S. auto industry, *Wheels*. Hailey wrote of "grimy Windsor" across the border from Detroit, "matching in ugliness the worst of its U.S. senior partner." According to press reports, Martin responded:

68   When I read this I was incensed . . . Those of us who live there know that [Windsor] is not a grimy city. It is a city that has one of the best flower parks in Canada. It is a city of fine schools, hard-working and tolerant people.

Martin's first point does tell against Hailey's appraisal, for a city with an attractive flower park cannot be completely ugly. But the Senator didn't continue building his case for Windsor's beauty (as he might have) by extolling its splendid rose gardens and miles of riverfront parkland. Instead he *changed the subject*. Fine schools and hard-working, tolerant people are no doubt an asset, but they have nothing to do with whether a city is fair or ugly.

The Senator's shift here is a common type of *red herring* move. Martin began his defense of Windsor on topic, then shifted to an associated point, not strictly relevant to the attack. Perhaps Martin interpreted Hailey's criticism of Windsor's physical appearance as part of a general critique of the city. That would explain his more general defense. It wouldn't alter the fact, however, that Hailey's comment was restricted to Windsor's appearance. Nor would it make the Senator's second point any less a distraction, inviting a step away from Hailey's claim. The effect, whether intentional or not, was to move the argument onto different ground to terrain much more favourable to Martin. (It's harder to document the allegation that the quality of life in a city is lamentable than it is to show that the city is physically grimy and ugly.)

A typical case of *red herring* as counter-attack occurred during the 1972 federal election campaign, when the Trudeau government faced its first re-election challenge. Prime Minister Trudeau and the Liberals had been swept to power in 1968, running on the slogan that they would build a "Just Society" in Canada. During the '72 campaign, on an open-line radio program in Regina, a caller asked Mr. Trudeau what had happened to the "Just Society" he had promised in 1968. Trudeau's reply was to suggest that his questioner ask Jesus Christ what happened to the just society that Christ had promised two thousand years ago.

Trudeau was probably trying to suggest that if it was impossible for Christ to keep His promise, the Liberals can be forgiven for failing to keep theirs. But his reply invites a shift of focus to the tenuous analogy. There is an enormous leap from the reasons a Canadian political party didn't keep a campaign promise in the mid-twentieth century to the reasons that the two-millenia-old Christian hope of peace on earth and goodwill towards men (and women and children) hasn't come about. Left behind was the caller's question about the social justice the Liberals had promised four years earlier.

Red herring might be defined in terms of the *intention* of the person who introduces the red herring to divert his or her opponent from the opponent's original line of attack. Because it is difficult to be sure about people's intentions, this definition would restrict our employment of the *red herring* tag. It would be an undue restriction, because we often want to mark a distractingly irrelevant response whether or not the person was *trying* to change the subject. However, to define the fallacy in terms of the *effect* a response has in diverting the opponent's attention to a different topic would mean that we could charge *red herring* only when the opponent was duped by the irrelevant rejoinder. Hence, the presence of the fallacy would depend on the cleverness of the opponent — an odd situation, since we'd want to say that the clever opponent exposed the fallacy or avoided it; we would not want to say, paradoxically, that the fallacy didn't exist because the opponent spotted it! Certainly a paradigm of *red herring* would be an exchange in which someone deliberately introduces a red herring to try to divert the opponent's attention from the point under controversy, and as a result the opponent is distracted by the red herring and follows it up, leaving behind the original issue. We find it more useful, however, to use the label for responses to attacks in adversary contexts that, because they are close but not strictly relevant to the topic, invite the opponent to digress, whether or not the distraction is intended or successful. More formally:

RED HERRING

1. In an adversary context, N has made a claim, Q, that is or implies a criticism of a position that M holds or identifies with.
2. M responds to Q by asserting R, which introduces an issue that is not relevant to the acceptability of Q, and thereby instigates in the exchange a shift of focus away from the question of Q's acceptability.

With *red herring*, we complete our list of discussion of fallacies of diversion. When evaluating an argument in an adversary context, you should be consciously on the lookout for these fallacies. It might be helpful in keeping them in mind, and also in keeping them distinct from each other in your mind, to be aware of how they are related. The following chart sets out their connections.

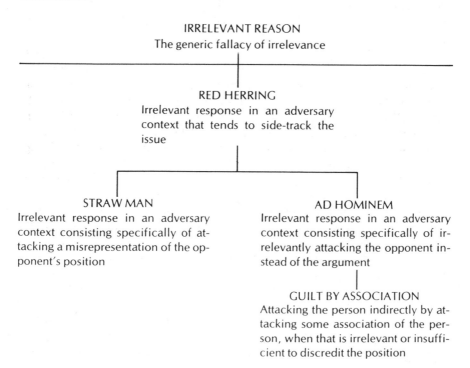

IRRELEVANT REASON
The generic fallacy of irrelevance

RED HERRING
Irrelevant response in an adversary context that tends to side-track the issue

STRAW MAN
Irrelevant response in an adversary context consisting specifically of attacking a misrepresentation of the opponent's position

AD HOMINEM
Irrelevant response in an adversary context consisting specifically of irrelevantly attacking the opponent instead of the argument

GUILT BY ASSOCIATION
Attacking the person indirectly by attacking some association of the person, when that is irrelevant or insufficient to discredit the position

Thus, the way our nomenclature works, any irrelevant response in an adversary context *that cannot be more specifically characterized* gets the general classification of *red herring*. When the irrelevant response takes one or another specific turn, it will then fall under one of the more specific categories: *straw man, ad hominem,* or *guilt by association*. Note that *guilt by association* is in fact a special case of *ad hominem,* for it is an attack on the person (instead of the argument), but an indirect one — via some (alleged) association of the person.

We can illustrate how this chart can help you to get a precise fix on the nature of a mistake in argument by offering a few examples.

In November 1975, a government official responsible for investigating and prosecuting misleading advertisements gave a talk on the subject to a group of Windsor businesspersons. He pointed out that, since 1969, 28,000 new files had been opened on misleading advertising, and he cited a wide variety of cases. His speech left the impression that much advertising is unreliable. One of his listeners responded during the question-and-answer period:

69   It would be far better if you didn't go around making speeches and discouraging people from entering this business.

The point of the talk was the reliability of advertising and whether business people were upholding their responsibility to provide reliable information in their advertising. But the critic's objection had nothing to do with reliable advertising. Why not, then, call this a case of *irrelevant reason*? We prefer *red herring* because the context is adversarial. The critic's accusation that the official's objections to misleading advertising "discourage people from entering this business" might, therefore, tempt the official to follow the false trail (e.g., by responding, "I'm not discouraging anyone") instead of keeping the exchange on track (e.g., by rejoining, "Are you arguing that misleading advertising should not be prosecuted?").

The next example emphasizes the blurry boundary between *red herring* and *ad hominem*. Its setting was a meeting of a group of touring Ontario (Conservative) cabinet ministers and local citizens at Sault Ste. Marie. An NDP supporter charged that the "Government was too slow to act on mercury poisoning in the Kenora area and lung cancer dangers facing uranium miners in Elliot Lake until the NDP 'screamed for action'" (*The Globe and Mail,* September 1975). According to the newspaper report, Ontario Health Minister Frank Miller responded that he was

70   tired of people complaining about health hazards facing Indians in Northwestern Ontario while the complainers go on killing themselves with what he called diseases of choice by exercising too little and smoking too much.

"I get a bit cynical about reactions of society that totally ignores my warnings about smoking and wearing seat belts, killing more people every day than mercury ever will," he said.

Was Ontario slow to act on the dangers of Minamata disease from mercury poisoning and of cancer from uranium radiation? Mr. Miller's reply was clearly irrelevant to the accusation. It invited a digression onto the topic of the consistency of the government's critics or even to the extent to which people were heeding warnings about smoking and seat belts. Thus, it seems to qualify as a case of *red herring*. Yet Mr. Miller was also launching a personal attack against the critics of the Government (charging inconsistency) instead of responding to the merits of their case. Thus, the fallacy meets the conditions of *ad hominem*. Since *any* irrelevant rejoinder in an adversary context tends to distract attention from the original issue to the unrelated rejoinder, if we label Mr. Miller's attack *ad hominem* we do not give up that point. What we do, instead, is add to it the specific way Miller's attack *is* digressive — namely, by turning the discussion toward the issue of the inconsistency of his critics. Hence, we would favour accusing Mr. Miller of the more specific logical fallacy, *ad hominem*.

Finally, consider an example where the choice is not between two fallacy labels, but between *red herring* and no fallacy at all.

D.C. of St. Lambert, Quebec, wrote a long letter to *The Montreal Gazette* (February 1975) in which he made a case against some suggestions for gun control laws. He began:

71   Reading your editorial "Drop those guns," made me 'do a slow boil.' It is quite evident you know very little about game laws, and even less about sport shooters, i.e., target shooters.

There is far more ammunition used each year on targets, either paper or clay, than on living things. You say nothing in your editorial on this point.

[D.C. next argued against a proposal to have licensed rifles kept at target shooting ranges. He proceeded:]

I believe John Diefenbaker had the best idea, when he said that people who commit crimes with guns, should get an automatic five years prison term, with no parole, in addition to any other sentence received for the crime.

Please start blaming the people, not the guns.

Also, *why is so much time and effort spent on this subject recently? How about the people killed on snowmobiles each year? How do their numbers rank with killing by guns? Much higher. And how about traffic deaths? Drunken drivers? Why not do something about them?* (Emphasis ours.)

The last paragraph looks like a *red herring*. What has the number of people killed in snowmobile and traffic accidents got to do with whether guns should be controlled? D.C. seems clearly to be changing the subject. On the other hand, it cannot be denied that most of the letter responded to various arguments for gun control. Why not give the letter this interpretation: first, it dealt with the arguments favouring gun controls; then it suggested that there are other, more pressing, problems for public attention. The fact of the matter is that in D.C.'s letter we have a prime example of expression of opinion that has not been articulated and developed into argument. Instead, it is characterized by hints or suggestions about possible lines of argument which are never taken up and played out. Perhaps the best judgement here is: no fallacy because no argument.

We end the chapter with a reminder: by trying to identify these fallacies and defend your charges you should be led to a deeper understanding of the argumentative interaction in adversary contexts. If you treat the charge of fallacy as an incantation with which to strike down the person you criticize and end debate, you reveal yourself as a name-caller who is hostile to the rationality of argumentation.

EXERCISES

Directions

Determine which, if any, of the four fallacies of diversion occur in each of the following passages. Be sure to argue in defense of each fallacy charge. A passage may contain more than one fallacy, or none.

1. *Background:* In late February, 1981, President Ronald Reagan flew from Washington, D.C. to his ranch in Santa Barbara, California, at an estimated cost to U.S. taxpayers of $52,000. This at a time when Reagan was attempting to get members of Congress to agree to slice the federal budget and show fiscal restraint. Many were upset by Reagan's trip and argued that it was not justifiable on grounds such as these: (1) Reagan should be expected to practice what he preaches, i.e., restraint; (2) Camp David (Maryland) is close by, available and would cost less money. Here follow letters to the editor of the *Los Angeles Times* (March 8, 1981), making reference to earlier rounds of letters. Appraise the logical merits of each.

   (a) If President Reagan does the job for the country he proposes to do, he deserves everything we can give him, including a ranch on the moon with a ring around it! And free travel, too!

   What have the "complainers" gone without in order to help the inflation picture? An unnecessary trip? A new suit? Or perhaps a new automobile or TV set? How about one less trip to the race track?

(b) This is an angry letter. I am referring to your printing seven letters faulting Reagan for taking time for R&R at his ranch. Who are these writers? . . . The answer is self-evident. They are, one and all, inconsequential people. No matter what they do, whether they live or die, has no consequence to the world at large. Not so with the President of the United States. What this man does, and the decisions he makes, has direct bearing on the welfare of every single person on the face of this earth. And Presidents are humans, which means that their decision making powers are directly affected by their personal mental and physical conditions. They become fatigued, and harried, and impulsive and irritable, just like anyone else. But the consequences of these negative states, the decisions that come out of them, are of the greatest possible pertinence to us all. All right, then, if President Reagan has the need to spend his weekends in Tierra del Fuego, or even at the North Pole — fine. No matter what the expense, as long as he returns refreshed and restored to a state of calm and correct judgement.

(c) Has Reagan been so blinded by the glamour of Hollywood that he cannot see the stark reality of abject poverty? Has he no heart or soul that he can so readily cut out things like nutrition for the young children while he freely spends $52,000 getting away from the very thing he fought so hard to obtain?

2. *Background:* Geoffrey Stevens is a columnist for the Toronto *Globe and Mail.* In 1979, he devoted several columns to the problems in South Africa (Zimbabwe-Rhodesia) which elicited this response from an associate professor of history at the University of Western Ontario (Toronto *Globe and Mail,* August 8, 1979):

Not all of Mr. Stevens' recent writing on southern Africa has been . . . praiseworthy. It is enlightening to contrast some of Mr. Stevens' criticisms of the Republic of South Africa with points made by Dr. L.H. Gann and Dr. Peter Duignan in their book, *South Africa: War, Revolution or Peace?* For example, Mr. Stevens states that "blacks are still denied access to good jobs in business and industry," whereas Gann and Duignan write correctly: "Africans now occupy an increasing number of skill and even submanagerial positions."

Similarly, Mr. Stevens dismisses as "nonsense" the view that there are fewer police in South Africa than in New York City, whereas Gann and Duignan point out: "The proportion of policemen to civilians in South Africa is smaller than it is in the United States."

3. *Background:* In 1982, the issue of nuclear deterrence and the idea of a nuclear freeze surfaced in North America with great force. Here is an excerpt from an opponent of the freeze movement, Benjamin Stein, "An Example of 'Junk Thought'" (*San Francisco Chronicle,* May 16, 1982):

> We have known that nuclear war is horrible ever since there have been nuclear weapons. For the proponents of the freeze to act as if they had discovered something new is a sign of almost staggering ignorance of the history of the last 37 years. For all of that time, the United States' paramount goal has been to maintain freedom and avoid a nuclear war. To imply otherwise is not only specious but insults the speaker as well as the listener.
>
> If no one is eager for a nuclear war, the demonstrators and senators are doing no more than uttering a cliché: "We do not want nuclear war." The nuclear freeze petition signers are uttering a truism that is embarrassingly hackneyed. Of course, no one wants nuclear war. Are the proponents of the freeze doing anything more than satisfying themselves by uttering a momentarily satisfying, but empty banality? No. And that's what makes junk thought.

4. *Background:* Those who travel from one country to another know the problem of exchanging currency. This writer opposes the position of the editorialist referred to in the first sentence: (*The Windsor Star,* September 10, 1977):

> Pat Whealan says the Canadian reputation is at stake because some merchants are cheating on the dollar premium. This is just rubbish. All Americans have to do is change their almighty dollar to Canadian funds before leaving their own country. Then they will get full value for their dollar.
>
> Americans, I notice, did not make any waves when their dollar was below the Canadian. In fact, trying to spend a Canadian dollar in the U.S. was like trying to spend play money (never mind the refund) and I didn't hear anyone then speaking out for the Canadian shoppers. [3]

5. *Background:* In 1973, the city of Windsor, Ontario, was considering the expansion of its airport. In August 1973, S.L., the president of a Windsor

---

[3] When this was written, the US$ was worth about $1.10 Canadian.

firm, wrote to the *Star*: "As a citizen of this community, speaking no doubt for the silent majority of Windsor and Essex county residents, I wish to express my full support for . . . plans to expand the present Windsor airport facilities." F.W. responded:

> In his letter, Mr. S.L. lavishes praise on the . . . expansion plans for the airport of Windsor, while purporting to be "a citizen of this community, speaking no doubt for the silent majority of Windsor and Essex county."
>
> Mr. L. certainly displays no careless habits of accuracy. He is not a citizen of the community of Windsor, but resides according to all records in the bucolic splendor of Colchester [a town near Lake Erie, about 25 miles from Windsor]. If he has no doubts at such a distance, I have them at close proximity. I doubt, for instance, that Mr. L. has a mandate from any majority, and I also doubt that any majority would remain a silent one once Mr. L. joined it.

6. *Background:* In the fall of 1974 the government was considering regulating Canadian content in print media. One of the guidelines called for any new *Time* Canada company to be 75 percent controlled in Canada. It must also be substantially different from the foreign-owned original. In a telephone interview (as reported by James Farra-bee, Southam News Services, in *The Windsor Star,* November 1974), Stephen Larue, president of *Time* Canada, said that his company was rethinking what it might do to exist in Canada, but the question of government control of content was a major stumbling block:

> No editor is willing to turn his product over to a government or anyone else to decide what's in it.

7. *Background:* Bob Talbert writes a daily column for *The Detroit Free Press*. He covers a variety of local activities and issues. Like most columnists who receive letters from their readers, Talbert devotes an occasional column to the response. Here is one letter he received (August 1972) from someone who used the pseudonym "Sam Detroit," along with Talbert's reply:

> S.D.: The danger of writing a witty(?) column such as yours is that eventually, being in the public eye, hob-nobbing with celebrities, you begin to acquire a false sense of importance, which some psychiatrists call delusions of grandeur. Come down off your white charger and try writing an amusing article for a change.
> B.T.: Wonder what psychiatrists would call hiding behind a pseudonym?

8. *Background:* With reference again to Arthur Hailey's charge that Windsor is ugly, here is the response of another Windsor politician, then-Minister of National Revenue and MP for Windsor West, Herb Gray:

> I don't think Hailey's impressions are correct. The fact that thousands of people choose to live in Windsor even though they work in Detroit, and that even larger numbers of Detroiters come to Windsor for shopping and entertainment, shows that the negative aspects of life in Detroit, fortunately, are not found in Windsor.

9. *Background:* In the 1972 Olympics, the black nations of Africa stated they would boycott the games if Rhodesian athletes were allowed to compete. The International Olympic Committee subsequently voted Rhodesia out of the games. In an editorial entitled, "Racism in Black Africa, too," (August 1972), the Detroit *News* stated:

> The black nations of Africa, citing racism by the white supremacist Rhodesian regime, almost wrecked the Olympic Games opening this weekend by using their political muscle to force Rhodesia out of the games. It was coincidental that the day they won their point, Uganda, one of the leaders of the movement, confirmed its own brand of racism by spelling out the details of its arbitrary ouster of Indians and Pakistanis who have for generations lived in Uganda.
>
> Racism is clearly a two-way street.

10. *Background:* This is an excerpt from a column by Peter Brimelow entitled, "The world, according to churches' double-think: freedom is slavery." It appeared in *The Financial Post* on March 17, 1979. The article begins by quoting the Most Reverend Edward Scott, Primate of the Anglican Church of Canada, on the question of whether homosexual activity is sinful. Scott reportedly said: "It is not my job or the job of the church to be always defining and judging things." Brimelow responds:

> Whatever Archbishop Scott's hesitation about homosexuality, which is after all specifically condemned in the Bible, he has absolutely no doubts about capitalism, which is not mentioned there. He is against it and, by implication, against the democratic political systems with which it is inextricably linked. And so, apparently, are the hierarchies of the Canadian Roman Catholic, Lutheran, Presbyterian and United churches. Admittedly this message is not trumpeted from the pulpit of Timothy Eaton Memorial Church [a United Church in Toronto with a very wealthy congregation] or when helping elderly parishioners make their wills.

But it is stated vehemently and in detail in the "Leader's Kit" circulated in support of Ten Days for World Development, the annual foreign-aid campaign sponsored jointly by all five churches. "People go hungry in the Third World because our standard of living is high in the developed world," the kit tells the "leaders." "Citizens of developed countries are also oppressed by an international economic system which is not designed to fill human need. Its purpose is to create scarcity for profit; race and sex distinctions for profit; a devastated environment for profit; war for profit." Before capitalism, in other words, we were all beige hermaphrodites.

CHAPTER FOUR

FALLACIES OF IMPERSONATION

Introduction

It has been held that all fallacies impersonate good arguments. No doubt a significant feature of most fallacies is that they counterfeit sound patterns of argument.[1] As such a widely shared characteristic, this masquerading role played by most of them wouldn't normally be expected to set apart one particular subgroup of fallacies. However, the three we discuss in this chapter exhibit this feature more than any other. Three of the most common and useful kinds of argument in public discourse are: (1) arguments from analogy, (2) appeals to fairness and precedent, and (3) arguments about causal claims. *Faulty analogy, two wrongs* (and its variant, *improper appeal to practice*), and *questionable cause,* respectively, impersonate these three types of argument.

Faulty Analogy

An analogy is a comparison between two things, or situations. It may serve a variety of functions. Thus, an analogy may be used to describe: "He looked like death warmed over." Or to explain: "To show that a fallacy has been committed is like producing enough evidence to convict the accused in a court of law." Or to state a point in provocative language, as James Eayrs

---

[1] See the title of W. Ward Fearnside's and William B. Holther's book: *Fallacy, The Counterfeit of Argument* (Englewood Cliffs, N.J.: Spectrum Brooks, Prentice-Hall, Inc., 1959).

did when he wrote (in a column about the demise of the Allende regime in Chile in September 1973):

72   Like a group of bystanders unconcernedly gazing at a mugging, the world's democracies stood to one side last week as one of their number was brutally beaten to death . . .

An analogy can also be used in order to persuade, and it is strictly such uses — *arguments* employing analogies — that we are concerned with here.

Here's an example from a letter by E.P. to the *Winnipeg Free Press* (August 1974):

73   . . . I believe the citizens of this province, whether they be drinkers or dry, might consider it only fair that liquor sales revenue be further increased to cover the costs to society of the extra costs that seem to fall in the wake of imbibing. In other words why cannot the full costs of the effects of drinking be met by the sales tax on alcoholic beverages *just as the cost of highway maintenance costs are met by the sales tax on gasoline?* What would we expect this additional revenue from liquor to cover? For openers, about $10 million is the annual provincial loss through absenteeism from drinking workers. (Emphasis ours.)

Notice what E.P. has done here. He or she has taken an accepted belief — that the cost of highway maintenance should be met by a sales tax on gasoline — and used it to pave the way for the proposal for an increased tax on liquor. The argument says: the two situations are comparable (i.e. analogous), so if you accept the principle in the case of gasoline taxes, you should also accept it in the case of liquor taxes. One's acceptance of the conclusion based on this argument depends entirely on the adequacy of the analogy.

Does the analogy support the conclusion? We don't think so. It is true that the revenue from taxes on gasoline is used in part for the maintenance of roads and highways. That's fair enough, since virtually everyone who buys gasoline contributes to the wear and tear on thoroughfares, and roughly in proportion to the amount of gas purchased. It is quite true, as E.P. pointed out, that drinking, like driving, can cost society money. But the analogy supports E.P.'s conclusion only if drinkers are responsible for the social costs of drinking in proportion to their purchases of alcohol — the way drivers are responsible for the costs of road repair in proportion to their purchases of gasoline. However, not everyone who uses liquor contributes to the social costs due to the consumption of alcohol; only those who *drink too much* are responsible for those costs. The respect in which the two situations (gasoline and liquor consumption and attendant costs) must be analogous to support E.P.'s conclusion is this:

$$\frac{\text{amount of gas consumption}}{\text{responsibility for roadway wear and tear}} = \frac{\text{amount of liquor consumption}}{\text{responsibility for social costs of alcohol abuse}}$$

The two situations are not similar in this respect, so the analogy does not support the conclusion. E.P. has committed **faulty analogy.**

Another example. In August 1975, Thomas Middleton wrote an article for *Saturday Review* calling for stricter gun control legislation. A reader responded:

74   I wish to protest the article written by Mr. Middleton. Can Mr. Middleton be so naive as to really believe that banning ownership of firearms would significantly reduce murders and robberies? Did banning booze significantly reduce drinking?[2]

Standardizing this argument helps make the role of the analogy explicit:

75   1. Prohibition did not significantly reduce drinking.
MP   2. Banning ownership of firearms is analogous to banning booze in precisely the respect which led to the failure of prohibition.
         3. Banning ownership of firearms won't work either.

The analogy is contained in the missing premise. Does it support the conclusion? The answer requires a brief look at why prohibition failed. There was a host of reasons: it didn't have the support of most people; liquor, beer, and wine are relatively easy to make in one's own home; it was difficult to enforce. The question is, would banning private ownership of firearms be subject to the same limitations? Hardly. While gun proponents are vocal, they are relatively few in number; it would be very difficult to manufacture guns in one's home or secretly; given the need for factories for gun manufacture, firearm distribution should be much less difficult to police than booze distribution was. So, although it is undeniable that prohibition was a failure, the reasons it failed do not apply in the case of gun control. The analogy does not support the conclusion.

The conditions for the fallacy are these:

FAULTY ANALOGY

1. An analogy is offered in support of the conclusion of an argument.
2. The two things* being compared are not similar *in the respect required to support the conclusion.*

---

*By "thing" we mean to allow for the inclusion of events, situations, etc.

---

[2] Thanks to Brian Savard for bringing this example to our attention.

The analogy may be explicit (as in Example 73), or implicit (as in Example 74). Usually, the exact way the two analogues must be similar, if the analogy is to support the conclusion, is not made explicit. The first steps in arguing that *faulty analogy* has been committed are, correspondingly: (a) identify the two things being compared and (b) figure out the *precise* respect in which they must be similar if the analogy is to support the conclusion. The last step is to argue that the two things are *not* similar in that particular respect.

In typical cases, the *faulty analogy* gets its plausibility because the two things compared are indeed similar in some respects. So you needn't try to argue that they are in no way alike. And obviously, since they are *two* things being compared, they will be dissimilar in many respects. Hence, it won't be enough to argue that they are not alike in some respects. What you must do is *zero in on the particular feature that the two things must share for the analogy to lend support to the conclusion.*

To illustrate this one last time, we will take an argument from analogy and present two attempts — one bad and one good — to charge the argument with *faulty analogy*. The example comes from a letter from J.S. in New York City in *Time* magazine (October 1971) that appeared when the United States was still actively engaged in the Vietnam war:

76   Contrary to your article, the events that are taking place in South Vietnam's presidential election offer the best opportunity for the U.S. to make a "decent" exit from Southeast Asia. Under the existing circumstances, the U.S. should declare that South Vietnam is unable to sustain a political democracy, that there is no reason for us to remain there, and that we should withdraw our remaining forces. By doing this, we would leave the image of a patient who died despite the extraordinary efforts of a good doctor.

First, we standardize:

77   1. By withdrawing from South Vietnam with the declaration that South Vietnam can now be seen to be unable to sustain political democracy, the U.S. would be acting like a good doctor, who, despite extraordinary efforts, lost the patient.
      2. No one would blame a doctor whose patient dies despite the doctor's extraordinary effort.
      3. No one could blame the U.S. for withdrawing from South Vietnam under the circumstances.

First look at an *unsatisfactory* attempt to show that J.S. committed *faulty analogy:*

78   The U.S. and South Vietnam cannot be compared to a doctor and his patient because a doctor receives pay for his services and the U.S. did not receive any pay from South Vietnam.

Although it's true that the U.S. did not receive any pay, this attempt to defeat the analogy seizes upon a minor feature of the analogy and overlooks the important ones. Even if the U.S. had been paid by South Vietnam, the analogy would fail, for, and here we begin what we regard as a satisfactory defense of the charge,

79   in order for the analogy to be applicable, the analogue of the patient's life would have to be a democratic South Vietnam, and the analogue of the doctor's extraordinary fight to save that life would have to be the U.S.'s extraordinary efforts to create (or sustain) a democratic South Vietnam. The record is clear, however, that the U.S. was willing to tolerate clearly undemocratic regimes in South Vietnam so long as they were fairly stable. Both the Diem and the Thieu regimes, though patently undemocratic, were sustained and supported by the U.S. with little effort to make them more democratic. The analogy fails, then, in the respect relevant to support the conclusion: the doctor did not make an extraordinary effort to save the patient's life.

It also fails because the doctor-patient metaphor has certain built-in assumptions not warranted here. It assumes South Vietnam was a single patient, but that assumption is questionable. The war there can be interpreted as a civil war, with the United States in the role of a doctor treating Siamese twins, one of whom does not want the doctor. Finally, whether the U.S. can reasonably be termed "a good doctor" in terms of this analogy is open to question. A "good doctor" here would be one who sought to make democracy a workable form of government. In fact, U.S. foreign policy throughout the 1950s and 1960s can be interpreted as more anti-Communist than pro-democratic — witness the U.S. support of the undemocratic regime of Batista in Cuba, of the military dictatorship in Greece, and so on.

We said at the outset of this section that *faulty analogy* labels, exclusively, bad *arguments* from analogy. We also noted that analogies function outside arguments — to describe, for instance, or to explain. A particular analogy may be a poor one for any of those other purposes, too; that cannot make it a logical fallacy, however, since in those cases there is no argument present.

Two Wrongs

The fallacy we're calling **two wrongs** is a logical fallacy employed primarily in ethical arguments, and appealing to very strong emotional and psychological factors. This deceptively simple manoeuver is one most children are capable of mastering and using. Remember when your father or mother criticized you for hitting your little brother or sister and you defended yourself by saying, "But she (or he) hit me first!" The idea is simple and attractive, isn't it? You were wronged (your brother or sister slugged you — something they shouldn't have done) and that act, you reasoned, justified you in returning that wrong (hitting back). The fallacy of *two wrongs* seeks in effect to elevate the instinct to retaliate into an argument. Let's look at a few examples.

Our first needs a bit of background. In July 1974, a group of militant Indians took possession of a small park on the outskirts of Kenora, Ontario. They claimed that they had exclusive rights to its use. The occupation made national headlines because the Indians were armed, so there was the possibility of violent confrontation. An agreement was eventually reached and the occupation ended peacefully. It stirred a great deal of comment in the press, and the following passage is from a letter by J.G. to the *Winnipeg Free Press* (August 1974), defending the actions of the Indians against the criticisms which had been aired:

80   The occupation of a 14-acre park by the native people in the Kenora area is completely justified. After all, what's a mere 14 acres when they have been robbed of 14 million square miles — the entire North and South American continents.

Notice the pattern here; it is a recurrent one. It begins with the criticism of the action. There follows a defense which takes the form of citing some other wrongdoing, the implication being (in this case it is explicitly stated) that *the act which comes under criticism is justified.* If we standardize this compact argument, we get:

81   1. The Indians were robbed of North and South America.
        a. The Indians were wronged long ago.
          1. The Indians were justified in occupying the 14-acre park in Kenora.

Clearly, an implicit premise or assumption operates behind the scenes here, but what is it? J.G.'s reference to "a mere 14 acres" suggests that he or she is thinking of some version of the principle that persons who suffer wrongdoing are entitled to compensation. The idea would be that 14 acres is little enough compensation, given the magnitude of the original wrong done to the Indians. In claiming that the Indians were justified, J.G. would no doubt concede that the seizure of the park by just any group would, in normal circumstances, be wrong. Thus, the complete idea behind the argument is this: an instance of an action, that would be wrong if done in ordinary circumstances, is declared to be permissible. The ordinary judgement that would apply to an instance of this action in normal circumstances is overruled, or does not apply, so it is alleged, because in this case the agent already suffered some wrong done by the person whom the action is affecting. The first wrong is said to justify the second one, and to make it, in just this instance, right: two wrongs make a right.

Such arguments seem plausible because they appeal to our sense of justice and fair play; they model legitimate arguments. They go wrong, however, because they involve either a misapplication of the principles of justice, or because they involve unwarranted assumptions, or both.

In the case of J.G.'s argument, the wrong that was unquestionably done to Indians in the Americas by the encroaching Europeans does not serve to justify the occupation of the Kenora park by the local Indians. Even if the non-Indians living in Kenora today had stolen land from the Indians living there, that would not justify the park takeover, because the mere suffering of a wrong from someone cannot warrant acting outside the law to try to redress it. If that principle were embraced, then private feuds would disrupt peaceful society. There would have to be other factors present such as, for example, that the Kenora band had tried every legitimate means to get its land back and was refused any sort of fair hearing, plus perhaps that the occupation of the Kenora park seemed the most effective way of drawing attention to their grievance and getting a fair hearing. J.G. mentions no such additional factors in his argument. Do not infer from what we are saying that the Kenora park occupation was wrong. Our argument has only been that J.G.'s defense of that takeover, based as it was solely on the appeal to a past wrong, does not succeed. It remains an open question whether the takeover was justified on other, or additional grounds, such as those we've just mentioned.

We should say a word here about an ancient principle of justice, the *lex talionis:* "an eye for an eye, a tooth for a tooth." The point of that law (which defined a sort of combination of retribution and compensation) was that *no more than* an eye could be taken for an eye. It placed a *limit* on compensation, or retribution. The law did not stipulate that the person who suffers the wrong be the one to exact retribution from the wrongdoer. That was usually left to the state.

The next example arises from the recent debate about whether or not to restore capital punishment. Taking issue with the abolitionist viewpoint, A.P. wrote to the *Edmonton Journal* (December 1974):

82   Mr. E. stated "capital punishment is legal vengeance based on emotion instead of logic." Really! *What kind of "reason and logic" do killers use who snuff out the lives of innocent people?*
I don't think any murderer can produce a logical reason for taking a life. So why should society be hesitant to give him the same treatment he meted out to others? . . . (Emphasis ours.)

A.P.'s meaning is less than fully clear. Is he arguing that just as a murderer cannot produce a logical reason for taking a life, so too society should act without reason and logic in return? Surely not. Perhaps his point is that capital punishment is society's emotional response to murder, but that is all right, because murder itself is an act of emotion (no logical reason for taking a life being imaginable). A.P.'s reasoning, in this case, would seem to be that an emotional reaction to murder, namely the desire to impose capital punishment, is justified since murder itself is a crime based on emotion. The trouble with this reasoning is that it does not yield defensible results consistently. Emotional acts are often best defused, and prevented in the future, by coolly reasoned responses. Our "gut" reactions to wrongs we and others suffer, the impulse to strike back at the wrong-doer, is often counterproductive or futile. So A.P. must find some other pattern of reasoning to defend capital punishment. The manner in which murders may be carried out cannot justify reacting to them in the same manner.

The next two examples bring out interesting variations on the pattern we've been looking at. They're close enough in spirit to *two wrongs*, we think, to be considered here.

In early fall of 1974, Minister of Agriculture Eugene Whelan came under a good deal of criticism because the government agency responsible for storing eggs had bungled and over 27 million eggs had been allowed to spoil. In an interview reported in the *Windsor Star* (September 1974), Mr. Whelan, taking issue with his critics, stated:

83   I wouldn't call that a surplus. It was only two days consumption for the whole province of Ontario. *They think that's a lot, but how many billions, and I means billions, of potatoes were dumped in Prince Edward Island years ago. Nothing was said about that.* (Emphasis ours.)

The *two wrongs* motif is evident here. Whelan has been (indirectly) criticized for wasting eggs (a misguided action), and he defends himself by pointing to another bad situation (the potatoes dumped in P.E.I.). His argument differs from the two we've seen already because Whelan does not appear to be arguing that the earlier wrong somehow justifies the present one. Instead, he's saying: nobody jumped all over the P.E.I. people, so why are you all jumping on us now? Whelan's point is that he and his agency are being subjected to *unfair* criticism. Our sense of justice and fair play is being appealed to: similar cases should be treated similarly.

If the two situations were indeed similar, then Whelan would have a legitimate grievance. But what follows? Not that the egg marketing board was wrongly or even unfairly criticized, for it truly goofed. What follows from Whelan's appeal to fair play is that the P.E.I. people should have been criticized, but weren't. That they weren't does not mean we should repeat the oversight; the way to correct the situation is not to compound or double the wrong by withholding criticism here. How strange the principles of justice and consistency would be if they required us to blind our eyes to obvious wrongdoing, simply because similar wrongdoing had once escaped detection and criticism in the past!

Our second variant on *two wrongs* is exemplified in a situation that involved a philosophy professor at an Ivy League college in the United States. To supplement his income, Professor M. took on a second teaching job at another university, in violation of his contract with the first university; and he did not inform either institution of his dual role. An extremely able and mobile person, he apparently managed to do a competent job at both institutions. Alas, he was discovered and promptly lost both jobs. According to a report in *Time* (March 1972), he admitted a mistake, but not a fault; and in a 15-page letter, reminded the president of the Ivy League institution that:

84   . . . *there are faculty members who spend time doing extensive consulting, who write bestsellers, introductory textbooks or columns for popular magazines* — all of which do not contribute to scholarship or teaching, but which earn substantial amounts of money while requiring large amounts of time. (Emphasis ours.)

Professor M.'s argument here is that since other faculty members do outside work which takes time from their teaching and scholarly work without blame or penalty, his taking an outside job should not have been blamed or penalized.

This argument serves as an example of a feature often present in *two wrongs* arguments. Prof. M. is drawing an analogy between his holding two jobs and many other faculty members' consulting and writing novels, textbooks, or opinion columns. He is assuming that all their actions belong to the same general class, which could be described as "doing outside work that takes time from teaching and scholarly work." It's possible, then, to commit *faulty analogy* in the process of committing *two wrongs*, and we would argue that Prof. M. does commit *faulty analogy* when he puts writing introductory textbooks on a par with moonlighting. First, his contract explicitly prohibited him from taking another job, whereas the activities he mentions were not then prohibited. Second, introductory texts can be contributions to teaching, and they can also include conceptual innovations that are contributions to scholarship, so that people occupied with them aren't necessarily doing outside work. Writing a newspaper column can hardly be compared, in terms of the time it requires and the sort of effort that goes into it, with holding a second full-time job. So the analogy is faulty.

Quite apart from that, however, Professor M.'s reasoning is fallacious. If faculty members are not doing their work because outside work is interfering, then they should be dealt with in the appropriate way. The existence of such wrongdoing, even when it goes undetected and unpunished, is no reason for letting Professor M. off. These other wrongs can't be used to justify his conduct.

Clearly, *two wrongs* is a fallacy to look for in the adversary context, when someone is attempting to defend some action (or course of action) against criticism. The conditions for the fallacy are these:

TWO WRONGS

1. *M's* action, *X*, has come under criticism.
2. *N* (or *M*) tries to defend either *X* or *M* by citing *Y, Z,* or *W* —allegedly similar actions (the wrongness of which is granted or at least not challenged).
3. *Y, Z* or *W* are not relevant to, or not sufficient for, the defense of *X*, or of *M* for having done *X*.

Two wrongs is a fallacy, at least in the paradigm versions, because it is an argument move offering no more reason to cause us to put aside our standard condemnation of a given type of action than the fact that the agent had previously received an injury from the victim of his or her action. This by itself must always be insufficient evidence, and it may be irrelevant, at least in a morality like ours where vengefulness is not a virtue and where the society has taken the right to punish out of the hands of the injured individual for a very large number of actions. The variations on the basic pattern of the fallacy don't go quite so far. They are attempts to excuse, or to mitigate blame, or to block criticism. They don't try to justify the wrong. But their appeal to an earlier wrong remains insufficient or irrelevant. The precedence of the earlier, admittedly wrong act, does not by itself make the present, similar act excusable, or blame for it less in order, or criticism of it less appropriate.

To show that *two wrongs* has been committed, you need to identify the two actions involved in the defense, and to sort out just what kind of defense is offered. Does the argument attempt to justify the act (as in Examples 80 and 82) or to mitigate the blame or censure (as in Examples 83 and 84)?

We've already indicated why *two wrongs* is an *impersonator;* that is, its plausibility and air of respectability come from its apparent similarity to various principles of justice. The defense of the Kenora occupation imitates the principle of retributive and compensatory justice that when a wrong has been done, the victim deserves compensation. The Whelan example trades on the principle of justice that similar cases be treated similarly. Both of them warp the principles of justice in the naive belief that the interests of justice can somehow be served by either compounding or ignoring wrongdoing.

Improper Appeal to Practice

You've surely heard (or used) this line of defense before: "But Honey (Officer, Mom), *everybody's* doing it." To rebut or defuse a criticism of the action a person is appealing to some common practice. A variation is to appeal to the weight of tradition or past practice: "But . . . this is the way it's *always* been done." Appeals to practice to justify an action or to mitigate criticism are not necessarily fallacious, but they easily can be. The fallacious ones look much like the ones that are sound, and by this impersonation can get past the inattentive consumer of arguments.

Consider this example, which is an extension of the excerpt from Vincent Theresa's reminiscences which we alluded to in Chapter 2:

85   There are plenty of good things about [mobsters] . . . most are [patriotic]. We don't think about undermining the government. We corrupt politicians, but that's only so we can do business. *We cheat on taxes, but let's face it, there isn't a damn business executive who doesn't.*

Theresa here offers a defense of the Mafia's cheating on taxes: all business executives cheat on their taxes. Put aside the probability that this claim is a *problematic premise.* The gist of Theresa's defense is that cheating on taxes is a common practice, at least among business executives, and that therefore it is not culpable. We think that this appeal to practice is improper. It won't do for the reason that no one contends that the practice of cheating on taxes is a legitimate one. Those who do it are placing their personal interests (more money) above their legal (and moral) obligation to pay for the services the state provides for them and their fellow citizens. They are trying to get a free ride. The arguments against tax evasion are not undermined by the fact that numbers of people evade taxes. Hence, the commonness of the practice does not make it right. Theresa, then, commits here what we term the fallacy of **improper appeal to practice.**

The Theresa example involved an appeal to a practice that, no matter how widespread, is conceded to be wrong. There can be a different kind of appeal to practice. The arguer may contend that, although the action *used to be* considered wrong, the fact that it is now widely practiced is grounds for ceasing to consider it wrong. Especially when there is no objection to a new practice, it may in time come to represent the norm and be granted legitimacy. Such arguments have been used to defend actions as diverse as pre-marital sex and cancelling classes the Friday afternoon of a holiday weekend. Since we do, and indeed must, figure out how to proceed in life by learning the customs that have been established to give some order, an appeal to these customs to justify actions — in the absence of any controversy about their propriety — is relevant. We may not appreciate this in our own society, because we've grown up with its customs and they are second nature to us. Move to a different culture, though, and you will find yourself at a loss about how to behave until you discover what conduct is considered appropriate there.

Though an appeal to practice in such arguments is relevant, it is not by itself sufficient, for one must also show that the practice is, or has become, accepted, and that it is not being challenged. When a practice is in the midst of change, or if there is a dispute about its propriety, clearly an appeal to that practice would be question-begging.

For example, if a person is arguing that she should not include the promise "to obey" her husband in her wedding vows, on the ground that such a promise is inconsistent with the roles she wants for herself and her husband in their marriage, she is implicitly challenging the tradition of including this promise in the wedding vows (as well as the past practices built into the marriage roles which it reflects). It would be irrelevant in that situation for her traditionalist parents to argue that she should follow the standard service and make the promise "to obey," on the ground that this is part of the traditional and customary wedding service. In appealing to the tradition they assume its legitimacy when that is just what is in question. So for this sort of *improper appeal to practice*, what makes the appeal improper is that it is a case of *begging the question*.

Here is an example that illustrates this form of the fallacy clearly. D.W. wrote to the *Edmonton Journal* (January, 1975) opposing gun-control legislation, and using the following argument:

86   The people in Canada are accustomed to living in a state of individual liberty. *Part of our heritage is the privately owned firearm* . . . (Emphasis ours.)

This heritage (or the myth that there is such a heritage in Canada) is precisely what proponents of stricter gun-control legislation want to put an end to. D.W.'s appeal to tradition takes for granted what is at issue, so he *begs the question*. What he needs to do is produce reasons why the tradition should be continued that answer the present objections to it.

We can, then, distinguish the following different types of appeal to practice used to defend an action against criticism. *Case 1:* There is an appeal to a practice that is generally thought to be wrong (bad, improper, etc.). This is an *improper appeal to practice. Case 2:* There is an appeal to a practice when that practice itself is what is, directly or indirectly, under criticism. This is a *question-begging appeal to practice. Case 3:* There is an appeal to practice to argue that values or expectations have changed. If the arguer establishes that the new practice is generally accepted and unchallenged, then the argument in that respect is not fallacious. If he fails to show that the practice has become established, then he makes an *improper appeal to practice* that is a special case of *hasty conclusion*. The conditions of the fallacy are as follows:

IMPROPER APPEAL TO PRACTICE

1. M defends an action, X, against criticism by arguing that X is widely practiced or is a custom or traditional practice.
2. The existence of the practice of X is either not relevant, or not sufficient, to justify M's defense of X.

Let us end this section with an example that we find tricky to analyse. In 1974 the city of Regina was debating whether to build a new city hall. The city council favoured the idea, but not all ratepayers shared its opinion, as the following letter V.M. wrote to the *Regina Leader-Post* (September, 1974) attests:

87   A new city hall will cost many millions of dollars and that cost will increase the mill rate as well as other taxes.

In the opinion of many tax-payers it is undemocratic for the mayor and city council to bypass the public on this important issue. *Past councils would never have gone ahead with the scheme until the people had approved of it.* (Emphasis ours.)

In the last sentence V.M. is appealing to the past practice of the Regina city council. Let's assume she is right, and there was in Regina the custom that when big civic expenses that would increase the mill rate were proposed, the council checked with the citizens of Regina (e.g., by holding public hearings, or a plebiscite). In that case, V.M.'s argument is a strong one, we think, though not yet complete. For she would need to show also that no one on council had raised objections to the city's practice and that there was no particular reason to amend it. (One could imagine such an objection. A city council, after all, is elected by the citizens to run city government and plan for the city's future. That will often involve making commitments for expenditures. Councillors have the legal authority to do this, and, by virtue of having been elected, the moral trust of the majority of citizens to make such decisions. Hence, a city council would be abrogating its responsibility and wasting time and money if it went back to the electorate between elections.) So, as it stands, we think V.M.'s argument contains an *improper appeal to practice*. However, in this case the flaw is minor and easily repaired by providing the assurances we asked for above — that the Regina city council practice had not, explicitly, been objected to.

The *improper appeal to practice* is a cousin of *two wrongs*. Both involve seeking to deflect criticism by citing as precedent the actions of others. Such an appeal is sometimes appropriate and sometimes not, and that is what makes these fallacies tempting to commit and tricky to identify.

Questionable Cause

Think, for a moment, of some of the hotly contested public issues of the past few years. Should capital punishment have been abolished? Should pornography and marijuana be legalized? How should we fight unemployment? inflation? Should something be done about the violence on TV? To be able to give intelligent answers to these and scores of similar questions, we must make judgements about *causal relationships.* For example: Does capital punishment serve as a deterrent to murder? Does the open availability of pornography decrease the incidence of sexual crimes? Does marijuana have detrimental long-term side effects? Do tax cuts increase spending, hence increase production, hence increase jobs? Does violence on TV lead to violent behaviour in viewers? Obviously a good deal of the discussion about public policy, and the persuasive argumentation directed at the consumer connected with it, must consist of or presuppose arguments about causal claims.

Roughly speaking, a *cause* is an event which produces another event, its *effect.* Causes are, as it were, the moving forces of the world. We refer to them in various ways: we may say that one event leads to another, produces it, brings it about, makes it happen, forces it, stops it, prevents it, stems it, increases it — the list could go on to some length. No one or two or three terms can be depended on to cue causal arguments. You will have to judge from the context whether a causal claim is involved.

A systematic account of causal reasoning is beyond the scope of this section. Indeed, the theory of causal inferences is still much debated in philosophical circles. As it happens, however, detection of the kinds of mistakes typically found in causal reasoning does not depend on theoretical subtleties. Moreover, causal fallacies are best understood through the examination of concrete examples. Our approach is to work through a healthy sample of representative errors in arguments employing causal claims, introducing the necessary theoretical background information as we go. These errors, we shall say, constitute cases of the fallacy, **questionable cause.**

A distinction between *arguments to causes* and *arguments from causes* is useful to keep in mind. The former are intended to establish that one thing is the cause of another. The latter take it as a premise that one thing is the cause of another, and go on from there to argue for some further claim, usually a recommendation for action or policy. Of course, the two may be combined, so that someone argues first that X causes Y, and second proceeds to argue that, since X causes Y, something should be done to prevent or bring about X, on the ground that Y is undesirable or desirable. Keeping clear about the distinction between arguments *to* and arguments *from* causes can aid in spotting flaws. For instance, it may be true that X is a cause of Y, but not the only one. Hence, an argument, based on the assumption that X causes Y and concluding that preventing X will therefore prevent Y, is clearly a case of *questionable cause,* for the other causes of Y will still be operative, even if X is stopped.

Although most arguments found in the public domain involving causal claims push recommendations that an action be taken or that a policy be implemented, and thus are arguments *from* causes, their flaws are usually due to some error in reasoning *to* a causal claim. Therefore, in the inventory of examples that follows, we focus primarily on arguments *to* causal claims and the typical ways they can go wrong.

Arguments to causes can be subdivided into two groups. Some deal with the causes of particular events — events unique in time. Belonging to this group of *particular causal claims* are arguments about the causes of World War II, the causes of the rise and fall of the Diefenbaker government, the causes of the emergence of rock music in the 1950s, and so on. The other kind of argument to causes covers *general causal claims,* claims about the causes of recurring types of events, such as cancer, revolutions, inflation, rape, and so on.

As a rule, particular causal claims must invoke general ones and consist of showing what general causal laws work in the particular case in question. So, for example, in looking for the cause of someone's lung cancer, the doctor would seek to find what general cancer-causing factors were present in that medical history. This model is less clearly applicable when dealing with social events. In arguing about what brought about Joe Clark's victory at the 1976 Progressive Conservative Party leadership convention, one would have to look for the sort of factors that would influence this kind of party, given the kinds of circumstances it found itself in at the time, to prefer a young, relatively unknown backbencher to the sorts of leader the other available candidates represented. Yet all of these conditions are likely to be unique, and certainly their juxtaposition is. The bearing of general causal claims on Clark's victory is not so obvious.

Particular causal claims. The following examples will illustrate some of the variants of *questionable cause* possible in arguing to the causes of particular events.

In the spring of 1975, government weather reporting went metric. Among many who complained was a gentleman from Cape Breton Island:

88   Ever since we changed over to Celsius, the weather has been unusually irregular.

The implication is that the switch from Fahrenheit to Celsius *caused* the irregular weather. We can smile at this inference, but the *kind* of mistake he made is not always without dangerous possibilities. In the context of defending RCMP surveillance of university campuses in 1963, Commissioner C.W. Harvison alleged that criticism of the RCMP was communist-inspired. He argued as evidence that prominent Canadian Communist Party leader William Kashtan had spoken at an international communist conference in

Prague the previous summer on how to combat anti-communism and that, "It was only a short time after his return that we began to see increased criticism aimed at the RCMP."[3] Harvison's inference was that because criticism of the RCMP increased following the return to Canada of a Canadian communist who wanted to combat anti-communism, the former was caused by the latter.

What is wrong in both these arguments is that the mere existence of a before-and-after sequence is never by itself sufficient foundation for any causal claim. For a number of events immediately precede any effect, yet not all can be its cause. The inference about the irregular weather was silly, we know, since we are familiar with the kinds of hypotheses meteorologists employ to try to explain weather changes, and the influence of the units of temperature measurement is not among them. Commissioner Harvison's claim was not silly, for the hypothesis that a Communist activist freshly returned from the inspiration of an international meeting could generate a round of criticism of the militantly anti-communist RCMP is very plausible. But the Commissioner's causal argument was still unsound, since it was also possible that given the circumstances at the time other hypotheses were even more plausible, and Mr. Kashtan's return merely coincided with independently inspired sources of RCMP criticism. (As it happened, the clearly non-communist Canadian Association of University Teachers had responded to revelations of RCMP surveillance on university campuses with a resolution urging its members not to cooperate with such investigations.)

Such arguments are said to commit the fallacy of *post hoc ergo propter hoc*: "after this, therefore because of this." What gives this reasoning its appeal is that often a cause of an event immediately precedes it. Looking for an event just prior to the one whose cause is being sought is therefore quite appropriate. What is fallacious is moving straight from the fact that *X* came immediately before *Y* to the conclusion that *X* caused *Y*. It is necessary, further, to have some hypothesis connecting the two events and, finally, to rule out alternative hypotheses as less plausible.

Someone we know received the following chainletter in the mail:

89   "Trust in the Lord with all your heart and knowledge and He will light the way." This prayer has been sent to you for good luck. The original copy came from the Netherlands. It was sent around the world 9 times . . . . You are to receive good luck within 4 days of receiving this letter. This is not a joke. Don Elliot received $60,000, but lost it because he broke the chain. While in the Phillipines (*sic*), General Walsh lost his wife 6 days after he received the letter and failed to circulate the prayer. Please send this letter (20 copies) to

---

[3] House of Commons *Debates* (May 31, 1963), p. 513. The incident is reported in Lorne and Caroline Brown, *An Unauthorized History of the RCMP* (Toronto: James Lewis & Samuel, 1973), p. 104.

people you think need good luck and see what happens on the 4th day after . . . . Take note of the following: Constantine Diary received the chain in 1933. He asked his secretary to make 20 copies and send them out. A few days later he won the lottery of $4,000,000 in his country. Carlos Broodt, an officer employer, received the chain, forgot it and lost his job. He found the chain and sent out 20 copies. Nine days later he found a better job. Aaron Barachilla received the chain and threw it away; 9 days later he died. For no reason whatever should this chain be broken . . .

No harm done in sending the prayer and letter on, right? After all, why take a chance? Well, this sort of superstition will readily intimidate those who have no defense against the *post hoc* version of *questionable cause*. (Actually, even a prior consideration is the reasonableness of these claims. How could anyone have access to all this information? How could anyone follow the progress of the chain?) Assuming for the sake of argument that the information is correct, what we are given are some cases of "good luck" and some cases of "bad luck" all consisting of before-and-after sequences. The numbers can have no significance unless compared to the total number of people involved in the chain. (And if it's been going since at least 1933, that would include a lot of people.) Also, no connecting hypothesis is offered, unless perhaps it is the implicit suggestion that God will reward those who circulate the prayer and punish those who do not. But no reason is offered, or obvious, why God might take such an interest in this chain letter. This is a good example of how *post hoc ergo propter hoc* can underlie superstitious beliefs.

What about this example (from the *Edmonton Journal,* December 1974)?

90   In Australia, where seat belt use is mandatory, hospital occupancy, one of the highest prices society pays for traffic accidents, has been reduced by 25 per cent.

The implication is that the use of seat belts caused the decrease in hospital occupancy, and the sole basis seems to be a before-and-after sequence. It is clear why wearing seat belts might be expected to cause a decrease in serious injuries, thereby reducing hospital occupancy. This intervening principle might save the *Journal* from the *post hoc* version of *questionable cause*. But what about the reductions in speed limits that occurred widely at about the same time, partly as a result of the world-wide fuel shortage? They too could be responsible for fewer accidents. The *Journal* doesn't mention whether that could have been a factor in Australia.

A more careful statement on the same subject was reported by Canadian Press in July 1976:

91   Staff Supt. John Marks of Metropolitan Toronto police said in an interview, "there is absolutely no doubt that the seatbelt law is working." [Use of seat belts became mandatory in Ontario on January 1, 1976.]

"Our sharp drop in death and injury statistics has more to do with seat belts than it does with lower speed limits. Our jurisdiction does not include the major provincial highways, where speed-limit reductions have played a major part in lowering accident statistics."

Here, Staff Supt. Marks acknowledged the alternative hypothesis, and explained why it was unlikely to have been a factor.

Another kind of mistake in arguing to causes consists of treating an explanatory hypothesis as an account of the cause of an event, without sufficient evidence. Here's an example from a *Time* magazine story some years back. The city of El Paso, Texas, is about one-third the size of Dallas, but the number of El Paso residents found in state mental hospitals was then one-seventh the number of Dallas residents in such institutions. Other things being equal, one would expect roughly similar proportions, so how might the difference have been explained? A University of Texas biochemist offered this explanation:

92   . . . El Paso's water is heavily laced with lithium, a tranquilizing chemical widely used in the treatment of manic depression and other psychiatric disorders. Dallas has low lithium levels because it draws its water from surface supplies.

An intriguing hypothesis: El Paso citizens were ingesting amounts of the tranquilizer in their drinking water, which helped to prevent or remedy the symptoms of mental disorders for which they might otherwise have sought treatment in a state mental hospital. But more investigation was needed. Were there other cities with high lithium levels in their water supply? If so, how did their mental hospital admission rates compare to those of El Paso? Also, how did admissions from Dallas compare with those of other cities with similar lithium levels? Furthermore, could there be alternative explanations? Did life in Dallas tend to put great pressures on its citizens? Did the considerably smaller El Paso have a more serene pace? Without investigating further the correlation between lithium intake and mental hospitalization and without checking alternative explanations, the biochemist would be guilty of *questionable cause.*

As it happened, *Time* had come across a competing hypothesis:

93   . . . State mental health officials pointed out that the mental hospital closest to Dallas is 35 miles away from the city, while the one nearest El Paso is 350 miles away.

We shall not commit *questionable cause* ourselves by asserting that the health officials' explanation provides us with the cause of the higher incidence of mental hospital admissions from Dallas. But, since the biochemist ignored that possibility, he can be charged with the fallacy.

Here's another example, from a Canadian Press report (August 1973) from London, England:

94   A 16-year-old youth dressed in white overalls, a collarless shirt, high boots and a bowler hat, kicks a younger boy unconscious, smashing his ribs and disfiguring his face. Why did he do it?

In the opinion of a British judge, who sentenced the attacker to a term in reform school, it was simply because he had watched a "wicked film," Stanley Kubrick's *A Clockwork Orange.*

The judge noted that the young man had launched his attack while wearing clothes similar to those of the "violence-crazed" characters in the film.

The judge did not argue in *post hoc* fashion. He reasoned from the fact that the crime resembled acts committed in the film and that the youngster was obviously imitating in his manner of dress the style of characters in the film. Still, the judge made a causal claim of a sort that is difficult to substantiate: a claim about the cause of a person's behaviour. We cannot play this youth's life back over again to see what would have resulted had he not seen Kubrick's film. Moreover, as the liveliness of the current debate attests, there exists no established general causal claim about violence in films or TV causing violent behaviour in their viewers. Finally, the judge's claim, that the youth had committed the crime "simply because" of seeing the film, is unclear. Does he mean that it was the *sole cause,* or that it was one of the contributing causes?

The clothing, style, and manner of the attack do suggest a connection with *A Clockwork Orange,* but we must consider alternative hypotheses. Perhaps the movie started a clothing fad, and it was due to the fad that the youth was dressed in that particular way, and not to his having seen the movie. And perhaps the violence of his attack could be explained as plausibly or more plausibly in terms of factors unique to that youth. Did he have a history of outbursts of uncontrollable temper? Was he acutely sensitive on some point and had the boy teased him about it? Was he acting under peer-group pressure to meet some misconceived standard of manhood? Had the judge offered his opinion merely as a possible and reasonable hypothesis, he would have been on safe ground. Since he asserted it as an unqualified causal claim, without assessing alternative possibilities, he was guilty of *questionable cause.*

What the *Clockwork Orange* and the El Paso lithium examples have in common is the premature elevation of one possible explanation to the status of the cause. In both cases, alternative hypotheses were available and should have been investigated. A more thorough check might have revealed one of three possibilities: (a) one or more of the other hypotheses correctly described the cause; (b) the factor proposed together with one or more of the other hypotheses all operated as independent but mutually reinforcing causes; (c) the hypothesis proposing the causal factor did indeed describe the sole cause. So *questionable cause* may be seen to be a special case of *hasty conclusion* — in the two examples above, the hasty jump to (c) without checking out (a) or (b).

We turn now to an example of an argument to a *general* causal claim. The following passage is from an article published a few years ago:

95   Psychiatry kills. It kills because of the ruthless, unprovable treatments used on those entrusted to its care . . . These are just a few of the facts. The bodies of no fewer than 21 people have been discovered in shallow graves in California — all killed with machete blows and knife thrusts by one man in a period of less than two months. The murderer, a Mexican-American, had previously been committed to a mental hospital. Sixteen people were shot to death by a student from the top of the Texas University Tower. The student had previously received psychiatric treatment. The Manson family killed seven in brutal murders in California. Manson had previously received psychiatric treatment . . .

The article went on to multiply instances of people who had previously received psychiatric treatment and later engaged in some form of violent, anti-social behaviour.

Note that the article is not *assuming* that what had caused such behaviour in each case was that these people had received psychiatric treatment. On the contrary, it is using these cases to establish a correlation between psychiatric treatment and violent behaviour. This is the correct move to make in trying to establish a general causal claim. If events of type X cause events of type Y, then when instances of X occur, instances of Y will tend to be found. Hence, to establish that Xs cause Ys, the first thing to look for is such a correlation.

Be careful not to make excessive demands of such a correlation. The claim is not necessarily that psychiatric treatment *always* causes people to become violent. More likely, and more typical of general causal claims of this sort, what is being argued is that psychiatry *can* cause violence. Nor was the article claiming that psychiatry is the *only* cause of violence. In fact, it's a claim of the same variety as the assertion that smoking cigarettes in sufficient quantity causes lung cancer. Pointing out such counter-instances as that Somerset Maugham smoked four packs a day for most of his life, yet died a natural death at 91, does not refute the latter claim. Nor would showing cases of people who received psychiatric treatment but did not commit murder refute the former claim. And just as the fact of other causes of cancer besides smoking does not show that smoking isn't also a cause, so the fact of other causes of violent behaviour besides psychiatric treatment would not show that psychiatry is not an additional cause of violence.

Does the article then establish that psychiatry is a cause of violent behaviour? Clearly not. To show precisely why not, however, we must say more about the method of establishing this kind of general causal claim, and it will help to use the example of the established general causal claim that cigarette smoking is a cause of lung cancer.

To establish that claim, researchers first had to demonstrate by carefully systematic studies that the incidence of lung cancer is significantly higher among the smoking population than among non-smokers. By "significantly" is meant, roughly, that the difference is too striking to be explained by chance. It was reasonable, therefore, to hypothesize a causal link between cigarette smoking and lung cancer. To corroborate this hypothesis, however, researchers had to rule out other factors that might have coincidentally been related to smoking, and have been the actual causal agents — e.g., cigarette paper, or the fumes from the match or lighter. Experiments were run in which these factors were present but the tobacco was absent, and the correlation with lung cancer disappeared. The experiments were refined until it was established that the nicotine and tar in cigarettes are the causally operative factors. Researchers have not yet succeeded in discovering the precise mechanism at work (largely because they do not yet know enough about cancers generally), but it's considered a well-established causal claim that smoking is a causal factor in contracting lung cancer.

We can now take stock of the differences between the article's argument that psychiatric treatment is a cause of violent behaviour and the argument establishing smoking as a cause of lung cancer.

1. The psychiatric treatment–murder correlation is inadequately established. The evidence is anecdotal, not systematic. What should have been done (the sort of study done to establish the smoking–cancer correlation) is this: obtain representative samples of those who have and those who have not received psychiatric treatment. Check each group for its incidence of subsequent violent behaviour. Only if there is a statistically significant difference between the two groups, with the treatment sample showing the higher incidence of violent behaviour, has a correlation worth further consideration been established.

2. Additional correlations that might turn out to signify causal connections are not ruled out. (In the cancer example, the tar and nicotine were isolated as the causal factors, and the cigarette paper, match fumes, etc. eliminated.) For instance, what led the people cited in the article's examples to seek or be referred for psychiatric treatment? Chances are good that some underlying disorder first showed symptoms that resulted in their receiving psychiatric treatment and in spite of that treatment later resulted in the

murderous behaviour. At the least, the article did not produce evidence to rule out such an additional correlate as a causal factor in these murders.

On these two counts, then, we consider the article guilty of *questionable cause* in arguing to the general causal claim that psychiatric treatment can cause violent behaviour.

We have been concentrating on these examples as *arguments to causes*. However, in almost every case, the argument was intended as the background for a further inference based on it. The gentleman from Cape Breton was suggesting that perhaps we ought to return to Fahrenheit degrees; the RCMP Commissioner was proposing that criticism of the Mounties be dismissed; the point of the arguments about seat belts was to commend their use; the London judge went on to urge the censorship of movies like *A Clockwork Orange;* and the psychiatry article argued that people ought to avoid psychiatric treatment. (We're not sure whether the Texas chemist was making any recommendations about the introduction of lithium into water supplies.) It's possible, now, to compile a rough catalogue of mistakes found in *arguments from causes,* using these examples as a starting point.

First, arguments from *particular* causal claims:

A. The recommendation is based on a pure *post hoc ergo propter hoc* inference, without even any connecting hypothesis proposed. (Cf. the Cape Breton gentleman's anti-Celsius argument and the chainprayer, Examples 88 and 89.)

B. The recommendation is based on a hypothesis offered to explain a spatio-temporal connection, but alternative, equally plausible hypotheses exist and have not been ruled out. (Cf. the *Clockwork Orange* and the El Paso lithium examples, 94 and 92.)

Second, arguments from *general* causal claims:

C. The recommendation is based on a claim supported only by a spotty correlation, one that hasn't been systematically established.

D. The recommendation is based on a claim supported by a correlation only, without other correlations checked out and found not to account for the cause. (Cf. for C and D the "psychiatry kills" example, 95.)

We have not yet fully discussed another fairly common error in arguments from general causes:

E. The recommendation is based on mistakenly taking what is merely one cause among others to be the *only* cause or the *main* cause.

There are two quite distinct versions of E. First, what is one among several independently operative causes is taken to be the only or the main cause. Here's an example, from a letter to the *St. John's Evening Telegram.* The writer was concerned about vandalism in the city:

96   The real problem was pointed out recently by assistant police chief
Brown in the talk to the St. John's Kiwanis Club. He pointed out
that the main cause of all this vandalism in the past 20 years is permissiveness in the families and in the schools.

The writer went on to urge an end to the "permissive" treatment of children as the way to end vandalism. But even supposing that permissiveness is a cause of vandalism — and that is certainly conceivable — it doesn't follow that ending permissiveness will eliminate vandalism. For it's very likely that the phenomenon has other causes as well — for example, drunkenness, resentment against authority, or youthful bravado. (Vandalism has not been restricted to the "permissive" 1950s and 1960s.)

The other version of the mistake of taking one cause for the only cause consists of the failure to see that factor as merely one component in a set of causal factors, all of which operate together to bring about the effect. Here is an example, from a letter by S.L. to the *Detroit Free Press* (April 1974):

97   This is written in reply to the dogma espoused by the *Free Press* and other gun control proponents — the claim that the availability of firearms is the root cause of all the killings in the land. I was born in 1913 and was 15 years old before I was anywhere within 100 miles of anyone who was shot with a pistol and that was a thief who was shot by police. Everyone we knew had guns in their home and knew how to use them . . . . If the availability of guns is the cause of the killings, why weren't we all murdered back in those days? Guns were everywhere.

The *Free Press* position was that the availability of guns was one factor that fitted together with others to result in murders, and hence by removing guns from the scene (the aim of gun control legislation), that causal set would be broken up and a major cause of murders removed. S.L., however, took the *Free Press* to be holding that the availability of guns *by itself* led to murders: this was the position he or she was arguing against. It's a case of *straw man* because S.L. confuses necessary with sufficient causal conditions.

Necessary and Sufficient Conditions

Philosophers and scientists have developed a convenient terminology for describing S.L.'s error. They distinguish between **necessary** causal conditions and **sufficient** causal conditions.

By a *sufficient causal condition* is meant an event or factor that suffices to bring about another event. "*X*" is a *sufficient causal condition* for *Y*" means "If *X* occurs, *Y* occurs." A burnt-out bulb, for example, is a sufficient causal condition for a light not to go on. So is a broken switch, or a burnt-out fuse, or a power failure. The occurrence of any one of these is enough to cause the light's failure.

A *necessary causal condition* is an event or factor whose absence prevents another from occurring. "*X* is a *necessary causal condition* for *Y*" means "If *Y* occurs, *X* must have occurred." So, for example, an unbroken electrical circuit is a necessary condition for a light to go on. If the light does go on, the electricity must be flowing through an unbroken circuit. And if this condition is absent — if the current is broken — then the light is prevented from going on.

Many causes consist of a collection of factors where each one is causally necessary, and all together are jointly causally sufficient to bring about the effect. To speak of "a cause" in such a situation is to refer to one of the necessary conditions. This was the *Free Press's* position on the way the availability of firearms was a causal factor in the increased frequency of murders. The availability of guns, it held, was a necessary condition, but not alone a sufficient condition, for the increase in the murder rate. S.L. mistakenly took the *Free Press* to be arguing that the widespread possession of guns was a sufficient condition for the murder rate increase.

So the second version of treating one cause as the only cause can be described as confusing a *necessary causal condition* with a *sufficient causal condition*.

We hope our discussion of these examples will serve as a useful indication of the complexities to be found in causal arguments, of the varieties of causal claims found in daily discourse and of the sorts of critical question to which you should subject them. We can summarize in a general way the conditions of the fallacy we've been discussing as follows:

QUESTIONABLE CAUSE

1. A causal claim, *Q*, appears in *M*'s argument, either as a conclusion or as a premise.
2. (a) *M* argues to *Q*, but fails to provide adequate support for it;
   or (b) *M* argues from *Q*, without supporting it, and there are grounds for questioning the acceptability of *Q*.

In detecting instances of *questionable cause,* the first and most important step is to ferret the causal claim (or implication) out into the open. Once that is done, the rest is a matter of looking at the sort of evidence that has been proposed for it. To defend your charge, it is not necessary that you prove that *X* is not the cause of *Y*. You need only show that the case for the causal connection hasn't been adequately made. An argument that can or might be strengthened by further evidence, so that the causal claim turns out in the end to be true, can still be guilty of *questionable cause.*

EXERCISES

Directions

Determine which fallacies occur in the following passages. You may decide that some passages contain explanations rather than arguments. You may also decide that some of the fallacies are more accurately classified under labels from Chapters 2 and 3 than those from Chapter 4. You may discover fallacies that do not seem to be accurately described by any set of conditions set out up to this point. Finally, you may decide that some passages are innocent of fallacy. Always argue carefully in support of your judgements.

1. *Background:* Several years ago, a New York City police officer was fired from his job when he was convicted of adultery. He filed a $1.6 million lawsuit against the New York City Police Department for damages. Part of his reasoning was:

   > Extra-marital relations are rather commonplace in Nassau County and New York. The laws against adultery have not been enforced in 50 years, insofar as any person is concerned, including, but not limited to, the former governor of New York, Nelson Rockefeller.

2. *Background:* In November 1981, the Catholic bishops of the United States spoke out against abortion. In a syndicated column in the *Detroit Free Press,* Harry Cook criticized their position on the ground that they were not qualified to speak about abortion since the bishops were men, unmarried and childless. In a letter to the *Free Press,* P.D. responded to Cook's column as follows:

   > Cook's claim that the Catholic bishops are unqualified to speak on abortion because they are male, unmarried and childless is like saying that a physician who has never had tuberculosis is unable to cure a patient with tuberculosis — which is, of course, nonsense.
   >
   > Indeed, the bishops made several pronouncements in their annual meeting. I fail to see any objection from Harry Cook on their pronouncement on the arms race, despite the fact that none of the bishops ever attended any of the military schools or the army war college at Ft. Leavenworth. Does their lack of expertise in this field disqualify them from making a pronouncement that the arms race is immoral?

3. *Background:* Some time ago, *The Windsor Star* introduced a new feature: Stargazer Girls, which brought a very mixed reaction from the community. Some charged the *Star* with being sexist; others could see no reason for the fuss. Here is one letter:

Why all the fuss? Can the male authors of these letters (opposing the Stargazer feature) declare positively that they have never bought or perused a girlie magazine? Can the female authors of these same letters declare that they have never worn a skimpy bathing suit on a public beach, fully aware that men could see them?

Why have these letter writers not commented on the "companions wanted" column? Or Ann Landers? Or Dr. Donohue? The Windsor prudes could have a field day with these.

Is "Pet of the Week" exploitation of animals?

"Today's Child." Good grief, you are exploiting children, too?

4. *Background:* In the late 70s, a number of ministers and priests organized musical bonfires, in which teenagers were asked to toss records which they felt unleashed their carnal appetites. One minister observed:

> There's a rhythm to our bodies and when we hear music with a similar rhythm we respond to that beat. Too much of this can affect you in the wrong way. Out of 1000 girls who became pregnant out of wedlock, 984 committed fornication while rock music was being played.

5. *Background:* An alderman from the city of Windsor, Ontario, proposed to the council that cats be licensed, just as dogs are. In an editorial, "The Last Free Spirits," *The Windsor Star* argued:

> Cats are free spirits, the last really independent creatures around. You can no more license cats than you can license the wind. Dogs may submit to bureaucracy. Cats won't. The same spirit tends to rub off on cat owners. They have enough trouble being pushed around by their cats without being asked to submit to man-made laws. Besides, there's an economic factor. They've never had to buy licenses, so why start? No . . . it just won't work.

6. *Background:* In an editorial in September 1975, the *Toronto Star* made the claim that abortion is a matter entirely between the woman concerned and her doctor, and that "making this change needn't violate the consciences of those women and medical practitioners who are opposed to abortion." Several weeks later, J.D. of Walkerton argued:

> Your concept of conscience is indeed narrow.
>
> One who is opposed to smoking, for instance, is not content to leave the matter between the child and the tobacconist. Indeed he or she seeks to have glamorous advertising of the product banned and tries to make smoking as difficult as possible (i.e., forbidding it

in schools, in food establishments, etc.) to create a deterrent to immature as well as casual smokers . . .

Similarly, one who is opposed to abortion cannot possibly leave this matter between an often immature or panic-stricken woman and a doctor often too busy and too materialistic to oppose her wishes.

7. *Background:* An observation by an Australian about the absence of some politicians is worth recording:

> While the Prime Minister, Mr. Whitlam, was overseas, the country was beset by two tragedies at Darwin and at Tasmania. Since the Premier of Queensland, Mr. Bjelke-Petersen has been overseas, the weather and most things have been perfect. I therefore conclude that Mr. Whitlam should stay in Australia and keep it safe, and that Mr. Bjelke-Petersen should stay overseas and keep Australia peaceful.

8. *Background:* The Chicago Bears had just lost for the sixth time in seven games during the 1981-82 NFL season when James Tulley, of Rockford, Illinois, filed a complaint in the small claims court, claiming that the Bears were guilty of false advertising and consumer fraud. He reasoned:

> The Bears advertised a professional football game but they don't play a very professional game. They make too many mistakes and don't live up to their advertising. It's like if Barry Manilow came on stage and suddenly got laryngitis and couldn't talk, I'd get a refund. If the Rolling Stones came to town without Mick Jagger, that would be misrepresentation.

9. *Background:* An excerpt from an advertisement for numerology contained the following claims:

> We have found that numerology is a very useful tool in producing good luck. For example, the letters in the alphabet have assigned numbers. Singer Dionne Warwicke took the advice from her numerologist and added an 'e' to the end of her name. Her numerologist told her that this would bring about the correct, fortunate combination.
>
> She immediately skyrocketed to fame. She has revealed this fact on the Johnny Carson show twice.

10. *Background:* In May, 1982, a columnist for the *Toronto Star* advocated the idea of parental leave (a policy which would allow either

the mother or father of a newborn child to have nine months leave from the job at 90% pay). After presenting the reasons for this, the columnist anticipated an objection: "But aren't thousands of lazy men and women going to idle away the months, having babies at our expense?"

No. That is just what was predicted when Canada brought in the baby bonus, and our birth rate has steadily fallen. In Sweden, after a decade of parental leave, the birth rate has dropped below the replacement level, and only 12% of Swedish men take the leave.

11. *Background:* Responding to the above column, J.D. of Toronto wrote (*Toronto Star,* May 15, 1982):

Rejoice! Michele Landsberg is back with her amusing emotional illogicalities, jumping to her *post hoc, ergo propter hoc* conclusions as usual.
She solemnly declaims that introduction of the baby bonus caused a reduction of the birth rate, as if there were a causal relationship between them. Burning witches at the stake restored milk to cows, no doubt.

12. *Background:* From the *Detroit Free Press* (June 29, 1982):

Two genetic researchers analysed 170 San Francisco couples who were married seven years ago, fifty-two of whom have since divorced. They determined that couples with similarly sized forearms enjoy better chances for domestic harmony than partners whose arms don't match. The best candidate for a rocky relationship is a long-armed man and a short-armed woman.

13. *Background:* Ontario is the only province in Canada that has a Grade 13 in the secondary system of education. There has been continuing debate about the wisdom of having Grade 13. Here is what one person said in a letter to the *Toronto Star* (June, 1982):

I'm a Grade 10 student who completely agrees that Grade 13 should be abolished. Five years of high school is not at all necessary. Ontario is the only province that has this extra year tacked on.[4]

---

[4] From *An Informal Logic Workbook,* ed. by Kate Parr (Windsor, 1981), p. 52.

CHAPTER FIVE

FALLACIES OF SLEIGHT OF HAND

Introduction

Much attention has been focused in recent years on the state of language and language use in North America. Writers like Edwin Newman, Joseph Safire, and John Simon have been campaigning for linguistic reform, calling attention to doublespeak, jargon, etc. In this chapter, we too shall be concerned with language, primarily insofar as it results in logical miscues rather than other forms of linguistic malfeasance.

Loaded Term

To start, let's consider a few "emotive conjugations":

98   I am firm, you are obstinate, he is pig-headed.
I am righteously indignant, you are annoyed, he is making a fuss over nothing.
I have reconsidered the matter, you have changed your mind, he has gone back on his word.

The moral of these conjugations (first developed by the philosopher, Bertrand Russell) is that we are often inclined to describe behaviour in one way when we are engaged in it, but in quite different terms (harsher and more judgemental) when someone else is. The very same behaviour can alternately be described as "firm," "obstinate," "pig-headed." But these

126

descriptions are not equivalent, as you can plainly tell. "Obstinate" and "pig-headed" carry an *evaluation* with them; far from being neutral, these are what we shall call **loaded terms.** If they are to be justifiably employed on a given occasion, there will need to be adequate evidence to support the evaluative component. If not, the fallacy called *loaded term* lurks in the background.

Naturally, the terms one chooses in constructing one's argument will reflect one's point of view. From the British point of view, the U.S. colonists who dumped tea into Boston Harbor in 1775 would probably be described as "terrorists" or "revolutionaries," while the colonists themselves would have described such people as "patriots" or "freedom fighters." And the same holds true of our current instances of political strife. Are members of the PLO to be described as "terrorists" or as "freedom fighters"? The answer to this question is a function of both evidence and of political point of view; and one of the problems is that people of diametrically opposed viewpoints are often unable to agree on just what is to *count as evidence.* So loaded terms like the ones we've mentioned get thrown around in political debate with very little thought given to their applicability.

The same phenomena recur in less volatile situations. Herb Caen, a columnist for the *San Francisco Chronicle,* noted that "Republicans have associates, the Democrats have henchmen." Terms like "voodoo economics," "chauvinist pig," "reactionary," and so on, lace the fabric of contemporary rhetoric, and the watchful consumer needs to become aware of the logical abuse involved. The logical point is not that the language of argument must be neutral or bland or lacking in punch. But when an arguer sees fit to employ highly charged particles in his argument, the arguer incurs the obligation of justifying his use of them. When he fails to do this, he commits the fallacy we call *loaded term.*

Here is an example from the ongoing debate about capital punishment. In an article, "No answer in noose" (*Windsor Star,* February 1976), Sandra Precop writes:

99   . . . Canada needs to abolish the death penalty. The arguments from both sides have been repeated so loudly and for so long that it would be a waste of ink to go over them again. To me it always comes down to one basic equation: a murder plus a murder does not equal justice.

Reconstructing Precop's reasoning here, we have the following argument:

100   1. One murder cannot justify another murder.
        a The state ought not to engage in murder.
        b When the state executes a murderer, it commits murder.
    c Canada should abolish the death penalty.

Certainly we will accept 1 and a. The problem here concerns b. That is, can we justifiably apply the term "murder" to the state's action when, presumably in acccordance with the laws of the state, it puts a criminal to death? There may be an argument for this position, but Precop (perhaps because she considers that the argument is well enough known) hasn't presented it. "Murder" here is therefore a *loaded term.*

Our second example comes from an advertising supplement circulated in a number of Canadian magazines like *Maclean's* and *Saturday Night* by the Imperial Oil Company. Esso was arguing for more "realistic" — i.e. higher — prices for petroleum products. The pamphlet contained a section called "Prices in perspective," which read, in part:

101 Over the past quarter century, because world prices for crude oil have been *depressed,* and because of intense competition, petroleum energy has been available in Canada at *bargain* prices. The price of energy generally in Canada has been so low that, in the words of the Ontario Government Advisory Committee on Energy, it has been taken for granted and regarded almost as a free commodity. (Emphasis ours.)

The thrust of this passage in the overall argument is that since prices in the past have been lower than they could justifiably have been, it is not unwarranted of Esso and the petroleum industry to demand and expect higher prices now. Note how that argument gains support from the classification of world prices for crude oil over the past 25 years as "depressed," and the classification of the prices of petroleum energy in Canada as "bargain." If world prices for crude oil were *depressed,* that implies they are lower than they ought to have been; if we've been getting our petroleum energy at *bargain* prices, that implies we've been getting it more cheaply than we have a right to normally expect. But these classifications are questionable. Economic dogma, at least, has it that fair market prices are established by competition. In arguing that world crude prices have been "depressed" by *competition,* Imperial would appear to be undercutting its own commitment to a free market economy. Further, we note that Esso is arguing that Canadian petroleum prices have been a "bargain" just at a time when it wants money for more exploration to come out of higher prices instead of out of retained earnings. Gasoline and heating fuel had hardly been "almost free" — despite what the Ontario Advisory Committee on Energy might have said. Our point is that the case needs a good deal more support; without that further support it's questionable to classify these prices as "bargain." Given that these classifications are used to support the intended conclusion that petroleum prices should be increased, Imperial in this ad is guilty of *loaded term.*

Clearly the conditions of this fallacy fall into two parts, each of which must be satisfied:

LOADED TERM

1. *M* labels something, *X* (a person, act, event, situation, etc.), in a way that is either debatable or else false.
2. *M* uses that classification of *X* without defense as support for some conclusion, *Q*.

The fallacy, we repeat, occurs only when the *loaded term* functions in a premise in an argument. A *loaded term* which occurs outside an argument is not a fallacy, although of course that doesn't mean you should accept it.

We must emphasize that *loaded term* is a special case of *problematic premise.* Essentially what you are doing in locating a term which has questionable application is pointing to a premise which requires defense; that is, the arguer needs to provide some reason for thinking that the term does indeed apply. Therefore, a charge of *loaded term* must not be pictured as a devastating rebuttal of an argument. It's more appropriately seen as exposing the argument's weak or tender spots. There is no presumption that the arguer cannot produce the needed defense of the classification that is questioned. For instance, Imperial Oil may well be able to demonstrate that, despite the questions we have raised, all the evidence taken together does justify their describing world crude oil prices as "depressed" and Canadian petroleum prices as "bargain."

. Next we quote what we take to be a rather typical example of the use of loaded terms. This letter was occasioned by the article written by Sandra Precop which we analysed earlier in this section:

102   Well, I see one of your esteemed columnists has added her name to the list of *bleeding hearts* concerning capital punishment.

Ms. Precop, and her band of *pseudo-intellectuals,* and politicians in general take the attitude that the public is, at best, near imbecile, and must therefore be led around by the nose mentally all their lives.

Let's put an end to all this rhetoric once and for all, place the subject on the ballot for a public referendum, and let the *do-gooders* busy themselves sending CARE packages to Millhaven. (Emphasis ours.)

Evidently the writer of this letter is in favour of capital punishment and finds Precop's position unconvincing. The writer uses three loaded terms to signal this disagreement: "bleeding heart," "pseudo-intellectual" and "do-gooder." The logical problem with the writer's position is that it lacks real substance. The loaded terms function as a *substitute* for argumentation.

When the writer describes Precop as a "bleeding heart," he presumably means that she lacks the moral fortitude necessary to assess the evidence. That would seem to be the core idea of this *loaded term;* and if the term were accurately applied here to Precop, then the writer would have scored a point in favour of his position. But the writer produces no evidence at all which would suggest that the application of "bleeding heart" is warranted here. The same is true of the use of "pseudo-intellectual," which we take to mean "lacking in tough-minded analytic skills." If those who oppose capital punishment can be justifiably so labelled, then there is reason not to accept their arguments. But this is something which must be shown by a careful review of their arguments, showing just where they break down. But the writer does not produce such an evaluation; and the use of the term "pseudo-intellectual" *substitutes* for such argumentation. Indeed, if the writer could and did produce the required evidence to justify the use of these loaded terms, there would be no objection to their use. Then, too, there would probably be little point to using them.

The salient point about the use of loaded terms is that they violate the spirit of argument and rational persuasion. Tagging your opponents' views with terms like "bleeding heart," "pseudo-intellectual," and so on is hardly an invitation to the reasoned pursuit of truth. Indeed, loaded terms tend by their nature to appeal to the converted, to those who already share your socio-political views. Describe a particular course of action as "communist" in front of a meeting of the Moral Majority and you will get one reaction; that same course of action described as "communist" at a meeting in Soviet Russia will produce the opposite reaction.

Loaded terms are not necessarily restricted to political contexts. The letter below (*The Windsor Star,* July 1982) does a nice job of pointing out a *loaded term:*

103   At the present time, cigarettes are advertised as "mild," "extra mild," etc., with the implication that, because they are mild, they are harmless. Whereas they are nothing of the kind and the tobacco interests should be forbidden to speak of them this way.

In sum, if people are going to use highly charged and evaluative words and phrases in their arguments, they are going to have to be prepared to *justify* that usage. At the same time, the critic of argumentation has an obligation to be fair and even-handed. In this context, that means not jumping all over every piece of spicy rhetoric. First stop to think about whether or not the vivid language plays a central role in the argument and whether or not it needs justification.

Ambiguity

The word "ambiguous" is defined in the Oxford Universal Dictionary as meaning: 1. "Doubtful; not clearly defined," and 2. "Open to more than one interpretation; equivocal." The fallacy we discuss in this section takes its name from the second meaning.

Incidentally, is the word "ambiguous" itself ambiguous, since it has two meanings? Loosely speaking, perhaps it is. More precisely, however, words or phrases are not in themselves ambiguous. The ambiguity occurs only when a word or phrase appears in a context in which it can be taken in more than one way. So it's words-in-context that are actually open to ambiguity.

Nothing is logically wrong with ambiguity per se. It may confuse, but that's a literary flaw. The logical fallacy of **ambiguity** is reserved for the manoeuvre in argument of trading on the potential of a word or phrase for more than one interpretation. This strategy results in blurring the focus of the argument, often resulting in the creation of a *red herring* or a *straw man*.

Look at how it can work in practice. The first example comes from a speech by then-Justice Minister Otto Lang to "The Continental Action Assembly of Christians and Jews" in June 1975 (reported in *The Windsor Star*). Mr. Lang touched on the abortion issue and defended his view that the 1969 legislation permitting abortion should be interpreted in a strict way so as to keep the number of abortions to a minimum — to cases in which the health "in the life and death sense" of the mother is in danger. In rebuttal of the counterclaim that such a strict interpretation of the law would lead to many unwanted children entering the world, Mr. Lang said that in Canada there is no such thing as an unwanted child.

It will help to have his argument standardized:

104

1. There is no such thing as an unwanted child in Canada.
2. It is not true that a strict interpretation of the abortion legislation will result in unwanted children.

Mr. Lang went on to defend his premise, arguing, "There are many places where children are wanted. People are on waiting lists for years applying for adoption of a child."

It's clear from his defense that Mr. Lang meant 1 in the sense that in Canada no children are not wanted by *somebody* — if not their natural parents, then by couples who want to adopt a child. But is that the sense in which the pro-abortionists (whose claim Lang was trying to refute) intend the proposition that fewer abortions will lead to more unwanted children? Not at all. What they mean is that there will be more children who are unwanted *by their natural parents*.

What went wrong with Mr. Lang's argument may be seen by noting that 1 can be understood in two ways:

1_1: There is no child in Canada whose natural parents do not want to bear and raise it.

1_2: There is no child in Canada who is wanted by no one at all.

1_1 is the sense of 1 that must be true if it is to lend support to Mr. Lang's criticism of the pro-abortionist position; 1_2 is irrelevant to that criticism, given the sense of "unwanted children" at issue. But Lang's argument employs 1_2. As a result, what he had to say never really made contact with the position he was trying to refute. He committed the fallacy of *ambiguity*. The culprit was the term "unwanted child."

For another example of *ambiguity*, consider the following argument:

105   The fact that there are laws of nature shows that God exists. For the existence of a law implies the existence of a law-giver, and God is the Supreme law-giver in the Universe. So, far from disproving the existence of God, science, in detecting the laws of nature, actually proves that God does exist.

Standardized, the argument may be set forth as follows:

106   1. Science discovers the laws of nature.
       2. Every law implies a law-giver.
       3. God is the Supreme law-giver.
       4. Science proves that God exists.

The ambiguous word here is "law." This word has two quite different meanings. It may mean "an observed regularity in nature"; it may also mean "a prescription or mandate set forth by duly constituted authority." It has the former meaning in 1, but the latter meaning in 2. So although it looks like 1 and 2 work together to support 4, they do not. 2 is false if "law" means what it must mean in order for 1 to be true; and 1 is false if "law" means what it must mean in order for 2 to be true. The fallacy of *ambiguity* occurs, and we may conclude that this argument fails to establish the truth of the conclusion.

Another example. In 1967 the Progressive Conservative Party of Canada held a "Thinkers' Conference" at Montmorency, Quebec, in order to begin to shape party policy for the next federal election. From this conference emerged a policy statement that asserted, in part, "that Canada is composed of the original inhabitants of this land and the *two founding nations* with historic rights, who have been and continue to be joined by people from many lands" (emphasis ours). When the 1968 federal election campaign began, the phrase "two nations" (a translation from the French, *deux nations*) became a thorn in the PCs' side.

Liberal leader Trudeau asserted that there could be only one sovereign state in Canada, that sovereignty is indivisible, and that there could not be two nations and one nation at the same time. The Liberals attacked the Conservatives' position as a dangerous threat to Canadian unity. Their argument might be standardized along these lines:

107 1. The Progressive Conservatives endorse the concept of two nations in Canada.
2. There can be two nations only if there are two political states.
3. The PCs' policy of accepting the two nations idea is a threat to Canadian unity.

The Conservatives were furious with this argument. It traded, they charged, on the wrong meaning of the phrase "two nations." "Nation" can denote a politically sovereign state (a "nation state"), or it can refer to a cultural or ethnic group (as the English, Scots, and Welsh are three nations in the single state of Great Britain). What the PCs endorsed was the recognition of the two founding ethnic groups in Canada — the French and the British — as basic facts of national life. The Liberals were quite deliberately misrepresenting their position. Trudeau was right, they granted, that there can be only one sovereign Canadian state. But that was irrelevant as a criticism of the PCs' position. What the Liberals had to deny, to refute the PCs' policy, was that there should be no recognition of the two sociological groupings, French and English, in Canadian life. That, of course, they could not do.

We can make this point in terms of the argument as we've standardized it. 2 is true if it is taken to mean:

2_1: There can be two politically sovereign states in Canada only if there are two politically sovereign states.

True — but trivially true. Moreover, it requires the willful misreading (according to the PCs) of the Conservative position. What they meant by "two nations" was "two socio-ethnic groups." Hence, if the term used in the Liberals' argument were correctly interpreted, 2 would become:

2_2: There can be two socio-ethnic groups in Canada only if there are two politically sovereign states in Canada.

Both the Conservatives and the Liberals (unlike most separatists) take the position that 2_2 is false. So the Liberals were able to employ their argument only by distorting the Conservative meaning of "two nations," taking it in a sense not intended by its advocates.

If this is a fair analysis of the Liberals' position, then they clearly did commit the fallacy of *ambiguity*. For their part, the Liberals defended their attacks on the two-nations policy on the ground that the Conservatives themselves vacillated between both senses of the phrase, and so were themselves the perpetrators of ambiguity. "In Quebec they are talking about two-nations and about special status, and in the rest of the country they are talking about one nation and no special status . . . ," Trudeau charged. (He thus accused the Conservatives of the fallacy of *inconsistency*.) There is still debate about who was right. Both sides agree that the "two nations" issue hurt the Conservatives in the 1968 election and contributed to Trudeau's victory.

These are the conditions of the fallacy:

AMBIGUITY

1. A premise, Q, in M's argument contains a term or phrase, T, that is open to different interpretations in different contexts.
2. The sense of T in Q (giving Q_1) is different from the sense of T (giving Q_2) relevant to defending M's conclusion or refuting M's opponent.

Typically, *ambiguity* is found in adversary contexts, and M's argument is a rejoinder to a position held by someone else. That was the case in two of our examples, 104 and 107. What those examples also illustrated was that usually the argument that results from M's interpretation of the term or phrase is a plausible one. That's what gives the exercise its credibility. But when the premise is interpreted in its *relevant* sense, the argument usually founders.

What you must do to prove *ambiguity* is locate the key term or phrase and identify the role its ambiguity plays in the argument. Standardizing the pertinent parts of the argument helps, as does identifying the two senses in which the ambiguous premise may be understood. You have then set down the necessary details for showing that the two conditions have been met.

One last example to tie all the pieces together, from a letter to *The Ottawa Journal* (August 1974):

108   A small number of self-appointed loudmouths in Women's Lib, intoxicated with the exuberance of their own verbosity, have partially forced on the public a humorless demand that the word "man" shall be replaced by "person."

I offer a suggestion that would save thousands of dollars in printing . . . Drop "man" and "woman" and use the wartime slang word "bod" for everyone; e.g., "sales bod" instead of "salesperson" . . . "Boditoba" instead of "Personitoba" (Manitoba); "ebodcipation," "bodifesto" and "Bodilla" — the capital of the Philippines . . .

The bod who wrote this letter was having great fun playing on an ambiguity. Bod's implicit argument can be standardized as follows:

109   1: Some persons in the Women's Liberation movement have
         suggested that the word "man" be replaced by the word "per-
         son."
      2: This suggestion would lead to such ridiculous consequences
         (which substituting the word "bod" where the Women's Lib-
         eration advocates would put "person" serves to dramatize) as:
         "Personitoba" for "Manitoba," "epersoncipation" for "eman-
         cipation," "personifesto" for "manifesto," and "Personilla" for
         "Manilla."
      3. The suggestion to replace "man" with "person" should be
         ignored.

Of course, Bod's argument gets off the ground only if 1 is understood in the
sense of:

   1_1: Some persons in the Women's Liberation Movement have
        suggested that wherever the particular ordered sequence of
        letters "m-a-n" occurs it should be replaced by the particular
        ordered sequence of letters "p-e-r-s-o-n."

However, that certainly isn't the intention of the Women's Liberation's suggestion, which would render a very different sense of 1, namely:

   1_2: Some persons in the Women's Liberation Movement have
        suggested that where the word "man" is used to designate a
        male or female indifferently, it should be replaced by the
        word "person."

That's the sense in which 1 is true, but then it has nothing to do with Bod's 2
or 3: Bod is guilty of *ambiguity*. Also, since Bod's letter distorts and attacks
the Women's Liberation position by using this ambiguity, we suggest that
Bod be found guilty on a second count: *straw man*.

Vagueness

The concept of vagueness deserves careful conceptual analysis. For our purposes, however, it will suffice to focus on one sort of vagueness that can
plague arguments. We'll concentrate on propositions that are vague in the
sense that you can't be sure what precisely they mean. You have no way
of knowing what they include and what they rule out. This is the sort of
vagueness often found in popular clichés. Here's a typical example:

110   You're the only one who knows what's right for you.

Sounds good, but what is it saying? "Right" in what sense? Morally right? The right size or fit? The right mix to suit your taste? It seems to rule out anyone else's knowing what is right for you, but that can't be, since others can know what size fits you, what flavours you like, and even what your moral duties are. Is it saying that no one else should tell you what you ought to do? Perhaps, yet that would rule out a parent or friend giving you well-meant advice. The guesses could continue; there are no doubt many other possible meanings of this cliché. Our point is that, taken as it stands, *no one can know what they are committed to if they accept it, nor what they have denied if they reject it.* Outside any context, it's incredibly vague; even when such clichés are encountered in actual use, the contextual furnishings merely reduce, but do not eliminate, their vagueness.

When such a proposition occupies the role of a premise in an argument, the support it provides for the conclusion will be diluted by its vagueness. When, on the other hand, the conclusion is vague, you cannot determine how well or poorly the premises back it up, since you can't be clear about what proposition they are intended to support.

We call **vagueness** a fallacy of sleight of hand because these indeterminate propositions don't *look* imprecise as they are slipped into the flow of everyday argumentation. Perhaps just because a variety of meanings can be read into them, we tend to gloss over them, probably assuming our own interpretation as we go. And there are those who have learned how to exploit vagueness for political and social ends. It takes a thinking reader or listener to notice vagueness; often it also takes a degree of courage to speak up (to think out) and wonder — not whether the emperor has any clothes — but whether there's anybody under the robes.

Consider now some actual examples of this fallacy. In September 1972 in an Ontario cabinet shuffle, J.D. McNie became Minister of Education. In an editorial about the cabinet changes, the Toronto *Globe and Mail* said:

111   Mr. McNie assumes his troublesome education post at a time when "individual initiative and free enterprise" are beginning to take on some of their old coloration, at least for the Ontario Government and people. His immediate charges — in college and university — may not yet have got the message; but the Government and the public are united in believing that there has to be a ceiling for education costs somewhere up in those airy clouds. Mr. McNie's task will be to see that not too many heads thrust through the ceiling when he finds it. It will be interesting to see if he has the strength to do it.

There seems to be an argument of sorts here, but the *Globe and Mail* has managed an adroit editorial waffle so that it's hard to determine precisely what the point of the argument is. Certainly one premise has something to do with a ceiling for education costs, and the conclusion has something to do with what Mr. McNie will do — or should do — to impose such a ceiling. Can we get a clearer picture? Is the second-last sentence a *prediction* ("Mr. McNie's task *will be* . . .")? If it is, then how can the editorial in the next sentence wonder if Mr. McNie will have "the strength to do it"? Does the *Globe and Mail* mean that Mr. McNie *ought* to put a lid on education spending? If so, why did it say "will be" instead of "should be"? And look at the main premise, the contention that there has to be a ceiling for education costs. We'll not quibble over the use of "has to be" where obviously "should be" is what's intended. The problem is that this contention, taken literally, is vacuous. What would it mean to *deny* that there should be a limit to education costs? Would it mean that schools and educators should get however much money they ask for, even if it gobbled up the whole provincial budget or required oppressive taxes? But who would take that stand? No, obviously there ought to be a limit to the amount spent on education; what is needed to assert anything significant is a statement of what that limit ought to be.

At this point, the ambiguity of the term "ceiling" in its use here blocks precision. Does "a ceiling for education costs" mean a limit to the total amount spent on education in any given year, or does it mean a limit to the percentage of the provincial budget in any given year? (And if the former, what amount? If the latter, what percentage?)[1] Or again, does it mean stipulating an absolute limit beyond which education spending may not go?

In short, we don't know at all clearly what the editorial is recommending. We do not know what would count as accepting or rejecting its proposal. We don't have any clear idea what it is telling Mr. McNie to do (or predicting that Mr. McNie will do). We charge the *Globe and Mail* editorial here with *vagueness*.

In the fall of 1974, *Saturday Night* magazine, running into financial woes, announced it would have to cease publication unless it could find $100,00 on short notice.[2] The anticipated demise of this venerable Canadian monthly, first published in 1887, was cited by many as further evidence of the harmful influence of the special status of *Time* and *Reader's Digest* on Canadian periodical publishing, and lent further support to the lobbyists trying to get the federal government to revoke the exemption from the foreign periodicals' tax enjoyed by these two American magazines. N.H. took issue with this position in the following letter to the *Edmonton Journal* (October 1974):

112   As far as I'm concerned, *Saturday Night* could have quit many years ago. When *Maclean's* and *Chatelaine* give up the ghost I

---

[1] Note that the ambiguity of "ceiling" here does not result in the fallacy of *ambiguity*. It merely contributes to the vagueness of the editorial's claim.

[2] *SN* did stop publication for a few months, but private capital was found to revive it, and as of this writing it is thriving.

won't know the difference until I read of it in the obituaries. What in the world have these magazines done for Canadian citizens? They are dull, prejudiced, their subjects are nothing but political (by radicals), the cost is high, and a free-lancer can't get in once in a century.

As usual, Canadians, who are incompetent, inefficient, lazy, miserly, and jealous, cannot compete with the U.S.A. in anything — be it sports, food production, manufacturing, films, popular songs, TV writing, publishing, or just plain work. Consequently they always want U.S. products and performers banned so they can produce the usual poor product.

I think *Reader's Digest* is an excellent magazine . . . . As for *Time*, not in 50 or even 100 years will Canada be able to produce anything comparable in coverage . . .

We take part of N.H.'s argument to be that the basic reason Canadian periodicals have trouble competing against *Time* and *Reader's Digest* is that Canadians aren't competent to produce magazines as good as these, and therefore the claim that *Time* and *Reader's Digest* have an unfair advantage shouldn't be credited. Now let us assess the premise here: "Canadians are incompetent, inefficient, lazy, miserly, and jealous." Wait a minute! *Which* Canadians was N.H. referring to? You? Us? We aren't too ready to accept these characterizations, and no doubt you aren't either. Certainly not all Canadians exhibit these traits. Yet no doubt some possess some of them, and possibly even some (a much smaller number) possess all of them. Before we can take issue with N.H.'s allegation, we must know which claim he or she was making. The charge is too imprecise: N.H. committed *vagueness*.

We might note two other common domiciles of vagueness: clichés, as we've mentioned already, and advertising. As an example of the latter, consider the slogan being used by Coca-Cola:

113   "Coke is it!"

It's short and sweet and says nothing at all (or anything you choose to get from it). What is the referent of "it"? We don't know. We aren't supposed to know. The function of this claim is not to state a truth but rather to allow them to call attention to their product. You couldn't really disagree with this slogan. We can imagine that the manufacturers of Pepsi-Cola, for example, believe that Pepsi is it — but this slogan is just as vague. We have more to say about the peculiarities of advertising claims in Chapter 11.

We can think of no rule for drawing attention to cases of *vagueness*. The examples we used illustrate a couple of common contributors, but there are many more. We have already met what might be called the "all-some" vagueness of N.H.'s letter in the sentence, "Canadians are . . . " Did

N.H. mean *all* Canadians, or only *some?* And if the latter, who? Unmodi-
fied general nouns are often vague in this way. We also have seen the
"must-ought" vagueness in the *Globe and Mail* editorial. When it said there
"has to be a ceiling on education costs," was it saying that this is in some
sense a necessity (something that somehow must be the case), or was it taking the view that such a ceiling is desirable? Other variants of this case are
the "will-ought" and the "is-ought" vagueness. The *Globe and Mail* said
that "Mr. McNie's task will be . . ." when pretty clearly what it meant was
that "Mr. McNie ought to . . . ." And you will have heard some teachers
say, "A student's role is to . . ." when they mean, "Students ought
to . . . ." Of course, there is no vagueness when you can discern from the
context which meaning is intended. But the looseness of these locutions can
contribute vagueness when the context is not determinate.

EXERCISES

Directions

Determine which fallacies occur in the following passages. Remember that
some may not contain arguments at all, some fallacies from earlier chapters
may be present, some fallacies may not be classifiable in terms of the labels
thus far introduced, and some of the arguments may be fallacy-free. As
always, present reasons for your assessments.

1. *Background:*   In the spring of 1970, the U.S. invaded Cambodia. This
   triggered a wave of protest on university campuses, the most famous of
   which was at Kent State University, where several students were shot
   and killed by the National Guard. At roughly the same time, the trial of
   the Chicago 7 was underway and there was much talk about the threat
   these events signalled for individual rights and freedom. Columnist
   John Roche stated:

   > Every society is, of course, repressive to some extent. As Sigmund
   > Freud pointed out, repression is the price we pay for civilization.[3]

---

[3] Cited in Kahane, *Logic and Contemporary Rhetoric* (Belmont, California: Wadsworth Publishing Company, 1971), p. 73.

2. *Background:* In 1971, the Ontario government was reviewing its policy of restricting state aid to Roman Catholic separate schools, in the face of considerable pressure to extend that aid beyond Grade 10. The Toronto *Globe and Mail* editorialized (August 1971):

> . . . aid should not be extended to the Catholic secondary schools.
> The reasons for this stand are several. The first is that in Ontario, which has put behind it the Orange era of politico-religious wars, it would be a tragic backward step to re-introduce a system which divided children on the basis of religion, which balkanized them by sects during their most crucial years of adjusting to a free and non-discriminatory society. If we have forgotten how bitterly and irrationally religion can divide, we have only to look at Ireland . . .

3. *Background:* From another contribution to the abortion debate (*The Windsor Star,* June 1975):

> Pro-abortion groups never refer to the true meaning of abortion. They use the phrase "termination of the pregnancy," they shy away from the term killing unborn babies. Perhaps the true meaning would not enhance their cause.

4. *Background:* This is an excerpt from a column entitled "Trudeau's view of Conscience vs. Law" which appeared in *The Windsor Star* in August 1971, in the aftermath of the debate about whether U.S. draft-dodgers should be allowed entry into Canada:

> Our sage philosopher-king, Pierre Trudeau, has again uttered some words of wisdom worthy of contemplation by all Canadians. Stating his support for draft-dodgers who come to Canada from the U.S., he explained:
> "I think that the only ultimate guide we have is our conscience and if the law of the land goes against our conscience, I think we should disobey the law. But because I am also a deep believer in the civil society, I think we should be prepared to pay the consequences of breaking the law — and that means either paying the penalty for it, or leaving the country."
> One is astounded by the individualism that this statement so pithily advocates. And that from a man who imposed the War Measures Act to deal with a handful of lawbreakers. . . .
> The point of the matter is that Mr. Trudeau has the business of conscience and law mixed up. Not conscience, but law, is the ultimate guide; without law there could be no conscience. When a

man thinks a certain law violates his conscience, it is only because there is some other law on the same subject that he believes should be followed.

5. *Background:* In June 1982, John Hinckley, the man who attempted to assassinate President Ronald Reagan in March of 1981, was found not guilty because (in the opinion of the jurors) the prosecution had not proved beyond a reasonable doubt that Hinckley was sane. Many objected to the verdict, among them U.S. syndicated columnist William F. Buckley who wrote "Voodoo law and a jeer for the jury," (*Detroit Free Press,* June 29, 1982):

> The word "expertise" means "a body of operative knowledge." If no such knowledge exists — for instance, on the question of whether Hinckley knew what he was doing and that it was wrong — then no one is by definition an "expert," except in the sense that he is devoted to trying to answer a question about which there is no expertise. If you attempt to play Rachmaninoff's Second Concerto, devoting your lifetime to the effort, but what comes out is disharmonious sounds, unrelated to what Rachmaninoff wrote, you simply have not mastered the Second Concerto. At least, however, we know that the concerto exists. What we do not know is whether there is any way in which Hinckley can be "proved" to have known what he was doing was evil and unlawful.

6. *Background:* In December of 1973, faced with mass resignations by high school teachers aiming to pressure school boards to negotiate favourable contracts, the Ontario government introduced a bill that would have outlawed such tactics during teachers' salary negotiations. (It was already illegal for Ontario teachers to strike.) The teachers protested that their collective bargaining rights were being denied them, and some also argued along the following lines. This is an amalgam of several letters to editors across the province at the time:

> The government ought to withdraw the proposed legislation.
> The bill it has introduced takes away teachers' right to resign. No government has the authority to force people to continue at a particular job if they wish to leave it. The bill interferes with a basic freedom of democracy: the right to choose your own job.

7. *Background:* In the fall of 1974, the Toronto *Globe and Mail* published a series of articles growing out of allegations by some citizens that Toronto police were guilty of brutality. One letter commented on these stories:

I am writing to express my deep regret at the publication of "Police Brutality" [the title of the series]. Sensational stories in your fine paper? Why have you turned to yellow journalism? You have done a great disservice not only to our superior police force but to the entire city.

8. *Background:* This is a letter to *The Windsor Star* (April 1976) concerning the petition by a group of francophones in the Windsor area for a French-language high school:

> Regarding the petition which stated "the French were here first, so why can't they have their own high school?", well, the Indians were here first and they don't have their own anything. Since it took all nationalities to make Windsor what it is, I think all nationalities should have equal say in what Windsorites need, and not just what the French want.
>
> You don't hear the French trying to speak English as readily as any other non-English, so that proves we don't need French high schools.[4]

9. *Background:* This letter to *The Windsor Star* from M.W. (September, 1982) takes issue with what the writer perceives to be a policy gradually developing at the newspaper:

> For several months I have observed with dismay a trend in *The Windsor Star* of publishing sensation photographs, regardless of their relevance and news value.
>
> The latest questionable choice of photographs occurred in your sports section. It showed a rider at the World Equestrian Championships suffering a fatal fall. Such a photograph might have a legitimate place on the sports page if it were related to an account of the World Championships — nations competing, riders, points, placings, etc. However, equestrian sports have earned not even a mention in your scores of columns previously, let alone an acknowledgement of the growing local participation in the sport. The photograph is not only unnecessarily sensational but gives a totally false impression of a sport where such freak accidents are extremely rare.

10. *Background:* In September, 1982, there were news reports about a meeting between Yasser Arafat and Pope John Paul, which prompted this response from R.T. to the Toronto *Globe and Mail* (September, 1982):

---

[4] Our thanks to Mr. John Sleziak for bringing this example to our attention.

The Pope and PLO leader Yasser Arafat in conversation? The Pope grants an audience to a bloody terrorist?

Are we Anglicans going to continue to support the Archbishop of Canterbury to have our Christian Church swallowed by the Roman Church? We, and I trust I speak for all Christian Anglicans, do not wish to have the Archbishop continue to talk with Roman prelates.

11. *Background:* From an ad sponsored by The Tobacco Institute (*U.S. News & World Report,* September 1982) whose lead was the question: "Do cigarette companies want kids to smoke?"

> No. As a matter of policy. No. As a matter of practice. No. As a matter of fact. No! . . .
>
> All of us need a time of "growing up" to develop the mature judgement to do so many things. Like driving. Voting. Raising a family. And knowing enough to make an informed decision about all sorts of adult activities.
>
> In our view, smoking is an adult custom and the decision to smoke should be based on mature and informed individual freedom of choice.

12. *Background:* In an article, "Red tape, rules, and repression," Professor Boris Schein recounted a number of experiences he had while an academic in the Soviet Union. One of the points he made was that academics have difficulty in obtaining books from libraries and in having access to photocopying machines. His article precipitated a letter from an entirely different angle of vision by Professor Cantelon of Queen's University, who wrote: (CAUT *Bulletin,* September, 1982):

> In carrying out my personal research in the USSR in 1973-74, I personally used photo-copying machines in Moscow, machines which were accessible to Soviet and foreign students alike. . . . I have received and sent articles to the USSR with none of the problems which Dr. Schein outlines. Why the disparity with your experiences, Dr. Schein? Could it be that your version of "the truth" is intended to pander to the anti-Soviet sentiments now in vogue in Reagan-America?

CHAPTER SIX

FALLACIES OF INTIMIDATION

Introduction

The three fallacies we take up in this chapter are called "fallacies of intimidation" because they work by attempting to put pressure on us to accept a conclusion. **Improper appeal to authority,** for example, attempts to pressure us by appealing to our sense of respect for those more knowledgeable than we are. The fallacy of **popularity** caters to our tendencies to be steamrollered by public opinion and "groupthink." The fallacy of **slippery slope** is an attempt to stampede us into the premature acceptance of a conclusion by making dire projections about the future.

Improper Appeal to Authority

Originally, at least, many of the beliefs we adopt are based on the authority of others. From our earliest days as children, our thoughts are influenced and fashioned by the opinions of parents, teachers, and others who know more than we do. Ideally, as we mature we become less and less dependent on others for our beliefs and become independent investigators and evaluators. And to the degree that we become rational believers, we realize that our beliefs ought to be based where possible on a direct and personal examination of all relevant evidence. In practice, most of us fall far short of this ideal — something the famous psychologist and philosopher William James noted when he said, "As a matter of fact, we find ourselves believing, we hardly know how or why."[1]

---

[1] William James, *The Will to Believe* (New York: Dover Publications, 1956), p. 9.

Although the best strategy for forming opinions is thorough review of the evidence and a clear head, very few have the time or the intellectual resources to implement this strategy in anything more than isolated cases. What are we then to do? Suspend judgement on the subject? There are times when this is clearly the best course to pursue. But at other times we must adopt some belief or other, without having the opportunity to review all the evidence. In such a situation it is certainly reasonable to rely on the opinions of those who have reviewed the evidence, who know what they are talking about, who, in short, are **authorities** on the subject in question. When we cite experts to establish a point in an argument, we are making an **appeal to authority.** In this section we provide some rules of thumb for distinguishing between proper and improper appeals to authority.

The mere mention of the word "authority" is enough to raise the hair on some people's necks. So let's be clear at the outset what we mean here by an "authority." We do not mean a person who is in a *position* of authority (priest, politician, teacher, boss) and who is therefore able to command others to act in certain ways, or to do certain things. We mean someone whose expertise in a particular area makes her assertions reliable — more likely to be true than false. More about this later.

Another misconception worth heading off is that any reference to the views of a knowledgeable person is necessarily an appeal to authority. That isn't so. Just above we quoted William James. But we weren't appealing to him as an authority. We weren't saying, "Believe this, because James — a famous philosopher and psychologist — said it." Our proposition was, "James has succinctly stated a point which we think you'll see on reflection is true." We quoted him because we liked his compact formulation of this basic truth. Standard practice calls for us to give credit for that statement to James himself. The mere mention of the views of an authority, then, does not necessarily constitute an appeal to authority. An appeal to authority occurs only when the purpose of such citation is to persuade you that the statement is true, or likely to be true, because an authority holds it to be such.

With these preliminaries concluded, we can move on to the important questions: What makes someone an authority? Under what conditions is an appeal to authority legitimate?

A person can be considered an authority when his contributions to a specified field of inquiry achieve widespread recognition, or when his expertise in a particular area is treated with respect by others — by others with knowledge of that field. It is a mistake to think, as some do, that being an authority is simply a matter of knowing a lot about a subject. Your Aunt Nora may have accumulated a great many facts about the birds in your county so that she is indeed knowledgeable, but until and unless her knowledge has been scrutinized and certified by others with knowledge of birds, she will not qualify as an authority.

So at least two other conditions must be met before someone can be considered an authority. First, one's scholarship and research must be submitted to the appropriate community of inquirers for appraisal. Generally, this means publishing one's results in the appropriate vehicles. To get an article published in a scientific journal, for example, it must first be judged and found acceptable by a board of referees who must agree that the article merits publication. So this step toward becoming an authority involves some judgement of the value of one's thoughts. The second additional condition, dependent on publication, is that one's peers must find that work to be of significant value. What made Einstein an authority on theoretical physics was not just the amount of knowledge he had, but the reaction to and the assessment of that knowledge by his peers. Ultimately, then, authority is conferred on an individual by the collective judgement of her or his colleagues.[2]

Our resumé highlights the crucial concept in the notion of authority: *knowledge*. Knowledge and authority go together. In effect, this combination means that appeals to authority should be restricted to those disciplines or intellectual endeavours that can be characterized as pursuing and arriving at knowledge and truth. Such subjects as physics, chemistry, and history would qualify. What they all have in common is that the knowledge-claims made within them are subject to testing and validation. There are agreed-upon criteria of truth and falsity. Moreover, the personal preferences of the investigator are not relevant to statements in the domain of knowledge. Findings are confined by the world that is inexorably out there — for the investigator and for others.

In some disciplines the notions of knowledge, truth, and fact either have no clear application at all or have a drastically qualified or limited one. In philosophy, religion, and art, reasonable and competent specialists differ on fundamental questions and there may be no way to adjudicate such fundamental disputes. The reason for such disputes is itself a controversial matter, but among the often-mentioned factors accounting for it are these: the absence of agreed-on methodology, a certain latitude for personal interpretation and preference, and a subject matter whose range and nature are themselves somewhat dependent on the judgement of the individual thinker. In such areas, then, no appeal to authority can be legitimate.

We must add one more important qualification. Although appeals to authority are restricted to fields of public truth and knowledge, that does not mean everything a *bona fide* authority says about such a field is true. Authorities are not necessarily right all the time, and appealing to an authority does not presuppose that the authority is infallible. In fact, then, the correct

---

[2] If you find this account too brief, we recommend the following two books: Michael Polanyi, *Science, Faith, and Society* (Chicago: University of Chicago Press, 1964), and John M. Ziman, *Public Knowledge* (Cambridge: Cambridge University Press, 1968). Polanyi states: "Authority is not equally distributed among scientists. There is a hierarchy of influence; but exceptional authority is attached not so much to offices as to persons. A scientist is granted exceptional influence by the fact that his opinion is valued and asked for" (p. 48).

schematic form of appeals to authority is not, "Q is true, because M (an authority) says so," but rather, "There is *good reason* to believe that Q is true, because M (an authority) says so."

When is it legitimate, in *an argument,* to appeal to someone as an authority? To answer this question, we are going to present five rules which specify the conditions of proper appeals to authority. If any one of these rules is violated, the fallacy of **improper appeal to authority** is committed.

> **Rule I:** If an authority is appealed to in support of a statement, *Q,* then *Q* must belong to some specifiable set of statements, *S,* which constitutes a domain of knowledge.

The force of this rule is to limit appeals to authority to those areas in which knowledge is achievable, in line with our previous analysis of authority. Consider some hypothetical cases. Suppose, for example, *Q* to be the statement: "Many chemical additives in food are more harmful than helpful to human health." In this case, *Q* belongs to *S,* the set of statements about the value of chemical additives, itself a subset of the science of nutrition. Such a statement could be the subject of an appeal to authority, therefore. Now suppose *Q* is: "Van Gogh painted *The Starry Night* at St. Rémy in 1889." Here *Q* belongs to *S,* the set of statements about Van Gogh, itself a subset of art history — which is a field of knowledge. Hence, it could be supported by an appeal to authority. Now suppose *Q* is this statement: "Van Gogh's *The Starry Night* is the finest painting ever done." What sort of statement is this? It is an aesthetic judgement, one which presumes to rank the finest works of art. Such a statement may be defensible in that one might show what one admired in Van Gogh's painting, and explain why one preferred it to other great paintings. However, the attempt to get others to accept one's judgement by appealing to an authority betrays a misunderstanding about this sort of aesthetic statement. There are no universally recognized standards of truth here; at best, one can explain the basis for one's personal preferences. Hence, this kind of aesthetic judgement does not fall within the confines of any domain of knowledge. The force of Rule I, then, is to limit appeals to authority in arguments to the sorts of statement which can or do fall within some established domain of knowledge.

Let's put the rule to work on a letter to *The Windsor Star* (February 1976) by R.H.:

114   The item in the Star noting the defection of General Electric engineers from the atomic energy program suggests that it might be profitable for some journalists to check up on what one of the pioneers in the field of atomic physics had to say about 20 years ago. Toward the end of his life, Prof. Milliken of the University of Chicago wrote his autobiography which appeared about the time that atomic energy plants were being projected. He makes the flat statement that as a major source of power, atomic energy has no future — "it is out." He did not elaborate but he must have had solid reasons for this opinion which he must have stated elsewhere, probably in professional journals.

Note, first, that R.H.'s appeal to Milliken is guarded. He says that "it might be profitable" to consider Milliken's views. Reading this letter, we can't be sure just what R.H. wants to establish by the appeal. Does he want Milliken's views simply considered, or considered true? Read further. The tone of the letter seems to be that the defection of the engineers is symptomatic of a serious problem in the development of atomic energy as a power source, and R.H. goes on to surmise that Professor Milliken "must have had solid reasons" for his opinion that atomic energy "is out." Thus, R.H. seems to think that atomic energy has no future, takes this view as true because Milliken had adopted it, and invites us to do the same.

Interpreted this way, R.H. is guilty of *improper appeal to authority*. He does not even know why Milliken believed that atomic energy is out; sufficient for him was the fact that Milliken, an authority, held that view. We can see that the appeal is fallacious if we isolate Q and consider it. In this case, Q is, "Atomic energy has no future as a major source of power." What sort of statement is Q? To begin with, it is not a statement from the domain of theoretical physics, Milliken's own field of competence. That's a flaw which we will deal with in Rule II. Nor is Q a statement that would belong to some branch of technology or applied science. In fact, Q is a complicated statement that presupposes judgements about technology, business and industry, ecology, and lifestyles. If anything, it is a statement of social policy. As such it needs the support of various kinds of hard evidence, but as well will involve numerous reasoned value judgements of a social nature. Since in this case there is no guarantee of consensus, R.H. has violated Rule I and is guilty of an *improper appeal to authority*.

> **Rule II:** If M is appealed to as an authority on Q, then Q must belong to a class of statements, S, on which M is an authority.

Note first that this rule is violated if M is not an authority on anything at all. We mention this point primarily because appeals to the "authority" of non-authorities are all too frequent. Think, for a moment, of the use of sports celebrities and entertainment figures in commercial endorsements.

The second thing which Rule II invalidates is the attempt to transfer authority, i.e. to use someone who is a legitimate authority in one field as an authority in some other field. Authority, however, is non-transferable, based as it is on the assessment of one's achievements by one's peers in one's field of knowledge. An authority on atomic physics may not be appealed to in order to support a biological claim (unless he or she is also an authority on biology). The Milliken example violated this rule, as well as Rule I, because the writer attempted to transfer Milliken's authority from atomic physics (where Milliken was an authority) to social policy on energy (where Milliken was not an authority — and indeed where no one is).

Don't misinterpret what we're saying here, and hang a *straw man* on us. In these times when many are busy debunking the "Cult of the Expert," we don't want to be misread. Certainly there is nothing logically wrong or objectionable with considering and quoting the opinion of an authority on a matter which lies outside his or her area of competence, but such opinions do not carry the weight of authority. A scientist who airs his or her views on political questions, for example, deserves to have those views listened to with the same respect and courtesy afforded anyone else. And that is the point — the same respect that would be given anyone else. Outside the area of competence, an authority's views are only as compelling as the evidence presented for them.

In our next example, we see how the respect that people have for intelligence and achievement can too easily lead them astray. G.P., in the excerpt following, is responding to an earlier writer who had accused some Christians of being dogmatic and narrow-minded (*The Windsor Star*, January 1975):

115   One naturally wonders how the writer would class the late Sir Winston Churchill, whose word conveys what he thought about Holy Scripture: . . . [G.P. then quoted Churchill as stating that everything in the Bible is literally true.]

G.P.'s argument seems to have been that it is not dogmatic and narrow-minded to claim literal truth for statements in the Bible, because Churchill said that the Bible expresses the literal truth. This appeal to Churchill's authority violates Rule II. First, it is not clear that Churchill was an authority on anything. He was widely admired as a statesman and influential as a politician; however, these are not qualifications for authority in any domain of knowledge. Second, even if we grant that Churchill was an authority on history (he did publish several historical works), his field of specialization was the English-speaking peoples and, more narrowly, World War II. He was not a Bible historian. Moreover, many of the statements made in the Bible belong to theology, not history — for example, that Christ is the son of God — and Churchill was not a theologian. Hence, although Churchill was an authority in one area of history, G.P.'s attempt to transfer that authority to a different area is improper.

Violations of Rule II are usually found in tandem with violations of Rule I, as we have seen in the Milliken example. Here is another. A.N. wrote this letter to *The Ottawa Journal* (November 1974):

116   May I bring to your attention the following statement of Dr. Joseph DeLee? He was one of the most eminent obstetricians of this continent, who devoted his entire life to the improvement of obstetrical care. He said: "At the present time, when rivers of blood and tears of innocent men, women and children are flowing in most parts of the world, it seems silly to be contending over the right of an annullable atom of flesh in the uterus of a woman. No, it is not silly; on the contrary, it is of transcendent importance that there be in this chaotic world one high spot, however small, which is against the deluge sweeping over us. If we of the medical profession uphold the principle of the sacredness of human life and the right of the individual, even though unborn, it will prove that humanity is not yet lost and that we may ultimately obtain salvation."

A.N., it would appear, is appealing to Dr. DeLee's authority as an eminent obstetrician to support the view that abortion is wrong. Dr. DeLee was undeniably an authority on obstetrics, as a check of *Who was Who in America* will show.[3] He was, for example, the author of four books on obstetrics, one of which, *The Principles and Practice of Obstetrics,* was originally published in 1913 and went through seven editions through 1938. Dr. DeLee was an authority on obstetrics, but that does not qualify him as an authority on the subject of the morality of abortion, which belongs to the field of ethics. Thus, A.N. violated Rule II. Furthermore, it is not clear whether the proposition that abortion is wrong can be a matter of knowledge. Since it is hotly disputed whether there can be *any* moral knowledge, there is no justification for taking it for granted that there can be an appeal to authority on this topic. So A.N. has violated Rule I as well.

The appeal to Prof. Milliken's authority used in example 114 is even more culpable than we've indicated to this point, for it violates yet another rule such appeals must honour:

> **Rule III:** If there is no consensus among authorities in *S,* to which *Q* belongs, then this lack of consensus must be noted in any appeal to authority about *Q,* and the conclusion qualified accordingly.

As we noted in our discussion of Rule I, when there is not even the possibility of a consensus, then no appeal to authority is valid. In areas where there is the possibility of consensus, but that consensus has not yet been reached, an appeal to authority is premature. The function of an appeal to authority is to provide a reason for believing the truth of some statement. When those who are in the best position to know have not yet reached a verdict, the appeal to any one authority rather than another cannot carry much weight. To refer to the Milliken example, then, even if the question of the use of atomic energy as a power source did belong to some particular domain of

---

[3] Cf. Vol. II, 1943-1950, A.W. Marquis Company.

knowledge (which, we have already argued, is not the case), the appeal to Milliken would fail to abide by Rule III, for equally competent scientists do not share Milliken's views.

In a letter to *The Windsor Star* (August 1974), W.C. criticized an earlier article about Down's Syndrome:

117   I believe the Star is doing a great service to the mentally retarded in the Windsor area by their recent articles on the subject of retardation, however, I wonder why David Gibson was quoted in this most recent article. His statements are not supported by other researchers in North America, Great Britain or Europe.

In an Editor's note, the *Star* responded:

118   Dr. David Gibson is a Canadian expert in his field. He is president of the Canadian Psychological Association, professor of psychology at the University of Calgary, editor of the *Canadian Psychologist* and has spent more than 30 years in active work with the mentally retarded.

Having recited Gibson's impressive credentials, the *Star* then added:

119   *There are those equally learned in the same area who disagree with him* — an occurrence that is commonplace in most professions. (Emphasis ours.)

The crucial phrase in the *Star's* attempt to defend its appeal to Gibson is in that last sentence. Since the *Star* had given no reason for citing Gibson's views rather than those of one of his "equally learned" colleagues, it violated Rule III. Where there are degrees of authority within an area, there is stronger justification for an appeal to a widely recognized authority than to one less well known. Where opinion among the top authorities is divided, as was apparently the case here, no appeal to authority can carry much persuasive force.

The rules listed thus far invalidate appeals to authority when the field in question is not a domain of knowledge (Rule I); or when it is, but the individual is not in fact an authority on that subject (Rule II); or when the domain is indeed one of knowledge and the individual properly equipped, but the appeal is vitiated by a lack of consensus (Rule III). Two additional rules are needed.

> **Rule IV:** The authority, *M*, whose judgement is appealed to, must not be in a situation of bias, or conflict of interest, about *Q*.

The very idea of appealing to an authority is that his judgement is likely to be true because it has been arrived at in a rational and competent way by someone familiar with the relevant evidence. Should there be a reason to think that bias, rather than rational review of the evidence, could have dictated the judgement, then the appeal to that authority is invalidated.

An example of such a violation occurs, apparently, in Gérard Pelletier's *The October Crisis,* quoted in Chapter 3. In reference to the FLQ, Pelletier writes:

120   When a marginal group tries, by using the most odious possible sort of blackmail (the threat to human life), to force the State to take actions contrary to principles on which it is founded, in most cases firmness is the only reasonable choice. (p. 95)

In a footnote, Pelletier quotes Quebec Justice Minister Jerome Choquette from a press conference of October 10, 1970, in which Choquette explained his reasons for refusing the demands of the FLQ. Choquette stated:

121   No society can consent to have the decisions of the judicial and government institutions challenged or set aside by the blackmail of a minority, for that signifies the end of all social order.

Is Pelletier appealing to Choquette as an authority here? Perhaps not, for he had already given his own reasons for thinking that political blackmail cannot be tolerated. There is, then, no need to appeal to Choquette. Still, the impressionable reader may think Choquette's office endows his judgement with authority. That would be a mistake. His office confers one sort of authority on him — the right to command people to act in certain ways. But it does not make him an authority on any domain of knowledge. Moreover, and to the point of our taking it up here, as Justice Minister, Choquette was himself involved in the kidnapping and the dramatic set of events which followed, so he was anything but a detached observer. His statement was, in fact, part of his attempt to justify the way his government responded to the crisis. So naturally he is disposed, or predisposed, to that viewpoint. Thus, Choquette, even if he were an authority, could hardly be impartial on this issue, and the appeal to his authority would violate Rule IV. Lastly, we're doubtful that this is an area that permits appeals to authority. Whether the state can both maintain itself in a position of public confidence and yield on occasion to blackmail by terrorist groups is, it seems to us, a judgement call rather than a matter of knowledge. If that is true, Rule I was violated here, too.

G.P., whose appeal to Churchill's authority we saw as a violation of Rule II (Example 115), provided in that same letter an example of why our final rule is needed. G.P. wrote:

122   If the grounds of the writer's accusations [against Christians for dogmatism] are justified, then he must include in his list of those deserving the stigma inseparable from those words, prominent men in all walks of life, past and present — many of super intelligence, highly trained and educated in their particular fields and respected the world over who . . . were and are immovable in their belief in the Bible as the inerrant word of God.

We might be willing to accept the testimony of these many alleged authorities — if we knew who they were and could assess their credentials! Since we don't we can't; and G.P.'s appeal to them remains bereft of persuasive force. This leads to a final rule.

Rule V: If M is appealed to as an authority on S, then M must be identified.

Should Rule V go further, and require that anyone using an authority list the pertinent qualifications? Or is it up to the person assessing the argument to do the legwork and check them out? We think the primary burden rests with the one who appeals to the authority. After all, that person is the one who is trying to persuade others. On the other hand, it's unfair to hold the arguer responsible when the authority appealed to is generally well known, so that failure to recognize that authority might be construed as culpable ignorance. Furthermore, even where it's a just criticism of the argument that the authority's credentials are not given, the critic cannot dismiss the appeal on the grounds of Rules II or IV without doing the necessary checking. To reply, for example, "I've never heard of Dr. DeLee and don't know of any contribution he has made to obstetrics, so the appeal is improper," is not only the lazy way out, it is also to commit *hasty conclusion*, if not *irrelevant reason*! If you are going to do more than put a question mark beside an appeal to authority, if you are going to charge it with violating Rules II or IV, the burden shifts to you. It may require a bit of time in the library to determine M's qualifications.

Here's a borderline example. Does the appeal in the passage quoted below violate Rule V? The background is that in 1972 a group of researchers at the Massachusetts Institute of Technology did a computer projection of the world's population and resources, published as the famous Club of Rome Study called *The Limits to Growth*. They concluded that, "If the present growth trends in world population, industrialization, pollution, food production, and resource depletion continue unchanged, the limits to growth on this planet will be reached sometime within the next one hundred years."[4] In an editorial entitled "Bad science, Good sense," *The Windsor Star* (November 1972) attacked the MIT projections by appealing to authority:

---

[4] Donella H. Meadows, Dennis L. Meadows, Jorgen Randers, William W. Behrens III, *The Limits to Growth* (New York: Universe Books, 1972), p. 23.

123   The latest criticisms of the MIT report were voiced in Windsor, by economist members of a panel discussion at the University of Windsor. One of the three speakers, himself an MIT professor, labelled the work "bad science," and two others agreed that the case had been grossly overstated. The criticisms should be welcomed by all those humans who are concerned about over-population and related problems . . .

The *Star* appealed especially to the unidentified professor of economics at MIT to defuse the conclusions reached by the Club of Rome. But who is this unnamed professor of economics? If we were intent on prosecuting this argument, it would be our job to do a bit of detective work, find out who was on the panel, then track down his or her credentials. We aren't as badly off here as we are in the advertisements which say "Doctors recommend . . . ." Yet the *Star's* appeal fails to persuade us precisely because it doesn't comply with the spirit of Rule V.

Another point brought out by this example: just because someone is a professor does not mean that he or she is an authority on any subject at all. The prestige that goes with academic titles can be deceiving. A person can, for instance, enjoy a modest and worthwhile academic career, do a good job of teaching, advance through the ranks — all without making that sort of contribution to her area which would qualify her as an authority.

Don't misunderstand. We are not suggesting that you dismiss what a professor says. What she or he is very often doing is conveying the findings of researchers, the positions and arguments of theorists, and the judgements of authorities. Part of that responsibility is to make you aware of what is authoritatively known and what is a matter of judgement and controversy. And part of this job will be to present the evidence on which opinions have been formed, so that you may develop independent judgement. You should accept a professor's competence as a conveyor of knowledge and as someone who knows the field well enough to recognize and distinguish between established truths and areas of contention. But unless your professor happens to be an authority in the subject, you should not accept what she says as true, merely because that professor says it.

Indeed, it is perhaps useful to distinguish various degrees of authority. In most areas where there is such a thing as authority, there is also a hierarchy of influence and recognition. Our analysis has been focused on the highest degree, attained only by the "top guns" in each field. Between the ultimate authority and the neophyte are the many competent specialists who have a great deal more knowledge than most, but whose contributions won't rank them with the best. Clearly, the more authority an individual has, the greater the weight attaching to an appeal to him or her. Sometimes, in verbal argument, a person will refer to someone (a friend, a local personality) as an authority. You should not dismiss that appeal outright, simply on the ground that the individual is not the ranking authority. On the other hand, the appeal cannot carry any greater weight than the degree of authority possessed by that individual. If you know the conditions required for the highest degree of authority, you can approbate appeals with that standard in mind, taking each case on its individual merits.

The five rules enable us to generate a set of conditions which define *improper appeal to authority:*

IMPROPER APPEAL TO AUTHORITY

1. *M* appeals — tacitly or explicitly — to the authority of *N* in supporting claim *Q* (which belongs to domain of assertions, *S*).
2. (a) *S* is not a domain in which authoritative knowledge can, or does, exist; or
   (b) *N* is not an authority about matters in domain *S* ; or
   (c) Although *S* is in general a domain of knowledge, there is among authorities in *S* a lack of consensus that such claims as *Q* are true; or
   (d) *N* has a special interest in *Q*'s being accepted; or
   (e) *N* is not identified sufficiently to enable one to check *N*'s credentials.

As you can readily see, first, an appeal to an authority in an argument can violate more than one of these conditions, however the violation of any *one* undermines the argumentative force of the appeal. Second, some violations are more grievous than others. If 2(a) or 2(b) is violated, there is no way to patch up that part of the argument: the violation of 2(a) means no appeal to authority can be appropriate in support of the claim in question, while the violation of 2(b) means no appeal to *that* person's authority can carry any weight on that point. The force of noting a violation of 2(c) will vary. If, for example, nearly all the authorities in the field agree on a standard theory from which the claim is drawn, and only one "maverick" in the field challenges this theory, then the appeal to authority will have a good deal of strength and the criticism alleging violation of 2(c) must be considered weak. On the other hand, if the field has as yet no established theory for claims of type *Q*, or if the field is in the midst of a revolutionary upheaval, so that formerly-assumed theories dealing with *Q* are now very much in question, then the appeal to authority for *Q* will have little force, and the criticism based on 2(c) will be fatal to that part of the argument. In the case of a violation of 2(d), one is registering merely the possibility that *N*'s judgement may be influenced by his interests, and the force of the criticism is to put a question mark beside *Q*, given that the appeal to *N*'s authority is the only support offered for it. Finally, if only rule 2(e) is violated, the effect is to postpone acceptance of Q based on N's authority until N can be identified and his credentials checked out.

The key to appraising any appeal to authority rests on your capacity to delineate carefully the general field or area, S, to which Q, the statement in question, belongs. You must then make a judgement about whether this is indeed an area of knowledge or not. Further, don't make the mistake of arguing against the truth of the claim which the so-called authority has been cited as support for. Here's an exchange which shows what we mean:

124   Psych. Major: Everything we do has some motivation, conscious or unconscious. Freud said so.

Logician: That's an improper appeal to Freud's authority. Lots of behaviour, like tying your right shoe before your left one, is just happenstance or habit.

We're not endorsing the Psych. Major's appeal to Freud, but the Logician's rebuttal takes the wrong tack. When someone appeals to an authority in matters of belief, that person is giving a kind of reason for the claim. To say the appeal is improper is not to say that the claim is false — it's to say that the reason (that the "authority" said so) is not a good one in this instance. So the relevant critique is to show why it's not — which is where our five rules are intended to help out. The Logician should have said that the Psych. Major's appeal to Freud here was illegitimate because authorities in psychology disagree about whether all behaviour is motivated and they disagree about the truth of the theory of unconscious motivation. In our terms, Rule III is violated. So here's useful advice: when charging improper appeal to authority, *attack the appeal to the authority, not the truth of the claim.*

Appeals to authority are perilous. They are often arguments of last resort. As the 13th-century philospher and theologian St. Thomas Aquinas aptly put it, "The argument from authority is the weakest of all arguments." Don't try to trip us up on the principles we've just listed, because (you guessed it), we aren't appealing to Aquinas's authority. You don't have to take his word for it — or ours, for that matter. With the five rules in hand, check out a few arguments from authority for yourself.

Popularity

We had occasion to cite the philosopher William James in this chapter. We're going to do so again here, this time for an example of specious reasoning that comes preciously close to the fallacy we take up next: **popularity.** An anecdote from James's *Pragmatism* (Lecture 2; Cleveland: Meridian Books, 1955) serves to illustrate the kernel of this fallacy.

James and a group of his friends had gone camping in the mountains. While James was out for a walk, the members of the party got into a heated dispute. James tells us what he found upon his return:

125   In the unlimited leisure of the wilderness, discussion had been worn threadbare. Everyone had taken sides, and was obstinate; and the numbers on both sides were even. Each side, when I appeared, appealed to me to make it a majority.

James, of course, did what philosophers are famous for: he drew a distinction which he thought resolved the issue. But suppose he had sided with one group rather than the other, would that have made its view the correct one? If you think so, then beware the fallacy of *popularity*, which consists of thinking that if most people or the majority believe something, then it is true. For many, the popularity or widespread acceptance of an idea is an index of its truth, while lack of acceptance is often construed as an index of its falsity.

In its purest and most blatant (and rarest) form, the fallacy of *popularity* occurs whenever an argument proceeds from the popularity of a view to its truth, thus:

126 $\Big\{$ 1. Everyone believes *Q*.
                 2. *Q* is true.

Instead of "everyone," the argument may refer to "almost everyone" or "most people" or "a majority." The flipside of the argument also occurs:

127 $\Big\{$ 1. No one believes *Q*.
                 2. *Q* is false.

Instead of "no one," the reference may be to "almost no one" or "very few" or "nobody I know of."

This move is so outrageous, when baldly stated, that *popularity* rarely occurs in this blatant formulation. You often have to dig below the surface to find it. For example, *M* expresses the belief that drugs are harmful and that people shouldn't rely on them. *N* counters, "Oh, come off it! Nobody believes that nowadays!" *N* has not actually said that because nobody believes it, it is false; but that is the clear implication. Or *M* says that women are inferior to men. *N* responds, "Surely you must be joking; that crazy idea went out with the '60s! Where have you been hibernating?" Again, *N* stops short of the explicit statement of the inference that because no one believes it, the view is false. The best way to counter such moves is to ask, point-blank, "Hold on, are you saying that because everyone (or no one) believes it, therefore it is true (or false)?"

Here's an example of the fallacy. It is from a letter to the St. John's *Evening Telegram* (October 1974) in which "Concerned" was arguing that laws should be more strictly enforced and that the courts should be handing out stiffer penalties:

128   *Every other person with whom one discusses this problem* will say
that the time has arrived when the lash will have to be re-introduced
in our courts. (Emphasis ours.)

"Concerned" stopped short of concluding that since this is what most
people believe, it is true. But if that is the implication, the fallacy of *popularity* has been committed.

To argue that a claim is true simply because a number of people think it's
true is outrageous. However, we doubt that most people who commit *popularity* are following this line of argument. Instead, we expect they reason
(implicitly) as follows: that many people believe Q is a good reason for
thinking Q is true. That's because, so the thinking goes, there would not be
popular acceptance of Q unless there were good reasons for thinking Q to
be true. Hence, the popular belief that Q is true is evidence of good reasons
for accepting Q. The key premise in this argument is that the widespread acceptance of Q entails the existence of good reasons for believing Q.

We are not about to propose that the popular acceptance of a belief is
never any reason for thinking it is true. Suppose you find that everyone in
a community you are visiting believes the fish in a nearby lake are contaminated. That would by itself be some reason for you to believe that the
fish truly are contaminated. So popular belief is not always irrelevant as a
basis for accepting a proposition.

However, the mere acceptance by numbers of people of a belief is usually not a very good reason for you to believe it. If people were generally in
the habit of arriving at their beliefs in a reasonable way (by considering all
relevant evidence, weighing it, etc.), then a consensus would be as impressive in ordinary life as it is in, say, the case of science. But the evidence
that people actually do this is scanty. Instead, people are persuaded by
bad arguments; they are duped by fallacies; they judge first and think afterwards; they fail to search out and review the evidence; they face the limits
of time and energy. If all this is true, the appeal to popular consensus, even
as an indicator of what is probably true, is fraught with pitfalls. Moreover,
rarely are the beliefs of others the only available basis for our own beliefs.
Almost always we can check out other more generally reliable grounds.

Of course, in arguing against the reasonableness of popular opinion as
a basis for belief, we are not for a minute supposing that the appeal to
popularity is usually intended as a reasonable argument. Most of the time
it's a tool of intimidation, an attempt to browbeat a person into accepting
some claim. Still, it gets some of its influence by hiding behind the façade
of good argument. So we need to be sure it is a façade, and not actually
legitimate.

In the absence of any strong connection between the quantity of people
who hold a position and its truth or probability, the appeal to popular acceptance is a fallacy. The conditions for it are:

For several reasons people find the appeal to popular acceptance attractive. In the first place, going against the grain of popular opinion is threatening to many people. (We haven't forgotten the "one in every crowd" sort who loves to disagree with everyone.) Peer pressure is difficult to resist.

But, second, two perfectly respectable principles provide perfect masquerades for *popularity:* "Majority Rule," and "Popular Sovereignty." A brief discussion of each of these may help you to detect *popularity* when it masquerades in the costume of one or the other.

Majority Rule is the political principle that what the majority of members of a decision-making group agrees to is what should stand as the decision of the whole group. The principle does not imply that the decision thus arrived at is true, or right, or the best one, but only that this is an effective way to carry on the group's affairs. (It could be replaced by a principle that calls for 75 percent in favour, or unanimity, before motions are passed.) There is a difference between this political principle and the logical principle on which *popularity* is based. The Majority Rule principle is a procedural one prescribing a procedure for decision making; behind *popularity* lies a criterial principle — one offering as the criterion of a belief's truth or probability the fact that most people embrace it. When the distinction is not marked, people invoke the Majority Rule principle as justification for an appeal to popular opinion.

Related to Majority Rule (and sometimes used to help justify it) is the principle that what most of the electorate of a body politic desires and agrees to is what the legislature should do — the principle of Popular Sovereignty. The foundation of this thesis is the idea that the people are sovereign, and that the views and attitudes of the people should be reflected in the laws of the land. Up to a point this is a sensible principle, because if the laws of a country stray too far from widely shared public beliefs about the sort of behaviour that ought to be legally permissible or prohibited, then people will as a matter of fact begin to lose sympathy with and respect for the laws. (The principle cannot serve without qualification: popular opinion on some issues changes more rapidly than the law can or should; also, it allows no role for legislators to give leadership to popular opinion.) The principle of Popular Sovereignty is different from *popularity*. The former makes no claims for the wisdom of the people — for the worth of their preferences — but only for their right to influence policy, to have their interests served. Popularity, in contrast, takes the further step of supposing that what the majority (or any large number) believes is true.

Against this background, consider this brief excerpt from an article in the Halifax *Chronicle-Herald* (January 1975) entitled, "Trudeau cabinet's 'bleeding hearts,'" in which Robert Coates (Conservative MP for Cumberland-Colchester North) stated:

129   There are many bleeding hearts in this nation, but they are substantially outnumbered by those who appreciate that the death penalty is a deterrent.

Is this an instance of *popularity,* or is this a disguised appeal to the principle of Popular Sovereignty? If Coates is arguing that capital punishment should be restored because a substantial majority want it restored (because they think it is a deterrent to murder), then he is appealing to the sovereignty of the people. He's saying that Parliament should follow the will of the people in this case. On the other hand, if Coates is arguing that the death penalty would be a deterrent and his reason for holding that opinion is that most people think it is, then he is guilty of *popularity,* for whether the death penalty is or is not a deterrent is an extremely complicated question not to be decided by appealing to what most people believe, but by careful consideration of the evidence.

As a concluding note, we add that something like an appeal to popular acceptance is found in many advertisements.

130   You'll find Maple Leaf meats and cheese in more than a million kitchens across Canada, day in and day out. *They're that popular.*

131   More than 250,000 hairdressers the world over believe in what L'Oreal Hair Colouring can do for you. What more can we say?

A quarter-million hairdressers can't be wrong! Here the assumption is that popularity is a criterion or index of the quality of a product, an assumption not far removed from taking popularity as an index of the truth of a belief. That assumption is questionable, although not necessarily false in these particular cases. (Chevrolet consistently outsells Rolls Royce. Which is the better-built car?) However, because advertisements have their own special logic, we will not multiply examples here, preferring to confront advertising in Chapter 11.

Slippery Slope

A common and perfectly legitimate style of assessing a policy or a proposed course of action is to draw inferences about its likely consequences. If a proposal can be shown to lead to undesirable consequences, then that becomes a strong (though not decisive) reason for not embracing it. Much debate and argument about social policy therefore takes the form of making causal projections. So long as the causal claims which lie at the heart of such projections are well-founded, there is no logical problem. However, it often happens that, in his haste to discredit a policy, the critic fails to provide close argumentation to support the causal claims. When the causal projection is weak because one (or more) links in the causal chain is dubious, and either not defended or insufficiently justified, then the fallacy we call **slippery slope** is the result. There are two typical forms of argument employing such causal forecasts. In one, the whole series of causal steps is included: "If we do/allow W, then X will follow; if X, then Y; if X, then Z. But surely we don't want Z. Therefore we should not do/allow W."

132   If abortion were legalized, it would become more widespread; if it were to become more widespread, respect for human life would weaken; if respect for human life were weakened, our form of civilization would be jeopardized. But surely we don't want to weaken our form of civilization. Therefore abortion should not be legalized.

In the second form, just the first and last chapters of the causal story are included in the argument: "If we do/allow W, then Z will follow. But surely we don't want Z. Therefore we should not do/allow W."

133   The legalization of abortion will be the first step along the road that can only end with the weakening of our form of civilization. Surely we don't want to jeopardize our form of civilization. Therefore we must not permit abortion to be legalized.

The following examples illustrate both forms of the fallacy. First the long form. The example comes from an editorial in the St. John's *Evening Telegram* (October 1974):

134   The federal proposal to switch cannabis from the Narcotics Control Act to the Food and Drug Act will probably be the first step leading to the eventual legalization of this "soft" drug. Under the drug act the possession of marijuana or hashish will be punishable with a fine rather than with a jail sentence as called for in the narcotics act.
        The penalties for trafficking, importing and cultivating the drug will still be stiff. However it is hardly likely that judges will take as serious a view of a drug as they do of a narcotic, and in time the penalty for trafficking or importing will probably be a light fine and a ticking off by the judge. Then, in turn, the fine for possession will

likely be dropped and it will be legal to have cannabis for personal use.

From there the next step is controlled manufacture and sale along the same lines as alcoholic drinks. Then the emphasis on the nature of the crime will switch to smuggling and bootlegging with the intention that the Crown gets its legitimate revenue from the sale of the drug. By that time, cannabis will probably be called joy candy or fun smoke or by some other euphemism.

If we seem to be moving too fast, remember that this is the usual way of softening up the law. We hope that when Health Minister Lalonde makes the change he will understand that he is opening the door to putting pot in every pocket.

The editorialist is clearly opposed to the federal proposal. In his view, it's going to lead — by a nexus of events which the editorialist spells out — to a clearly undesirable end (as far as the editorialist is concerned): "pot in every pocket" and "pot being called joy candy or fun smoke." Therefore, the argument implicitly concludes, the proposal ought not to be implemented. The strength of this argument against the Lalonde proposal depends entirely upon the plausibility of this causal projection. To get a clear fix, then, we must trace the nexus through its various stages, identify each stage, and scrutinize the links. We begin by spelling out the steps in the nexus, one by one:

135
1. Marijuana put under Food and Drug Act;
2. Possession punished by fine rather than jail; trafficking, importing, and cultivating punished stiffly;
3. Judges take a less serious view of offenses against this law;
4. The penalty for trafficking and importing becomes less severe — a light fine;
5. Penalty for simple possession dropped; legal to possess marijuana;
6. The manufacture and sale of marijuana controlled by the government;
7. Emphasis changes from possession and trafficking to smuggling and bootlegging;
8. Marijuana legal and in common use.

Note that few of these links are defended. Some are fairly obvious. The transition from 1 to 2 seems incontestable, but that from 2 to 3 less so. If judges are already disposed to impose heavy penalties for trafficking and importing, why would a simple reclassification of marijuana change that disposition? Step 3 wouldn't necessarily follow on the heels of 2. The transition from 3 to 4 seems straightforward. And if judges were to take a lenient attitude towards trafficking then it is likely that they would not penalize simple possession at all, so from 4 to 5 the link seems secure. If possession of marijuana did become legal, 5, then the government would probably set up controls on its manufacture and sale along the lines of liquor, to insure the quality of the substance and to increase the revenue base. If that did occur, 6, then the emphasis in enforcement would undoubtedly change to smuggling and bootlegging, 7, since possession would be legal, and trafficking would disappear. But does this mean that marijuana would be in common use (8)? That likelihood is unclear.

Weak links in this causal chain, then, appear in the inferences from 2 to 3 and from 7 to 8. There's reason to doubt both these steps, yet the editorialist asserts them without defense. Even assuming common use would be a bad thing, we cannot accept this as a clear consequence of the initial step — putting the regulation of cannabis under the Food and Drug Act. For these reasons, we think this is a case of *slippery slope*.

The next example illustrates the short form of the fallacy. In 1976, the province of Ontario made the use of automobile safety belts mandatory. Among the many who objected to this legislation was S.C., who wrote to *The Windsor Star* (February 1976):

136   If they can make us swallow this infringement of personal rights, what's next? A seat belt law for the bedroom, so we won't fall out of bed and hurt our little selves? Boy, when Big Brother watches us, he really watches us, doesn't he?

The argument here seems to be that the seat-belt requirement is the first step down an incline leading to a veritable 1984 ("Big Brother watching us"). But how precisely is this horror to come about? The intervening steps are not mentioned, except for the sarcastic reference to seat-belts in the bedroom. We are given the first and the last chapter but nothing in between. Most would agree that if the legislation were the first of a series of steps leading inevitably to the abdication of all individual rights, then that legislation is bad and ought to be repealed. But this outcome is far from obvious, and S.C. does nothing to persuade the reader of this chain of events.

Though it does not bear directly on the charge of *slippery slope*, we think worth pointing out the potential mischief of S.C.'s *classification* of the seat-belt law as "an infringement of personal rights." In one obvious sense, the law does take away a person's right: the right, if you will, to choose whether or not to use the seat-belt. On the other hand, it may be argued that no citizen has the right to take unnecessary risks when the consequences of that risk-taking must be borne by the rest of society. Since the evidence shows that the probability of severe injury and death is decreased when safety-belts are used, it could be argued that refusal to wear them constitutes an unnecessary risk. Second, the consequences of automobile injury and death — hospitalization, unemployment, compensation — have to be paid by other citizens. If this argument can be cemented, then the phrase "infringement of personal rights" is of dubious application here, and we have a case of *loaded term* too.

Another example of the short form of *slippery slope* occurred when in 1972 the Trudeau government let it be known that it was considering the possibility of issuing work permits to Canadian workers in order to prevent foreigners from taking jobs away from Canadians. (The unions had been complaining that foreigners were coming into the country as visitors, and then, against immigration regulations, taking jobs.) Union leaders responded to the proposal with unanimous opposition. Dennis McDermott, when he was Canadian director of the United Auto Workers, was quoted (in a story in *The Windsor Star*, September 1972) as responding:

137   They would run counter to our traditional freedoms and would be *the first step* toward a police state.

The implication is clear: No one wants a police state, so we should oppose any policy, such as issuing work permits, that would start us down the road to that repugnant outcome. One problem with McDermott's brief causal story is that we are given no idea what the intervening chapters are. However, it's not necessary to read McDermott's mind in order to throw doubt on his story, for work permits would not have to constitute any greater danger to our liberties than driving licenses or building permits do. Registration procedures and a system of inspection for work permits would seem to require no more police powers, no greater restriction of freedoms, than the sorts of bureaucracy that exist at present for getting and checking other permits and licenses. True, work permits could be introduced in such a way as to restrict freedom to change jobs. But there is no reason to believe that this would happen, if the purpose of issuing them were merely to reserve jobs in Canada for Canadians. Work permits in and of themselves would not start the ball rolling down the slope to a police state. By implying that they would, McDermott committed *slippery slope*.

The conditions for the fallacy are:

SLIPPERY SLOPE

1. *M* claims that if *W* is permitted, it will lead to *X*, *X* will lead to *Y*, and so on to *Z*.
2. *M* holds that *Z* is undesirable and therefore *W* should not be permitted.
3. At least one of the steps in the causal chain is unsupported and open to challenge.

In the short form, Condition 1 will have just the step from *W* to *Z* (the last one); in the longer form, the intervening steps are given.

Not every argument that involves a projection into the future is a case of *slippery slope*. The following argument by John Hofsess (*Maclean's*, October 1973) seems reasonable:

138   If you don't get into the habit of exercising regularly when you're young, you are less likely to keep exercising during your later 20s and your 30s, when career, home and family take up more and more time and interest. You'll then tend to become sedentary and physically unfit. That will set you up for various heart and lung diseases during middle age. No one wants to have a heart attack at 45 or 50, so to lessen that danger, you ought to get into the habit of regular exercise when you're young.

Hofsess's argument seems cogent to us. The launching pad for his causal projection (not getting into the habit of exercising regularly when young) is followed by a series of claims that are qualified by "less likely" and "tend to," so that his argument is a probabilistic one rather than one delivered with iron-clad assurances.

Slippery slope has to be distinguished from a form of legitimate argumentation which it resembles: the appeal to precedent. Decision-making bodies, especially in government, must take into account the effects of the policies they set. One of these is the setting of a *precedent*. Consistency and fairness require that if one case is treated in a certain way, similar cases must be similarly treated. For example, if your city council grants the Ukrainian community a parade permit for its national celebration, that sets a precedent. Other groups with similar requests will expect, and rightly so, to be granted the same permission.

Even the most judicious decisions can overlook important factors, so it is perfectly permissible to object to some plan or policy on the ground that it establishes an undesirable precedent. Such an argument will often be truncated, thus resembling *slippery slope,* but in full regalia it would be this:

139   1. If you do/permit *W,* that will set a precedent which will justify doing/permitting *X.*
       2. *X* is undesirable.
       3. Therefore you shouldn't do/permit *W.*

The acceptability of such an argument depends primarily upon whether *X* and *W* are similar in all relevant respects, for, if they are not, then P1 is false and the argument fails. The fallacy in that case is not *slippery slope,* but *faulty analogy.* The problem is not a causal chain with a weak link. P1 is false, instead, because the respects in which *W* and *X* are similar do not suffice to support the claim that if *W* is justified, then so too will *X* be. As we said, arguments from precedent are based on the requirement of consistency, that similar cases be treated similarly. These arguments break down when two allegedly similar cases are not similar in the relevant respect. Arguments harbouring *slippery slope* are based on empirical causal forces. They break down when a causal claim is unfounded.

Here's an argument using an appeal to precedent (and foundering due to a *faulty analogy*). At the end of June 1974, the spectacular Russian ballet dancer Mikhail Baryshnikov, touring Canada with the Bolshoi, defected and was granted asylum in Canada. A.S. complained in a letter to *The Ottawa Journal* (July 1974):

140   I am amazed that the Russian dancer Baryshnikov has been granted six months asylum in Canada.
      The minister of external affairs is notorious for his preference and admiration for special immigration cases who are no-goods, American draft-dodgers and American army deserters who came here while there was any danger of them having to defend their country. *We shall probably soon have some Palestine terrorists.* (Emphasis ours.)

We don't think A.S. is arguing that giving asylum to Baryshnikov is going to somehow cause Palestinian terrorists to seek and be granted entry into Canada. The point is that with the door opened for American draft dodgers and deserters and for Russians like Baryshnikov, a precedent has been set that will allow anyone entry into Canada, including undesirables like Palestinian terrorists. The Minister of External Affairs made a bad decision in allowing Baryshnikov's asylum, which only entrenched the undesirable precedent begun by letting in U.S. anti-war protesters during the Vietnam War.

A.S.'s argument is confused. These people do not belong to the same categories. American draft dodgers and deserters were allowed to immigrate to Canada only if they satisfied the qualifications any immigrant must pass, which do not require the listing of one's draft status in one's country of origin. Baryshnikov, on the other hand, sought political asylum — an entirely different means of entry into Canada. The policy of recent Canadian governments has been to grant asylum in cases, like Baryshnikov's, in which the petitioner would probably face prosecution at home were he or she turned back. Moreover, Baryshnikov's defection was not intended as a political act. He stated publicly that he wanted to come to the West for personal artistic reasons. So on many counts the analogy breaks down; the precedent does not apply, and the appropriate charge here is *faulty analogy*.

To end, the point we have been making in this discussion can be encapsulated in this slogan:

Bad causal chain arguments commit *slippery slope;* bad arguments from precedent commit *faulty analogy*.

EXERCISES

Directions

Identify any fallacies committed in the following passages. Always fully defend your claim, whatever it may be: fallacy; no argument; argument, but no fallacy; hitherto unclassified fallacy.

1. *Background:* This letter from E.L. to the Halifax *Chronicle-Herald* (August 1974) is another installment in the debate about the liberalization of abortion laws in Canada. The immediate occasion for this letter was then Justice Minister Otto Lang's opposition to any further liberalization. (See Chapter 5, *Ambiguity* for additional background.)

   > Some restrictions curtailing the birth of babies will soon have to be legislated in some countries. If this is not done at the individual level, then governments will have to act by passing certain measures. Otherwise, we will see nature revert to its first law, the one that was the sole arbiter before men came along: the survival of the fittest.

2. *Background:* E.N. might have changed her mind by now, but in 1974 she wrote to *The Windsor Star* defending then President Nixon's performance in office. This is an excerpt from her letter:

   > . . . Then on the home front, he isn't to blame either. On August 3 in *The Windsor Star,* Alan Greenspan wrote that 10 years ago, John Kennedy started the ball rolling towards inflation and we are suffering the consequences now. So why blame Nixon? As far as that goes, these conditions are in every country of the world, and more so in European countries.

3. *Background:* The following is an adaptation of a letter to *The Montreal Gazette* (September 1974) on the topic of amnesty for those who resisted participation in the Vietnam war:

   > A majority of the American people now believe that American participation in the Vietnam war was wrong. All Americans who resisted such participation were therefore patriotic and serving the American government, and all those who cooperated were unpatriotic and disserving the American government.

4. *Background:* In September 1982, Canadian historian Dr. Arthur Lower published a critique of the operation of the House of Commons in *Parliamentary Government.* Citing that critique in the Toronto *Globe and Mail* (September 1982), Michael Valpy wrote:

Dr. Lower links the degeneration of the Commons to the increasing democratization of the country — a democratization (one-person-one-vote) springing, as he says, from the "amiable but unsound philosophy" of Rousseau's eighteenth-century sentimentalism. . . . I am content to leave the linkage argument with the dean of Canadian historians.

5. *Background:* In 1981–82, Rev. Jesse Jackson began a campaign to force American business to open up greater opportunities for blacks. He threatened to have blacks boycott Coca-Cola unless blacks were granted more distributorships and management positions. William F. Buckley commented on this in a column in the *Detroit Free Press* (July 1982):

> Mr. Jackson's economic crusade strikes me as reasonably argued, though the obvious temptations (e.g. to veer in the direction of extortion) should be resisted.
>
> Speaking of temptations, Mr. Jackson has a number of things he should devote more time to avoiding. . . . His figures can be absolutely wild. He will inform you that 60 million black slaves were killed during the age of slavery. When you reply that this is difficult to imagine, given that only 650,000 slaves were brought to America, he says, you have your statisticians, I have mine. His turns out to be W.E.B. DuBois, a renowned black scholar who died a communist. My guess, without going to the Library of Congress, is that no one could simultaneously hold down a reputation as a scholar and as the purveyor of the 60 million myth.

6. *Background:* In early 1975 the Faculty of Physical Education at the University of Windsor was renamed the Faculty of Human Kinetics. *The Windsor Star* editorialized about this change (January 1975) as follows:

> Where's it going to end?
>
> Undertakers become morticians. Real estate men become realtors. Janitors become maintenance personnel. Garbage men become sanitary engineers. Reporters become journalists. Bartenders become mixologists.
>
> And now, Heaven help us, physical education students at the University of Windsor become kinesiologists. And the faculty of physical and health education becomes the faculty of human kinetics.
>
> George McMahon, dean of student services, has called the change "academic snobbery." Perhaps that should inspire the university senate to set up a new degree of Academic Snob (AS). And there should certainly be an honorary degree for Dean McMahon for his heroic if losing battle. Perhaps an honorary DPE — Defender of Plain English.

7. *Background:* An article in the Brandon *Sun* (August 1974) made reference to a decision by the Manitoba government which would force people to pay the tax on "free" car washes:

> For sales tax purposes, that scrubbing is assumed to be worth $1.50. And while you do not have to pay the price, you are required to cough up the tax bite. Which may be a small point. But think of the possibilities that are bound to come once the imaginative juices of the revenue boys really start to flow.
>
> How about a tax on savings, on the grounds that you would otherwise spend it on something taxable? Or how about assuming a value for tax purposes for do-it-yourself projects you sell to yourself? What about taxing the carwash you do in your driveway?
>
> Hell, why not go the distance and just assume a taxable value on dreams?

8. *Background:* In the mid-1970s there was a Canadian parliamentary study on the national immigration policy. The following reaction to the views of one of the Members of Parliament is taken from a column by Brian Kappler, then *The Windsor Star's* Ottawa correspondent (February 1975):

> The only politician still blithely calling for virtually open borders is Andrew Brewin, the Toronto New Democrat. Brewin, 67, is a knee-jerk supporter of all left-wing causes and is commonly known in Ottawa as the Honourable Member for Hanoi.
>
> On immigration, he says that Canada is a big country with lots of room. As usual, Brewin is out of touch with public opinion. Recent Gallup Polls show that well more than half of Canadians think the country is the right size — in population — right now.

9. *Background:* The following argument appeared in the *Canadian Public Safety* magazine some time ago:

(a) The average driver is not an expert.
(b) Racing drivers are experts.
(c) Racing drivers wear safety belts.
(d) Racing drivers agree that public highways are more dangerous than race tracks.
(e) You drive on public highways, therefore, why don't you wear safety belts?

CHAPTER SEVEN

THE CAUSES OF FALLACIOUS REASONING

Introduction

In the previous six chapters, we have paraded an assemblage of fallacies, accompanied by their defining conditions and by our analyses of examples. We have included those we believe to be important. What more is there to be covered? We are persuaded that no treatment of fallacious reasoning is complete which does not make an attempt, not merely to define and illustrate the forms of fallacy, but as well to diagnose their causes. Some logicians would claim that this question takes us beyond the scope of logic and into psychology. Why people reason fallaciously, it will be argued, is the proper concern of the psychologist rather than the logician, whose territory is that of matters of right and wrong in reasoning. However, since the purpose of this text is to help the reader both to detect fallacious reasoning and to reason better in order not to commit fallacies, we believe it mandatory to say something about the origin of fallacy. If that takes us into the realm of psychology, then so be it.

In Chapter 2 we said that one of the factors which causes people to reason fallaciously is letting one's emotions dictate one's thinking. Although very tempting as a diagnosis, we believe this view ought finally to be resisted as not going deeply enough into the problem. There are two reasons for this.

First, it presupposes a rather simplistic dichotomy between "reason" and "emotion." We say "simplistic" because it seems to us that the act of reasoning is rarely carried on in a situation which is without an emotional dimension and likewise because the emotions themselves are not bereft of reason.

To take the first point: few of us humans are like Mr. Spock of *Star Trek*. When we think about an issue, we do so because it attracts us, it has some interest for us, it strikes a chord in us — and all of these situations carry a residue of emotion. On some issues, we are inclined to be extremely vigilant and demanding, because the issue is one in which we have a personal stake. Typically where we have a stake, we have made not only a cognitive but an emotional commitment. Sometimes it is precisely because we have a stake that we undertake careful and rational review. And sometimes that review will take us to a different conclusion than the one with which we set out. The second point is that our emotions are not cognitively neutral or barren. For example, when one is irate about a situation — say the slaughter of the Palestinian refugees in Beirut in September 1982, or the possibility of a nuclear holocaust — one is irate precisely because one realizes (grasps intellectually) the horror of the situation. "Reason" and "emotion" seem to be abstractions, and artificial ones to a degree, from a single integrated experience or reaction; hence the attempt to segment or fractionalize seems ill-conceived.

But, second and more important, the contrast obscures the deep influence of the rationality of our emotional reactions. Why does one have just these emotional readings and responses? The answer seems to be that *they serve a function.* Emotional attachments themselves are symptomatic of what might be said to be either egocentric or ethnocentric commitments. To illustrate, many Americans who get very emotional and thickheaded about communism like to think that America has some special relationship to the values of freedom and liberty. Thus, in a widely syndicated column critical of Israel and the United States for their role in the slaughter of refugees in Beirut, Flora Lewis wrote (September 22, 1982):

141   Is it worse when Israel is involved, when America is somehow involved, than when Syrians massacre their own at Hama, than when Lebanese and Palestinians slaughter each other, than when Iranians install a reign of terror? Yes. It is worse because Israel and the United States *are democracies; because of the dedication to values of life and liberty;* because of the claim that what is done is in defense of these values; because by their nature both societies have accepted an obligation to live by higher standards than fang and claw. (Emphasis ours.)

The assumption that seems to operate here is that democracies have a special dedication to the values of life and liberty. This assumption is widely shared, but it is *ethnocentric* in the sense that it plays a certain role in the maintenance of a specific world-view. The problem with it is that it fails to take into account the fact that, for example, the Soviets also see themselves as committed to life and liberty. However, they construe these values differently. The problem with ethnocentric thinking is that it can blind us to certain realities, influence our thinking, cause us to see only certain sorts of items as evidence, overlook contrary evidence — and in doing all this, it can well sponsor fallacious reasoning.

This is no less true of *egocentric* commitments, those specific interests and involvements that individuals have as individuals. If, for example, you are an autoworker, you have a considerable investment in the United Auto Workers and will have a tendency to be very demanding of arguments which point the finger at the U.A.W. On the other hand, if you are a member of management for one of the automobile companies, you have a considerable ego investment in that company, and will be disposed to treat harshly anyone critical of that point of view. Here the term "egocentric" is meant to mark off those commitments which vary considerably from one individual to the next in the way that factors like nationality, sex and race do not.

All of this suggests that if we are to look carefully at the causes of fallacy, we are better off parting with the "reason vs. emotion" dichotomy, and taking a closer look at the *assumptions* which develop out of *ethnocentric* and *egocentric* involvements.

In what follows we will first discuss the attitudes involved in ego- and ethnocentrism. These attitudes are not themselves fallacious, though they often precipitate fallacy. Then we will discuss, under the title *dubious assumption* one particular fallacy that occurs when one or another of these attitudes intrudes into the realm of argumentation.

Ethnocentric Thinking

Here's one Canadian talking: "I am sick and tired of all the so-called Canadians who are saying the Russians are the greatest." (It's interesting how historical perspective exposes such chauvinism: the above was from a letter written during the 1972 Canada-Russia hockey series, after Canada had fallen behind in games.) Here's another Canadian, on a different subject: "Margaret Atwood, Margaret Laurence — never heard of them, so they must be Canadian."

Look behind these statements to the *attitudes* of the two speakers. The first speaker is decidedly pro-Canadian, as if to say: "*How dare* any Canadian even think that a Canadian hockey team could be inferior to the Russians!" The second speaker has just the opposite attitude toward Canadian literature: "How *dare* any Canadian think that a Canadian writer could be good enough to be well known!" At the risk of generalizing, we distill from these two comments the following underlying attitudes: "If it's Canadian, it's got to be good" in one corner; and "If it's Canadian, it can't be any good" in the other.

In this and the next sections we are going to discuss a basic attitude with a number of more or less familiar manifestations, known variously under the labels of *racism, chauvinism, sexism, nationalism, colonialism* and *provin-*

cialism. We propose to collect this host of attitudes under one roof and label them *ethnocentric thinking.*

A common denominator of many of these terms is that they suggest some form of *prejudice,* a concept worth having in mind as we proceed.[1] Like prejudice, *ethnocentric thinking* is easier to spot when someone else is the guilty party. In late 1974, the federal government circulated a "Green Paper" on the subject of immigration into Canada. *The Edmonton Journal* condemned the proposed policy in an editorial (October 1974). In early November, G.S. responded:

142   As the *Journal* said on October 30, the new immigration law will be racist and discriminatory . . .

I am from India and am inclined to think that people from the Indian subcontinent have a very high percentage of well-educated, hard-working, sincere and well-mannered people — comparatively speaking — and as immigrants, have tried to settle successfully by thrift and sobriety. (Emphasis ours.)

G.S. was arguing that the Green Paper's policy would have the result of limiting immigration to Canada from India, and that would be bad because Indians as a group have the traits highly desirable in immigrants. What we question is not the truth of G.S.'s claim, but the lack of any evidence to support this description.

There is some problem in deciding the sort of evidence that might lend credence to his claim: perhaps statistics comparing the education of Indian immigrants with those from other lands; carefully compiled interviews with employers who had hired both Indian and other immigrants, asking about their respective industriousness and courtesy. But G.S. produced no such evidence. Instead, he said, "I am from India and am inclined to think. . . ." That is, he seemed predisposed to think good things about his compatriots and to do so in advance of any evidence that might exist. A provincial attitude — a loyal identification with India — appears to have predetermined G.S.'s belief.

G.S. was guilty of *ethnocentric thinking* not simply because his beliefs about people from India were unsupported, though that was a contributing factor. A second detail was also necessary: the most plausible explanation of why G.S. advanced his challengeable claim without any supporting evidence was his strong identification with his native land and consequent tendency to extol the virtues of its people. This attitude is what we mean by *ethnocentric thinking.*

---

[1] The etymology of "prejudice" is revealing. It derives from the Latin prefix *prae* which means "before" and the noun *"judicium"* meaning "judgement." Thus, the literal meaning is "before judgement" — i.e., an idea or belief arrived at prior to and without knowledge and examination of the facts.

We would be negligent not to include an example arising from Canada's historic tension between francophones and anglophones.

In 1973, when the Queen was visiting Canada, Montreal *Le Devoir* editor Claude Ryan wrote an editorial giving his impression of the Quebec view of the monarchy. He said that the monarchy was a form of authority with which French Canadians "will never be reconciled," although most are willing to go along with it as the symbol of state authority for the present. In an editorial entitled, "A two-way tolerance," the Toronto *Globe and Mail* (August 1973) took issue with Ryan:

143   . . . he is definitely wrong in suggesting that Canada beyond Quebec should be asked by Quebeckers to relinquish . . . the monarchy.

English-speaking Canadians have not asked French-speaking Canadians to relinquish their visceral attachment to the French language and culture. Many of them have made valiant and successful efforts to become bilingual themselves. They have recognized that French-speaking Canadians should have their due place in the civil service, that business should recognize French across the country. They have contributed hundreds of millions to the extension of the French language and culture beyond Quebec, so that Quebeckers may feel at home in all of Canada.

The *Globe and Mail* editorialist's thinking seemed to be, "They're asking us anglophones to give up the monarchy! That would be equivalent to our asking them to give up their attachment to French language and culture. Not only have we not done that, we have worked very hard to respect and increase the status of French culture in Canada: witness 1 . . . 2 . . . 3. . . ."

Unlike the two examples discussed previously, the writer in this editorial produces evidence to support the premises. In many cases, ethnocentric thinking blinds one to the need for evidence. But ethnocentric thinking can occur even when evidence is cited. If only favourable evidence is selected from the total body of available data, and the selectivity stems from an ethnocentric attitude, then the fallacy of *hasty conclusion* results.

In the *Globe and Mail* editorial the belief that must be assessed is that English-speaking Canada has done its part to promote Canada's bilingual and bicultural identity. The editorialist mentioned four pieces of evidence supporting this claim; however, in every case only part of the picture is presented. Let's examine each in turn.

1. "Many English speaking Canadians have made an effort to become bilingual." What percentage of Canadians would this group account for? How many more have made no effort at all to become bilingual?

2. "They have recognized that French-speaking Canadians should have their due place in the civil service." How do French-speaking Canadians fare in terms of career progress in the civil service? What has "their due

place" turned out to be in practice? A professor of French at the University of Windsor recently stated, "When I go to talk about my taxes, sure they can usually find someone to speak French. But usually it is the janitor."[2]

3. "They have recognized that business should recognize French across the country." Can a francophone conduct business in French in Toronto? Vancouver? Calgary? Halifax?

4. "They have contributed hundreds of millions to the extension of French language and culture beyond Quebec." In what ways specifically was that money spent, and over how long a period of time? How receptive is the anglophone community in Canada to French plays and literature? How many read a French newspaper with any regularity, or make even a moderate attempt to learn about the culture and history of Quebec?

There exists, then, contrary evidence (and sometimes more than just the trickle we have hinted at) to each of the four points selected by the editorialist to advance the claim that English-speaking Canada has been active in promoting bilingualism and biculturalism. The editorial selected from the total body of evidence those portions that are favourable to its claim. A case for *hasty conclusion* is therefore in order here.

Ethnocentric arguments propound beliefs as true that are often little more than an expression of a visceral attachment to one's country, culture, race, special interest or sex. In some cases, it is difficult if not impossible to cite evidence which could conceivably count in their favour; for example, "My country is better than your country." In other cases, the beliefs may have evidence ("The people of my country are better educated than those in your country"), but the provincial eschew the difficult step of digging out and providing that evidence.

A noteworthy factor in ethnocentric thinking is the habit of thinking in **stereotypes**: Germans are industrious; North American Indians are lazy; Scots are stingy; the English are aloof; Newfoundlanders are simpletons; men are rational, aggressive, and out of touch with their feelings; women are emotional and illogical, passive and sensitive. There are several ideas behind the concept of a stereotype. It's an attribute that is based on a surface or warped impression falsely taken to describe the "essence" of a group. Accepted uncritically, the stereotype systematically distorts one's perceptions of people classified as belonging to the group — an arbitrary classification itself. Once they take hold of the mind, they become self-reinforcing and confirming. The examples that fit the stereotype are rated as evidence. Those that do not fit the stereotype are dismissed as exceptions. The result will be unreasonable beliefs.

Canada seems to be a mélange of attitudes about itself and "things Canadian." This fact brings us back to the opposite attitudes with which we began the section. On the one hand, Canadians are as capable as anyone

---

[2] Bill McGraw, "The Struggle to keep the Fleur-de-Lis blooming in the City of Roses," (*Detroit*, June 1, 1975), p. 11.

else of nationalistic pride and sentiment. Witness the remark of Robert McCleave (MP for Halifax-East Hants) during a debate in Parliament over the CBC policy of withholding some of its TV programs from Canadian border cities in the hope of later selling them to American networks. McCleave was arguing that the U.S. networks needn't fear that Americans would have already watched the programs on neighbouring Canadian channels:

144   If we examine the statistics regarding viewer preference of television stations, *the Americans, being much more parochial than Canadians and much more nationalistic-minded,* probably will not be seduced over to a Canadian station in any event. (Emphasis ours.)

Canadians, Mr. McCleave smugly implied, are above the parochial and nationalistic feelings so characteristic of Americans. A beautiful example of an ethnocentric denial of ethnocentric thinking.

On the other hand, Canadians are proficient at self-denigration, which surfaces most often when comparisons are made with the U.S. or Britain. Here, from an example we've used before, is a comment made as part of an argument about Canadian magazine publishing. N.H. wrote in *The Edmonton Journal:*

145   As usual, Canadians, who are incompetent, inefficient, lazy, miserable, and jealous, cannot compete with the U.S.A. in anything — be it sports, food production, manufacturing, films, popular songs and singers, TV writing, publishing, or just plain work. Consequently, they always want U.S. products and performers banned so they can produce the usually poor product.

There are many examples of this sort of colonial attitude in Canada. Numerous artists, musicians, and writers have had to achieve recognition elsewhere (usually in the U.S., Great Britain, or France) before Canadian critics could find much to get excited about in their work. We're not gainsaying the necessity of submitting artistic works to a wide range of critical response, both within and without the country; to go by local standards only is provincial. Yet to count exclusively on the judgement of American and British critics is colonialism. Times may be changing, but in Canada we still need to stand on guard against colonialism.

Egocentric Thinking

Thus far we have been looking at the way in which a person's ethnocentric commitments (to country, culture, race, sex) can take hold of the mind and result in fallacious reasoning.

In addition to the sort of broadranging investments we have mentioned, each person also possesses a stock of more individual attachments: to organizations, clubs, professions, etc. Unlike the other attachments (which are usually legacies of birth), these are usually chosen; hence our loyalty to them is likely to be that much stronger and the danger of having blinders on that much graver.

It is natural to rush to the defense of something or someone you love or value or identify with. Loyalty is an important trait. Unfortunately, loyalty can also interfere with rational appraisal of evidence and with the ability to face and respond to cogent criticism. Perhaps its clearest indicator is the tendency to discount in advance the possibility of evidence for a criticism, the refusal to face squarely documentation that is plainly evident.

Here is an example. In January 1981, in the Report of the Bertrand Commission, the commissioners alleged that oil companies had conspired to fix gasoline prices in Canada. In response, one individual wrote:

146 Bertrand and the commissioners must be out to lunch. In no possible way could he have one lousy shred of evidence to support their allegations. I can say this because I know that no price fixing occurred, and therefore no evidence for it could exist. My husband has been working for the oil company for 30 years and the company has always been good to him. To say that the industry my husband works for has been ripping off the public for years really irks me.

Two qualities stand out here. First, the fact that the writer has taken the position (we do not say concluded) that no price fixing has occurred, in advance of any review of the pertinent evidence. For this writer, the whole question of evidence simply does not arise. Second, the reason for this position seems to be found in the writer's egocentric investment: her husband is an employee of an oil company; he has been loyal to it and she is loyal to him. The egocentric nature of the reasoning is obvious here. One could of course charge the writer with *irrelevant reason,* on the ground that whether the company was good to her husband is totally irrelevant to the question of whether they have engaged in price fixing. But our interest here is less in the charge of fallacy than in its origin, which is plain in this case.

A classic example of *egocentrism* occurred during a controversy a few years ago surrounding an institution that's almost a litmus test of Canadian loyalty, the RCMP. In its July 1972 issue, *Maclean's* featured an article by ex-RCMP Corporal Jack Ramsay attacking the force for low morale, excessive image-burnishing, and rigid authoritarianism. Ramsay cited a fair amount of evidence for the conclusion that these faults were present in at least some parts of the force, and claimed that his examples were typical. In the September issue, *Maclean's* carried a letter from H.M., attacking Ramsay's allegations:

147   I am writing to tell you to cancel my subscription. I have never been
so angry with an article. Ex-Corporal Ramsay's confessions are a
disgrace to your magazine and I don't want another of your magazines in my house.

   Our son has been with the RCMP for 25 years and we are proud
of him. You really enjoyed yourselves trying to sabotage another
Canadian tradition.

This writer did not reject Ramsay's charges on the ground that his evidence
was mistaken or incomplete, as another writer did in that same issue, nor on
the ground that his evidence was not typical of the situation in the RCMP, as
did still another letter writer. The basis for H.M.'s rejection seems to have
been simply that she was proud of her son who had been a Mountie for 25
years, and that the RCMP is an honoured part of Canadian tradition. Her
blind, i.e. unquestioning, loyalty to her son and the RCMP interfered with
an objective and impartial examination of Ramsay's evidence.[3]

   H.M. displayed egocentric thinking by refusing to consider evidence that
was literally staring her in the face: after all, she did read the article containing Ramsay's allegations. In the next example the fallacy is committed in a
slightly different way, namely by ruling out in advance the very possibility
of any warrant for the criticism. We go south of the border and back in time
to the Watergate scandal. In July 1973, David and Julie Eisenhower — son-
in-law and daughter of then-President Nixon — appeared on a late-night TV
talk show. The U.S. Senate's Watergate hearings were taking place and conversation turned to them. Asked who he thought the most important
witnesses were, David Eisenhower replied:

148   The most important witnesses are the people who know most about
it. The importance or non-importance of the witnesses is irrelevant
if you believe as Julie and I believe that the president was not involved. They're all important, but the question is, can they be
believed?

It's not hard to understand what had happened here. Naturally loyal to President Nixon, David and Julie Eisenhower had made up their minds *in advance of the evidence* (which special prosecutor Archibald Cox and the
Senate Committee had only begun to accumulate) that Nixon was not involved. Nixon probably told them himself that he was not involved. Blindly
loyal to the President, Julie and David were not prepared to accept the
possibility of evidence indicating his involvement. The Eisenhower's
egocentric commitment to Nixon caused them to commit *hasty conclusion.*

---

[3] By the way, for a more sober assessment of the RCMP than you probably received in school,
we recommend Lorne and Caroline Brown, *An Unauthorized History of the RCMP* (Toronto:
James Lewis & Samuel, 1973), and Walter Stewart, *But Not in Canada!* (Toronto: Macmillan,
1976), Ch. 9, "Our Cops Are Cops."

A final example exhibits a typical blend of complacency tinged with a hint of racism. In August 1973, *The Windsor Star* ran an article about a local human rights officer and the evidence of racial discrimination (examples were given) she encountered daily through her work. That letter brought the following response from E.T.:

149   I have had much scope in knowing many, many white skinned people and never have I known one in Canada who felt superior to another because of skin color.

Often I have made a special effort to be friendly and kind to colored skinned people, and usually to find that they think it is condescension because many have an overwhelming inferiority complex which is revealed as a tremendous superiority complex, apparent disapproval and arrogance.

It is difficult for me to believe that any decent white skinned Canadian actually feels as this official indicates. All of us are judged in the working world according to character, ability, and potential and that goes for both colored and white skinned people . . .

I can't help resenting people preaching at white people against racial dislike when they know it is almost nonexistent in Canada. If they don't know, they are out of touch with "reality" or distorting actual facts.

E.T. refuses to give any credence to the human-rights officer's evidence, and suggests that she may be out of touch with reality or else actually misrepresenting the facts. Yet it's that officer's job day in and day out to investigate complaints of racial discrimination! And why does E.T. insist that racism is "almost nonexistent in Canada" — that the officer's examples cannot be representative of the attitudes of a significant (though not necessarily large) number of Canadians? Here we cannot be certain, since we must base our conclusion solely on E.T.'s letter. But the third paragraph of that letter evokes a rather smug image that many white Canadians have of themselves: "Racism is an American attitude; Canadians aren't racist." In our opinion, E.T.'s loyalty to that Canadian myth explains her response to the human rights officer's reports.[4]

A factor deserving special mention as a cause of egocentric thinking is friendship. Surely part of friendship is standing behind your friends when they are under criticism, lending them moral support.

The mistake people make is believing they must automatically take a friend's side in any dispute he or she gets involved in. What can happen is this: You accept your friend's description of the issues in the dispute and you

---

[4] If you're not convinced that this is a myth, may we recommend again as a salutary purgative, Walter Stewart, *But Not in Canada!* Ch. 12, "We Love Our Niggers."

see only his or her evidence that they are in the right and that the other party is wrong. Even if you get the other side's story, your sympathy and loyalty to your friend determine what sort of acceptance or non-acceptance you give to it. By getting involved in the controversy, you adopt your friend's orientation towards the situation, in terms of which you then filter and interpret the evidence. You give up your freedom to examine the issue reasonably, with an open mind.

A friendship that cannot brook criticism or tolerate disagreement is on shaky ground. True friendship requires the capacity to say, "Look, I'm your friend, but this time I think you're wrong."

Egocentric and ethnocentric attitudes are perennial problems for us all. What can be done about them? Obviously, one cannot rid oneself of them, indeed it would be folly to attempt to do so. Yet it is possible, and surely desirable, to become sensitive to one's own commitments. If, for example, you are actively involved in the right-to-life movement, you need to be aware of the fact that this commitment can cause you to make rigorous demands of pro-abortion arguments, while at the same time employ lax standards with anti-abortion arguments. Self-knowledge then is an important check against the possible narrowness of vision that may stem from one's commitments.

Worth mentioning in this connection is the exercise known as **reciprocity**: the ability to lay out in satisfactory terms the point of view to which you are opposed. This is not easy to do, as you will discover by trying. Find someone who takes the opposite viewpoint, preferably an intelligent and thoughtful person. See if you can lay out her reasoning in such a way that it is both recognizable and satisfactory to her. If you can do this without strawmanning that position, then you have avoided one of the main pitfalls of egocentric thinking.

Dubious Assumption

In the two previous sections, we put the spotlight on two attitudes that dispose people to fallacious reasoning. We did not introduce any new fallacies, since most of the logical miscues that ethnocentric and egocentric thinking sponsor are fallacies we have already dealt with. Thus, when an egocentric commitment leads the reasoner to accept without reservation a premise which really ought to have been defended, the appropriate charge will be *problematic premise*.

However, there is one fallacy that does need to be added to our inventory. This fallacy is often the result of an egocentric or ethnocentric pattern of thinking, but it is not limited to such contexts. It is the fallacy we shall call **dubious assumption.**

It is important at the outset to be clear about what we mean by an assumption, for this term is in common use and we shall be using it in a specialized way. For example, an assumption is often taken to be something that's not been proven and is open to question, as when someone says, "Wait a minute, you're making a big assumption when you say that . . ." A different use (and the one we have in mind here) is illustrated when the term is used to refer to something taken for granted by or underlying an assertion or a position, as when someone says, "The assumption underlying this policy is as follows . . . ."

So-called double-bind questions present a clear case of this sense of assumption. Someone asks you, "Have you continued cheating on your math exams?" or "Are you still doing dope?" How do you answer such a question if you've never cheated on a math exam or done dope? You're in a double bind, because if you say "No" you are implying that you used to cheat or do dope; and if you say "Yes," you are implying that you used to cheat or do dope, plus affirming that you are doing so now too. The problem here is that the question involves an *assumption* which is not legitimate; it makes a presupposition, so that the appropriate response is to challenge the assumption which underlines the question.

Roughly, then, we use the term **assumption** as follows:

> A sentence or position, Q, depends upon an assumption, R, just in case the truth of R is a necessary condition for the truth, or the intelligibility, or the appropriateness of Q.

In the double-bind questions, it is the appropriateness of the question which depends upon the truth of the assumption. Unless the assumption is true, the question is inappropriate.

Before we proceed with examples of the fallacy, we need to stress that our use of assumption rules out calling problematic premises assumptions, though in the ordinary sense of the term, it is tempting to do that. Consider the following example from a letter by G.T. to *The Ottawa Journal* (November, 1974), in which the writer urged the reappraisal of our foreign aid program:

150   Canadians are continually being urged to give money to feed starving children in India. While it is distressing to think of their suffering, it has to be remembered that *as much as three-quarters of all aid sent goes into the pockets of corrupt politicians and black marketeers.* (Emphasis ours.)

You might want to respond, "G.T. doesn't prove that charge, and it's quite an assumption to make." But the assertion we put in italics does not stand behind any other claim he makes; it's an allegation that stands by itself. You would be right in saying that it is quite a remarkable charge to make and that it ought to have been defended. However, the correct identification of this weakness in G.T.'s argument, following our nomenclature, is *problematic premise.*

Our interest in assumptions stems from and focuses on their role in arguments. We shall be looking at how the premises of arguments can be freighted with questionable assumptions. In this connection, we find it helpful and natural to include *missing premises* as a species of assumption. Recall from the discussion in Chapter 1 how missing premises work. This argument

151   Ellen is so irresponsible with money. Why, she spent her first month's salary from her new job on a dishwasher, of all things!

employs some such missing premise as this:

152   Anyone who buys a dishwasher before anything else is irresponsible with money.

The missing premise is an unstated link, needed to get from the stated premise to the conclusion, that is taken for granted. It is necessary for the *intelligibility* of the argument. As such, it may be called an assumption.

In summary, then, we'll be judging the reasonableness of either one of the following two sorts of assumption: (a) an assumption which underlies a stated premise in an argument; and (b) an assumption which underlies an inference from a stated premise to a conclusion — i.e., a missing premise.

Here are the conditions of the fallacy:

DUBIOUS ASSUMPTION

1. *M* employs an assumption, *Q*, in an argument where either *Q* is a proposition on which a stated premise depends for its truth, intelligibility or appropriateness, or else *Q* is a missing premise.
2. *Q* is open to reasonable challenge.

We can now review some examples. For the first one, we return to the exchange between former *Le Devoir* editor Claude Ryan and *The Globe and Mail* over Quebec's view of the monarchy where we found an instance of ethnocentric thinking (Example 143). The editorial said of Ryan's position:

153   . . . he is definitely wrong in suggesting that Canada beyond Quebec should be asked by Quebeckers to relinquish the monarchy.

English-speaking Canadians have not asked French-speaking Canadians to relinquish their visceral attachment to the French language and culture . . . it must be a two-way street. If Quebec's most basic desires are to be honored and supported, even when not shared, then Quebec must honor and support some similar desires in the rest of Canada.

Diagramming the argument in this portion of the editorial, we get:

154
1. Just as Quebec's most basic desires are to be honored and supported, similar desires in the rest of Canada are to be honored and supported.
2. English-speaking Canadians have not asked French-speaking Canadians to give up their language and culture.
3. French-speaking Canadians should not ask English-speaking Canadians to give up the monarchy.

Grant 1 and 2 just for the sake of argument, and look at those two premises alone. Don't look at the conclusion. By themselves they in no way force that conclusion. There must be an unexpressed premise in *The Globe and Mail's* reasoning connecting the point made about basic desires in 1, the assertion about French-Canadian language and culture in 2, and the English-Canadian attachment to the monarchy mentioned in 3 — some such missing premise as the following:

155
MP
a. The English-speaking Canadian desire to retain the monarchy is as basic to them as the French-speaking Canadian desire to retain their language and culture.

In other words, the editorial's argument makes the assumption that asking francophones to abandon their language and culture is analogous to asking anglophones to part with the monarchy. But this assumption has gaping holes in it. Relinquishing the monarchy would certainly effect changes in the self-conception of many English-speaking Canadians: it would alter the way they see themselves in relation to their cultural roots and historical traditions. However, the language and culture of Quebec are not just a part of French-speaking Canadians' self-image; they are the whole sum and substance of being French-Canadian. Their abandonment would constitute cultural suicide. *The Globe and Mail* argument makes an assumption that is clearly dubious. Indeed, the *dubious assumption* invokes a *faulty analogy,* as we have pointed out above. Now it is certainly possible (though this is speculation on our part) that *The Globe and Mail* editorialist was led to make this dubious assumption by the ethnocentric commitment he had made to English Canada.

Here is another example. During the time of the U.S. Senate's Watergate hearings, John J. Wilson, a lawyer for a White House staff member, was heard to refer to the committee member from Hawaii, Sen. Daniel Inouye, as "that little Jap." This remark created a furor when it was widely reported in the media. Attempting to defend himself, Wilson wondered aloud what all the hoopla was about, saying:

156   I wouldn't mind being called a little American.

K.S. wrote to the *Detroit Free Press* and neatly exposed Wilson's *dubious assumption:*

157   What is Sen. Inouye but an American? It is quite apparent that Mr. Wilson still believes that American is spelled "W-A-S-P."

Here again, we see how an ethnocentric commitment (the idea that real Americans are those descended from the English colonists) breeds fallacy.

The following letter to the editor of the *Halifax Chronicle-Herald* (August 1974) contains several fallacies, but can you spot the *dubious assumption* in it?

158   I am surprised that English Canada seems so undisturbed about Premier Bourassa's Bill 22, making French the official language in Quebec after the federal government's spending millions of our tax money promoting bilingualism for the benefit of Quebec. Unless Prime Minister Trudeau declares Bill 22 null and void, of which I have grave doubts as about half his support is from Quebec, then the other nine provinces should make the English language the only official language. Bill 22 is also another step toward separation. Since 30% of Quebec has already voted for separation, it may come sooner than most believe.

This argument is tricky for two reasons. First, it contains a number of cases of *problematic premise* which it's tempting to identify as *dubious assumptions*. Second, you need some knowledge of recent Quebec politics to spot the real culprit. You need to know that the statement, "30% of Quebec has already voted for separation," refers to the fact that the separatist *Parti Québecois* received 30% of the popular vote in Quebec in the 1973 provincial election there.

All that's recorded in the ballot count is how many people voted for each party, so all that is known is that 30% of the Quebec popular vote went to the PQ. Yet the writer asserts that 30% of Quebec voted for separation. He or she has a basis for the latter claim only if a vote for the PQ is automatically a vote for separation. In short, the writer is *assuming* that everyone who voted PQ favoured separatism.

However, a vote for a particular party is not necessarily an endorsement of all of its policies — and may not even signify approval of any of them, for you may prefer one party on balance over the others, considering the candidates running and the mix of policies. Also, a vote for one party may be a protest vote against another.

Both of these factors were said by observers to have been at work in the heavy PQ vote in Quebec. As well as being separatist, the PQ was the only democratic-socialist party available to Quebec voters in that election: the NDP ran no slate provincially. Voters with that preference had no other party to turn to. Also, the PQ had promised to make secession a question for a referendum, so a PQ vote was one step short of a vote for separation. Finally, observers believed no one thought the PQ had a chance of forming the government, so many voted for it as a way of lodging a protest against the ruling Liberal regime, without taking any risk of putting separatists in power. The letter-writer's ignorance of the political scene led to a *dubious assumption*.

In conclusion, it follows from what we have said in this chapter that a significant step in the avoidance of fallacious reasoning is self-awareness. If you are going to avoid the trap of being led into fallacious thinking you need to become aware of your own ethnocentric and egocentric commitments. Indeed, you need to understand the basis of these commitments and engage in critical thinking about them. Good logical critical thinking cannot and does not occur in a vacuum: both the force of personality and the complexity of the issue inevitably enter into any assessment of a process of reasoning. Logic alone is not enough; but awareness of the criteria of good argument, plus practice, plus self-knowledge and knowledge of the context — all of these must be integrated into the evaluation of argumentation.

In the next chapter, we switch the lens and look at arguments from the inside out; that is, the question of how one is to go about constructing arguments.

EXERCISES

Directions

This exercise is somewhat different from previous ones. Not all the passages here will be arguments; some are included in order to illustrate egocentric and ethnocentric thinking. Some passages contain the fallacy of *dubious assumption*. There may be other fallacies as well, or passages with arguments but no fallacies.

1. *Background:* The following is a UPI wire service story, titled "Women blamed," from Montes Claro, Brazil (August 1974):

> Saying that "in today's world it is the women and not the men who are doing all the seducing," Judge Emerson Pereia . . . acquitted Analindo da Silva of charges of seducing a minor, an 18-year-old girl.

"Reality shows us that the real seducers are the daughters of Eve who sashay their way through God's world with their miniskirts, low-cut and see-through blouses and tight-tight pants, for the sole purpose of exhibiting their curvaceous bodies to attract the attention and eyes of men," the judge's verdict read.

2. *Background:* In the mid '70s, the NBC-TV program, *Weekend,* featured a segment on racial tension in the city of Toronto, with particular attention devoted to incidents involving immigrants from Pakistan and East India. In the program, the claim was made that, "Toronto is a time bomb of racial tension." The following is a portion of an editorial response by *The Windsor Star:*

> Canadians are understandably upset at the charge by an NBC program that Toronto is a time bomb of racial tension. But Canadians should also be acquainted with the facts, should look at the gross exaggeration of the charge, and should not be too upset. A weekend visit to Toronto would provide the answer. . . .
>
> If anyone wanted to spend a few days in Toronto searching out prejudice, it would not be difficult. This is obviously what the NBC-TV program did, to come up with a scare report that Toronto is a time bomb of racial tension. To find the true picture would take longer and be a more difficult search. . . . They would have been better asking those of their countrymen who have first-hand knowledge of what the situation is. Let them ask the Vietnam war resisters and deserters. Let them ask thousands of Americans who crowd to Toronto on holidays, enjoying a clean, tension-free city where it's safe to walk the streets at night.

3. *Background:* From the *Temperance Education Journal:*

> Girls should never touch alcoholic liquors. The reasons are obvious. It is for them to steady the young men, and so maintain their dignity, their beauty, and their intelligence.

4. *Background:* Here's a passage from a Canadian history textbook which, while not an argument, is nevertheless persuasive and needs scrutiny.

> A good number of the *coureurs-de-bois* married Indian women and abandoned all trace of civilization; some even lowered themselves to the level of savages and became as ferocious as the Redskins when they took to torturing or killing enemy captives.

5. *Background:* In his book, *My Lai 4: A Report on the Massacre and its Aftermath,* Seymour Hersh recounted some of the reactions of some

Americans to the reports of the massacre in which U.S. troops killed over a hundred civilians. We paraphrase:

> Someone wrote to the Cleveland *Plain Dealer*, which had printed photos of the massacre:
> "I can't believe our boys' hearts are that bad. Your paper is rotten and anti-American."

6. *Background:* Charles Lynch, head of Southam News Services, wrote a column several years ago entitled, "Why Canadians fought Hitler." In it he stated:

> The idea that Canada went to war because of Nazi atrocities against Jews is a widely accepted rationale, but the fact is that the main cause of the Second World War was German expansionism, and the desire of other nations, principally Britain and France, to contain it.
>
> The German invasion of Poland was the last straw, and Britain and France declared war. Canada followed a step behind, and made a mighty contribution in manpower and munitions over the next five years, as she had during the Great War of 1914-18. But for Canada, as one reader points out, the war could have dragged on many more years, or even have been lost. Today's youngsters might be marching to a Nazi drumbeat, instead of "contemplating life and its meaning through the euphoria of pot and the cacophony of over-amplified guitars."

7. *Background:* In March 1982 *The Windsor Star* ran a column by syndicated columnist Allan Fotheringham in which he claimed that Canadian leaders, especially Prime Minister Trudeau and Conservative Party leader Joe Clark, were poor leaders and that this was partly because they use language poorly. Fotheringham wrote:

> Because Pierre Trudeau, in his retirement bound arrogance, and Joe Clark, in his leadership desperation, brutalize the language, it is no surprise that the unlettered public in irritation has shoved Ed Broadbent's NDP six points up in the Gallup poll.

The immediate occasion for the column was a Gallup poll which showed New Democratic Party leader, Ed Broadbent, running six points higher than in previous polls, whereas both Trudeau and Clark had lost ground.

8. *Background:* An excerpt from an editorial in *The Windsor Star* (October 1972), which ran shortly after a newspaper report of a decline of sexual crime in Denmark following upon that country's legalization of pornography:

Latest crime statistics from Denmark provide a striking illustration of the beneficial effects of that nation's experiment in pornography, and will provide a powerful argument for those favouring the legalization and open availability of pornography here in Canada.

9. *Background:* from the same editorial:

Whatever weight attaches to the moral or good-taste arguments against pornography, it seems doubtful that they will prevail, in the long run, over the increasingly liberal attitudes in modern society, particularly when the liberal position is buttressed by proof that legalized pornography leads to a decline of sexual crimes.

10. *Background:* The following conversation is reported by the Russian scientist Zhores Medvedev to have taken place in the mid 1960s between himself and a Russian bureaucrat named Filippova, when Medvedev was seeking approval to attend an international congress of scientists to be held in the U.S.A.:

"Comrade Medvedev, do you read the papers?"
"Of course I read them," I replied.
"Obviously you don't read them very well. You ought to know that they (the U.S.A.) are sending U-2 planes over and dropping spies by parachute. And you've been getting ready to go and visit them."
"It's not going visiting, it's a congress, and anyway, it's an international congress — not an American one!"
"Well, so it's international, but if this international congress were in West Germany, would you still want to go?"
When I tried to show that if Soviet scientists took part in international congresses, it would help raise the prestige of Soviet science, Filippova at once rejected my arguments: "We don't need recognition of American pseudo-scientists, we got our sputniks up first."

11. *Background:* At the Commonwealth Games held at Brisbane, Australia in the fall of 1982 new electronic sensing devices were used in the relay swimming events, to ensure that the swimmer in the water finished his or her leg before the teammate dove in to swim the next leg. As a result of these devices, several teams were disqualified in various relay swimming events. Canadian swimmers had several medals taken away, including two golds. Many swimmers from different countries complained that the devices were more sensitive than the human eye — too sensitive — so swimmers could not tell when to dive in, and had to delay too long. There was considerable dissatisfaction over their use, but some members of the Canadian team took the step of walking out

of the Games' closing ceremonies in protest. This act provoked a lot of criticism back home, including the following letter to the Toronto *Globe and Mail* (October 1982):

Well, we Canadians have done it again. We've let that insular attitude-bred insecurity of ours manifest itself as paranoid pique.

The recent disgusting display by one or two petulant pups at the Commonwealth Games should shame all Canadians. It's reminiscent of our hockey teams that have blamed the officials for their own shortcomings; of our skiers and skaters who've whined about poor conditions and poor organization when their performances have fallen short; . . . .

Not all our athletes and performers are bellyachers, of course. Not all need scapegoats and excuses. . . .

A federal Cabinet minister recently referred to Canadians as "a nation of bitchers." I seldom agree with this person, never politically, but this time he was right. How sad for all of us. . . .

CHAPTER EIGHT

CONSTRUCTING ARGUMENTS

Introduction

So far we have been talking about how to identify, display and criticize arguments. The examples of arguments we have used to illustrate the fallacies have been short, or else excerpted from larger bodies of argument. While letters to the editor are necessarily brief (many newspapers have a 200-word limit on letters they will publish), many arguments you encounter in everyday discourse, including the more serious and important ones, will be longer and more complex in structure than the letters or excerpts we have looked at so far. You will not be adequately prepared for logical self-defense until you have mastered the moves required by the analysis and critique of these more extended arguments. We shall offer our method for handling extended arguments in Chapter 9. First, however, we must pause for what might seem like a digression. There is another aspect of logical self-defense which we have as yet not dealt with, and it is one whose treatment will provide the essential background for analysing extended arguments.

We are referring to the ability to construct arguments. This ability is relevant to argument criticism, because you have no right to be confident of a critical evaluation of someone's argument until you yourself can produce a sound argument in support of your critique. To the extent that your ability to argue in support of your critical judgements is defective, not only are you going to have difficulty getting them accepted, but also they won't deserve your own confidence.

Your ability to construct arguments is indirectly related to knowing how to criticize extended arguments. Knowing how to build an argument entails understanding the dialectical pattern of argumentation, and understanding this full-blown structure of argumentation is necessary for the critical analysis of extended arguments. What we mean by "the dialectical pattern of argumentation" will emerge as we proceed in this chapter. Our present point is that it is only once you understand how argumentation as a process works that you will be able intelligently to make sense of extended arguments.

So we turn at this point to the business of constructing arguments in order, first, to help you learn to produce good arguments to support your critical judgements — and, in general, to support whatever defensible claims you may want to advance — and in order, second, to provide the necessary background for analysing extended arguments.

Argumentation as Dialectical

If you want to know how to construct something, whether it be an automobile engine or a sailboat, an after-dinner speech or an advertising campaign, you must first understand its purpose or function. The same goes for arguments. A survey of the uses to which arguments are put shows that they can have more than one function. Pre-eminently, arguments are used to persuade. But they also can function to reinforce beliefs whose truth their audience already accepts (e.g. political speeches at party fund-raisers, or religious sermons, for examples; literally preaching to the converted, yet where arguments are frequently found). Another use of arguments is for the purpose of inquiry. Here the person conducting the inquiry tests various alternative theses by seeing whether good arguments can be found to support them and whether the arguments that have been urged against them stand up. These seem to be the three main functions of argument. (We are not here concerned with the wide range of incidental uses to which arguments may be put — to browbeat, to impress, to seduce, to annoy, to frustrate, to bore, to delay, to amuse, to exercise the mind — to name just a few.)

Whether used to persuade, reinforce or inquire, arguments presuppose two related assumptions. First, they make sense only if there is doubt or question about the truth of the claim which occupies the position of conclusion. There is no point, as we have seen in our discussion of *problematic premise*, in arguing about the self-evident or the obvious. Second, arguments make sense only if at least two people (or roles) are involved. There must be the person who is the doubter or questioner, and the person who presents the arguments to answer the doubt or question. (In the case of solitary inquiry, one person must switch back and forth between the two roles of questioner and arguer.) An argument consists of reasons intended to show that a claim is worthy of acceptance. One person (or persona) must bring forward the reasons, another person (or persona) must require them.

(Nothing prevents there being many people occupying the two basic roles of questioner and arguer.) These two assumptions are central to understanding how to go about constructing arguments.

The second implies that when you construct an argument, you have some audience in mind, be it one particular person, a special group, or even any reasonable person whatever. The first implies that in constructing your argument, you must respond to the doubts or questions your audience may have about the claim you are arguing for. Thus any claim that you think is worth arguing for will have, on the one hand, reasons which lead you to consider accepting it, and on the other hand, reasons which have led others either to reject it or to question it. It follows that, if you remain convinced that the claim is worthy of acceptance, you must believe yourself able both to produce good reasons supporting it and to produce reasons for rejecting the grounds for criticizing or doubting it.

What makes your reasons for accepting the claim good ones? The answer must be that they themselves will stand up to critical scrutiny. This means that doubts or objections that can be raised against them can be resolved or countered. Similarly, what makes your arguments against the initial objections to the claim itself good ones is that those arguments too can stand up to criticism.

This is beginning to look complicated. It really isn't. The idea is this: when you argue fully for a claim, you in effect *make a case* for it. This case must consist, at its core, of arguments in support of the claim and the refutation of arguments against it. Thus the very simplest possible case for a claim will involve three arguments: (1) one argument which has the claim in question as its conclusion (the support for the claim); (2) the statement of one argument which has the denial of the claim in question as its conclusion (the argument against the claim); and (3) one argument which has as its conclusion a criticism of the argument against the claim (the refutation of the argument against the claim). A case can get much more complex than this, however the basic structure always relates back to arguments for the claim and arguments refuting arguments against the claim.

One way the case can get more complex is that there can be more than one argument in favour of the claim. (We call each distinct argument for a claim a *branch* of argument in the case for the claim.) Similarly, there can be more than one objection to the claim, and since each objection must be refuted, more than one argument in answer to objections.

A second complicating factor can be that the arguments in positions (1) or (3) can themselves come under criticism. This happens when, for example, after you present somebody with an argument for a position you are trying to defend, they find fault with your argument. If you are to maintain your position, you must proceed to try to refute that criticism. Or again, it can happen that, after you have argued against an objection to your position, someone finds fault with your "refutation" of the objection. At this point you must proceed to try to refute that criticism of your refutation. Since at every stage that you present an argument in the process of making your case there is always at least the theoretical possibility of a criticism of the argument, you can see that this process of criticism-reply, criticism-reply, could go on indefinitely (in theory, at least). In fact it rarely is necessary to go beyond a couple of moves before you have considered all reasonable objections to your arguments — assuming your arguments are sound ones.

Combine the two complicating factors — (A) more than one argument for the claim and more than one objection requiring refutation; and (B) criticisms of the arguments in (A), and the need to produce further arguments to refute those criticisms, plus possible objections to those further arguments and the need for replies to them — and you can appreciate that a complete case for a claim can be a lengthy and complex enterprise. Still, as you have seen, everything relates back to the basic structure of arguments for a claim, and the refutation of arguments against it. This whole pattern involved in making a case is what we call the dialectical process of argumentation.

Constructing Arguments

We have taken the time to spell out what is involved in dialectically making a case for a claim because this is the ideal or the model which should be the background you keep in mind when you construct arguments in support of claims you want to put forward. You will not have the time, or the need, to develop a full-fledged case every time you argue for a claim. However, you should always have this structure in mind, and be aware of just what move in it you are making, even when you are just making a partial case.

With a dialectically complete case as our model, then, we now offer some more specific advice about how to construct arguments.

Identify the Problem, Question or Issue

Make clear to yourself what the issue is, and be able to say why it is controversial enough to generate argumentation. You should be able to state the issue in a clause that begins like this: "The issue is *whether*. . . ." Here are some examples. (A) The issue here is whether capital punishment is justified. (B) The question is whether Jones's reply to Smith is a *red herring*. (C) The problem is to determine whether wage increases are the root cause of the recession. In each case you must be able to identify the controversy or the source of a question about the issue. For example: (A) There are many who want capital punishment reinstated, while others are convinced it should be abolished forever. (B) Smith was criticizing the provincial health-care system, and Jones in defense replied with an attack on the provincial education system, which on the face of it doesn't seem connected. (C) The unions maintain that the recession is caused by price-fuelled inflation; the business community agrees that inflation is the immediate culprit, but lays the blame for it on escalating wages. Identifying the question, and why there is a problem or controversy, will put you on the track of the points that need to be covered in your argument.

Making Your Position Clear

You should be able to state your position in a single sentence or in a clause which begins with the word "that." For example: (A) My position is that capital punishment should be reinstated. (B) Jones commits *red herring* in his defense, against Smith's criticisms, of the provincial health care system. (C) The cause of inflation, I shall argue, is a combination of price increases and wage escalation.

The most common mistake is to combine an argument, or a fragment of argument, with the statement of one's position. So you find people saying things like, "My position is that capital punishment should be reinstated because it is a deterrent to murder." That is false. The person's position is that capital punishment should be reinstated. He *also* intends to defend that position with an argument which has, as one of its premises, the assertion that capital punishment is a deterrent to murder. It is a mistake to combine the two, because when it comes time to consider objections, the confusion of position and argument will result in confusion between objections to the position and objections to the argument, which as we have seen are quite distinct.

Another mistake is to state two or more positions together, when each requires separate defense. Thus you will encounter this sort of statement of a position: "In my opinion, which I shall defend, capital punishment should not be reinstated, and those who are lobbying for its return cannot be the devout Christians they claim to be." These are two distinct propositions. Even if one of them is true, it doesn't follow that the other is too. Moreover, quite different kinds of evidence would be required to support each claim. Combining them at the outset invites nothing but confusion in the argument to follow. There is nothing wrong with holding and defending two or more distinct positions related to a single issue. But it is crucial to separate them and to defend them one at a time.

Presenting Arguments for Your Position

Only now does that actual "argument" start. Presumably you have some reasons for holding your position instead of the alternatives to it that you referred to in explaining why there is a problem or question here. This is where you state those arguments — the strongest ones you have.

You may have one or more than one argument for your position. If more than one, be sure to keep the different arguments separate. For instance, if you are arguing for the reinstatement of capital punishment, you may think it is justified on the ground that it is a deterrent to murder, and you may also think it is justified because you believe it is the punishment that a murderer deserves. These are different arguments, for one could be sound even if the other were refuted. When you turn to consider possible objections to your arguments, you will want to avoid the confusion that could be caused by mixing up an objection to one argument with an objection to another. So keep each argument clearly distinguished from the others.

Try to write out each argument as completely as you can. Spell out all the steps. If you will recall the difficulty you had in supplying missing premises for arguments you were trying to understand and evaluate in working through Chapters 2-7, you will recognize the importance of making your arguments as fully explicit for your audience as possible. So you might spell out your deterrence argument for capital punishment with the following sort of completeness: "The threat of execution for murder is likely to deter a person who might otherwise want to commit a murder, and the state should do whatever it can to reduce the incidence of murder, so the state should reinstate capital punishment as the penalty for murder." Since it is only the state that can legally institute capital punishment, you need to include the second premise to connect your deterrence premise with the conclusion. Spell out such connections.

Defending Your Arguments

Your arguments are no more privileged than those you have been evaluating up to this point in working with this text. Hence they, like any other argument, must meet the standards of relevance, acceptability and sufficiency. If your arguments are to be logically sound, they must be fallacy-free. So the next step in developing your case is to consider what possible objections a reasonable critic of your arguments might raise. Stop! We are referring now to objections that an opponent might make against *your arguments* for your position. This is importantly different from objections against your position itself (to which we turn in the next section). What you should be doing at this point is trying to strengthen your arguments for your claim by testing those arguments against criticisms that a reasonable but skeptical observer might level. There are at least a couple of ways you can put yourself into the position of a critic of your own arguments.

One way to assess your own arguments is to attend to the *kind* of argument you are offering, in each case, and see if yours meet the standards for arguments of that sort. Is it a causal argument, for example? If so, and you are arguing to a causal claim as your conclusion, have you established a systematic correlation between what you allege to be the cause and the effect? Have you considered and refuted alternative hypotheses? Is your argument an argument from analogy? In that case, are the two things you are comparing truly similar in the respect in which they must be in order to justify your conclusion? Have you appealed to an authority? In that case, does your appeal satisfy the rules for legitimate appeals to authority? If you are arguing in an adversary context, have you fairly represented the views of the person whose interests conflict with yours and with whom you disagree? You get the idea.

The other way you can put yourself into the position of a critic of your own argument is to pay attention to the points that have already been discussed and argued about in the controversy on which you are taking a position. These may pertain to premises in your arguments. You may have to do some research to find this out. In the capital punishment argument, for example, you ought to be aware of (or to find out) the fact that people have presented evidence which they contend shows that capital punishment is not in fact a deterrent. The data purport to show, for example, that when states have abolished capital punishment, the murder rate did not proceed to increase. This contention appears to stand in opposition to your claim that capital punishment is a deterrent to murder. Thus you will need to respond to it.

What is needed here, in general, is an effort on your part to detach yourself from your argument and look at it with an austere and demanding eye. Here the egocentric and ethnocentric attitudes we discussed in Chapter 7 will do their best to obstruct you. But it is really in the interest of your own position that you be a harsh critic of your arguments. Such criticism will expose to you their initial flaws, which you can then proceed to correct. In this way, your case will actually be stronger, not weaker, as a result of your own perceptive criticisms of it.

While the first move of defense is criticism, the second is further argumentation. Where your critique exposed an undefended premise that is open to attack (e.g., your "deterrence" premise), you can now move to provide the needed argument or counterattack. If you found that your conclusion was hastily drawn on the basis of a limited sample of the relevant kinds of evidence, you now seek out and present the additional evidence needed to nail down your case. If a premise was found to be irrelevant, you can move to supply the unexpressed assumption that was at work implicitly when you formulated the argument.

In some cases you will find the criticism cogent. This may call for a strategic qualification on your part. (Perhaps, on reflection, you would want to defend capital punishment only for first-degree murder; or you may find that you can provide sound arguments only for the conclusion that the wage-price spiral is one of several causes of inflation, and not the single cause.) In other cases, granting the force of a criticism will require you to abandon an argument altogether. Perhaps you got carried away and argued from a faulty analogy that cannot be repaired or qualified. In that case, you may need to look for another argument to replace the one you dropped, or you may be able to get along with the remaining ones if you had several in your arsenal to start with. Your case is strengthened, not weakened, by the addition of needed qualifications and by the excision of bad arguments.

Considering Objections to Your Position

Recall the pattern of dialectical argumentation. First, arguments for the position, and second, refutations of objections against the position. So far we have dealt only with the former. The second kind of move in making your case, distinct from producing your arguments for your position and defending them against objections, is to try to state the strongest arguments *against* your position that you can think of. These are arguments that will have as their conclusion either the proposition that your conclusion is false (or otherwise unacceptable), or else some other proposition which, if true, would be incompatible with your conclusion. (Here is an example of the difference between these two: suppose your conclusion is that capital punishment should be reinstated. There might be an argument with the conclusion that capital punishment should *not* be reinstated, perhaps on grounds that it is an uncivilized punishment. Alternatively, or in addition, there might be an argument for the conclusion that murderers should receive life imprisonment without parole, perhaps on the grounds that this would be a sufficiently harsh punishment, and one that is safe for society. If the conclusion of this argument were true, then of course your position, that capital punishment should be reinstated, is not; hence it is incompatible with your conclusion.)

These arguments against your position ought to be stated as fairly and fully as you can manage, for you want to avoid misrepresenting the position you disagree with and risk setting up straw men. But once you present these arguments, your next move is to try to show that they are not sound. Thus you will have to generate arguments which show that these objections to your position violate one or more of the standards of good argument, and consequently that they do not establish their conclusions.

Once again you may find some objections make good points that require you to qualify your position. However, if any of these arguments turns out to be sound, you will be forced to abandon your position, at least in its present form. For these are objections not against your present arguments for your position, but against your position itself.

Assuming that you have presented and defended strong arguments in support of your position, and that you have refuted strong objections against it, the result is a strong case that your position is worthy of acceptance — and this is what you set out to produce.

The Order of Presentation

In the last few pages we have reviewed the steps to follow when constructing an argument for a position you wish to defend. Let us distinguish between these steps in the dialectical process and the order of presentation you should follow when writing up your argument for presentation. It is probably a good idea to practice by following a set order, until the moves become automatic (which they do, in time). However, there is no heavenly edict that requires the arguments for a position to be set forth and defended first, and the arguments against it to be considered and refuted second. Sometimes it is more effective, rhetorically, to reverse that order. For example, when your audience believes there are clear arguments proving your position false, it may be wise to start out by presenting your attacks on those arguments, and thereby weakening the audience's predisposition to dismiss your position out of hand and making them more receptive to your later presentation of your arguments on its behalf. We suppose there is nothing in principle against a presentation that alternates arguments for and refutations of criticisms against, in sets of two. This does risk confusion, though, and your presentation will not be persuasive if it is not clear.

There is another way you might want to rearrange the steps you followed in putting your argument together when you get to the stage of organizing it for presentation. You initially worked through an argument for your position, objections against it, then your responses to those objections. The last move sometimes consisted of providing additional argumentation to make good the defects in the original argument. Having spotted those defects, there may be no point in repeating this whole process when you present your finished argument. Instead, it will usually be more effective to produce the strengthened argument at the outset. The only time this won't be a good policy is when the objection is a very common one, and you want to draw attention to it in order to make sure your audience appreciates that you have an answer to it.

Argumentative Inquiry

In the previous section we proceeded on the assumption that you had already settled on a position and had arguments to present in support of it. In a way, this is putting the cart before the horse. All too often what we do is fasten on (or cling to) a position without having considered its merits and defects in an open-minded way, and cast around for arguments to support it only after we have already decided to accept it. One might take the situation of the defending or prosecuting lawyer as analogous, and also as a precedent in support of this procedure. The lawyer must, it is true, make out the best case possible for the position she is called upon to take up, whether it be for the defense or for the prosecution. She is given her conclusion first, and only after that makes the best case she can to support it. However, there is this much that is different about the model of legal argumentation: *both* sides are given, in theory, the best possible case. The assumption underlying the system is that with strong arguments for and against the accused, plus a system of fair procedures, the truth will make itself evident in most cases. However, when you or we take up a position in advance of any review of its merits, and then seek out arguments that will support it, we do not assign an advocate to the other side. Moreover, so often we start out with positions that we have adopted out of egocentric or sociocentric attitudes, with the consequence that we have a strong personal investment in defending them, come hell or high water. We are not about to put them before any Court of Reason — and hire a lawyer to attack them too! So when we decide upon our position first, and only subsequently hunt up some support for it, we may have put our money on the wrong horse, and be tempted to follow that up by sending good money after the bad.

One happy feature of the dialectical argumentative pattern is that it can be used just as well when you have not made up your mind about a position, and when you are not sure what position is supported by the arguments that have been advanced on various sides of the issue.

Here is how to proceed. You follow the pattern in just the way we set it out in the section on constructing arguments. Only this time, instead of making your initial position one that you have already decided to accept, you take a position on the question or issue that seems to you to deserve serious consideration. And you "take" this position only in the sense that you treat it as a hypothesis. Then you work your way through the various steps, striving to find the strongest arguments you can, and open to finding out that in fact they do not support the position you started out with, but instead tell against it.

More specifically, you first state the position. Then you gather and present, in turn, the best arguments you can find in support of that position. Third, you consider these arguments one by one, from a critical point of view, trying to see what logical flaws they have. Fourth, you see if you cannot repair any flaws that you have found, either by qualifying the position or by producing further evidence or arguments. Finally, you look back over the criticisms of the arguments and the response to those criticisms, and see if the arguments stand up or have to be abandoned. Having thus considered the arguments for the position, you next turn to arguments against it. Now you first cast about for and state as fully and fairly as you can the arguments which go to show that the position is false or should not be accepted. Then you scrutinize each of these arguments for logical weaknesses. Third, you see if any weaknesses cannot be repaired. Fourth, you step back and assess the net force of these objections to the position.

Throughout this whole process you have withheld your personal commitment, for or against the position. Now, looking at the strengths and weaknesses of the arguments for and against it, you can decide whether it merits acceptance, and if so, how strong the overall case for it is. If it does not stand up to this dialectical inquiry, you are free to reject it and consider some alternative position on the issue in question. You can subject what strikes you now as a plausible position to a similar careful argumentative inquiry. In this way you can wait until after a careful consideration of the various arguments and positions on the issue before deciding which position seems to be the most defensible, and hence most worthy of your assent.

Once again, the foregoing describes a procedure of inquiry and not necessarily a structure for presentation. Nothing prevents you from presenting the inquiry to your audience in just the way you followed it along, and this can be an effective way of winning over a skeptical audience, for presumably the arguments that won you over from a noncommital position will also be seen by your audience to be sound. But nothing says you have to follow these steps in making your presentation. You may choose the organization you think most effective, so long as it is clear, and so long as the result is that your audience is given a full review of the arguments for the position, along with your defense of them, and the arguments against the position, along with your refutation of them.

An Example

It is time to illustrate the procedure for constructing arguments that we have been describing by working through an example using it. We won't take up a major controversy, because to develop a case for a position on a major issue, such as the morality of abortion or the merits of nuclear disarmament, would take more space than we have available. Our example would have to be severely truncated, and would risk leaving you with the erroneous impression that the procedure for constructing arguments results in a superficial treatment of the issues.

Our example comes from a minor dispute that ruffled our campus recently. A bit of background is in order. You need to know that our university runs an internal mail service, twice a day delivering mail from a central post office to departmental offices (where departmental secretaries sort it and file it in faculty mail slots). You also need to know that in our city one of the candidates for mayor in the recent civic elections, (we'll call her Dr. Gibson), is also a professor on campus.

Our student weekly newspaper recently ran the headline, "University unwittingly sends campaign mail — who's to blame?" According to the story, one of the people working for Dr. Gibson's campaign, a colleague in her department (whom we'll call Schneider), had sent through the university mail system to all the faculty a flyer and a letter asking for support and money for Dr. Gibson's campaign. All the costs of sending this material except those connected with the mail distribution were borne by the Gibson campaign. But the newspaper was taking the position that Prof. Schneider shouldn't have sent the letters through the university mail without paying. Was the paper right?

That is the question we shall examine. Prof. Schneider didn't think he had done anything wrong, at least not morally wrong. He was quoted as saying that he couldn't find any policy that prohibited sending campaign material through the university mail service. So we have a disagreement between Prof. Schneider and the student newspaper; we have a controversy.

We are not sure what to think about this issue, so we will treat our argument construction from the point of view of argumentative inquiry. It does strike us as plausible to think the newspaper is right, so we will begin by taking the position, at least for the purpose of starting the inquiry, that Prof. Schneider should not have sent the campaign literature through the university mail without paying for that delivery.

So far we have explained the issue and why there is a question, and we have taken a position. The next step is to formulate arguments in support of that position.

Here are a couple of arguments that occur to us as we think about what might be said on behalf of the newspaper's position:

159   *Argument A*

1 The university should not in any way take a partisan position on the city's politics.

2 By using his university connections, and not paying for the mailing of the Gibson campaign literature, Prof. Schneider has compromised the university's non-partisan position in civic politics.

3 Prof. Schneider should not have sent the Gibson campaign literature through the university mail without paying for it.

160   *Argument B*

1 By sending non-university material through the university mail system without paying for it, Prof. Schneider has set a precedent that will allow other university and non-university people to send non-university material through the university system without paying.

2 It is undesirable to have people, connected with the university or not, sending non-university material through the university mail at no charge.

3 Prof. Schneider should not have sent the Gibson campaign literature through the university mail without paying for it.

Notice that in both cases the conclusion of the argument is the position we are inquiring into.

The next step is to go through each argument, separately, to see if it stands up to critical scrutiny. We'll leave *Argument A* to you, and work through *Argument B* next.

First we check the connection between the premises and the conclusion. The argument seems to go like this: "If an action of yours sets a precedent, and it is a bad precedent, then you shouldn't have done it." To test this inference, we try to think of a counter-example to it: could there be a situation in which the premises were true but the conclusion false? Could an action that sets a bad precedent ever be justified?

Someone might object that if a great deal of good is done on a particular occasion by an action, then it should be done even it if sets a bad precedent. For instance, if someone not connected with the university saved a life by using university property (say, a fire extinguisher), then whatever the precedent thereby set, the action would still be justified because the gain was so great. (Here is the first objection to Argument B.)

Does this counter-example show that the inference from the premises to the conclusion in *B* is not sound? Here we move to the next step in our procedure, and try to reply to the objection. We think that in fact the example is not a counter-example. Using university equipment to save a life does not set a harmful precedent, but a most desirable one. So the example does not give us a case where the premises are both true — i.e., where the action sets a precedent *and* it's a bad precedent. We cannot think of any further objections to the move from the premises to the conclusion in *B*, so we declare it acceptable (pending notification of some as-yet-unconsidered objection).

Now what about the premises themselves? Take *1*. Does Prof. Schneider's action really set a precedent? If his action is not judged wrong in this case, does that mean other faculty, and non-university people, would have to be permitted to send non-university mail through the campus system without paying?

One might object, first, that Prof. Schneider is connected with the university, so his action does not open the door to non-university people having this right. However, in reply to this objection to premise *1* we would make the point that Prof. Schneider was acting in his capacity as campaign worker for Dr. Gibson's campaign, not in his capacity as a university faculty member. Sure, his faculty status was what led the university post office to accept and deliver the campaign literature without question, but as sender of this literature he acted as campaign worker, not professor. The objection does not, then, show that no precedent has been set for non-university use of a university service.

Another possible objection to premise *1* is that Prof. Schneider was sending material relating to Dr. Gibson, another faculty member, so the material is not unrelated to the university.

But a similar reply to our previous one works here too. Dr. Gibson is running for mayor in her capacity as private citizen, not in any connection with her faculty post or as representative of the university. Since her connection with the university is not related to her mayoralty campaign, the campaign literature mailed by Prof. Schneider on her behalf is non-university material.

We will leave our testing of the first premise here. You may think of further objections that would have to be countered by anyone trying to defend this argument. We move on to premise *2* of *Argument B:* it is undesirable to have anyone who wants to sending any mail at all through the university postal system without charge.

Is this really true? What would be the consequences if this were the policy? What problems would it create? It strikes us that the consequences will depend on the demand for this service. If outsiders want to use the university postal system for non-university business only once or twice a year, the burden on the mail delivery system will be unnoticeable. If such mail starts to go through the system every day, it might be forced to add staff or cut service. Thus looking at the precedent from the point of view of its consequences, we would say that one should reserve judgement until there is some concrete evidence that it is a burden on the mail system, or that it isn't. This basis for assessing premise 2 leaves us in the position of having to withhold judgement. Is there some other way to assess premise 2 that will give a definite answer?

Here is a possibility. If there is a policy allowing the free use of the university postal service by non-university people or for non-university purposes, then some people will not be paying for this service while everyone else is. It's unfair. So even if the harm is minimal or negligible in terms of cost to the university or restriction of service, there is an element of unfairness involved that makes the precedent undesirable.

As far as we can see there is no disputing that the Schneider precedent allows for a certain amount of unfairness. Let us consider how strong a point this is. If only a very few people take advantage of the policy, and do so only rarely, then although the unfairness exists, it is a pretty minor consideration. Thus if this is all that can be said in support of premise 2, the result is that *Argument B* is not a terribly forceful objection to Prof. Schneider's action.

Argument B gives us some grounds for accepting our position, though not overwhelming ones. Maybe *Argument A* will fare better under critical scrutiny. And there may be *Arguments C, D* and *E* that we have not had the wit to assemble. Begging limitations of space, we cut off here any further consideration of the arguments for our starting position, and turn now to arguments that might be framed against it.

Prof. Schneider himself offered one such argument, as he was quoted in the student newspaper, so we should consider it. It ran as follows:

161   *Schneider's Defense*

1 There is no university policy prohibiting sending political campaign literature through the university mail free of charge.
a When there is no policy against an action in a large institution, then that action is permissible.
2 It was not wrong for Prof. Schneider to have sent the Gibson campaign literature through the university mail without paying for it.

You will notice that we have supplied a missing premise, to make all the steps in the argument against our position explicit. We have tried to make the missing premise plausible by adding the qualifier "in a large institution." It seems particularly true in large institutions that one must be free to act except where a policy introduces a restriction; the alternative of being free to do only what a policy permits would be too stifling. If Schneider's argument is sound, then our initial position is false. We must now examine this argument.

The inference from premises to conclusion stands up, indeed we have supplied the missing premise to make sure it does. And we see no reason not to take Prof. Schneider's word for it that no policy forbidding his action could be found when he mailed out the campaign literature. So the question comes down to premise *a*, and this strikes us as a very weak link in the argument.

Our argument against premise *a* consists of pointing out that some actions can be dangerous, or wasteful, and for that reason alone should not be performed, whether there is any policy expressly forbidding them or not. Thus premise *a* taken as it stands is false. To avoid this objection we restate premise *a* as follows:

> a^1 When there is no policy against an action in a large institution, then *other things being equal* that action is permissible.

This rewording makes premise *a* acceptable, but we now have to add a further missing premise in order to get to the conclusion, namely:

> *b* In the case of Prof. Schneider's mailing the campaign literature other things are equal — i.e., there is no special reason for not going ahead, in the absence of a policy prohibiting it, and mailing the literature.

The trouble with this second missing premise is that it is pretty controversial. Our initial arguments, *A* and *B*, both offered reasons why Prof. Schneider should not have mailed the campaign literature the way he did. We cannot then grant premise *b* in Prof. Schneider's defense without giving up the initial position we are investigating, so going along with *b* requires us to beg the question. Since *b* cannot be granted, then this argument fails to establish its conclusion that Prof. Schneider did nothing wrong.

We have, so far, considered and rejected one objection to our position. Perhaps there are other arguments against the position that will fare better. If our inquiry were to be complete, we would have to search for them. However, we will break off the inquiry at this point, since we believe it should have illustrated in a fairly thorough way the dialectical procedure to be followed in trying to work out a position on an issue. Since this is the same procedure to follow in making a case for a position, you can look back over our discussion of this example as if we had initially commited ourselves to the *position* that Prof. Schneider was wrong to have sent out the campaign literature for Dr. Gibson through the university mail without paying for it.

Conclusion

A good deal more could be said about the construction of arguments, but in this chapter we have addressed what we believe is the most important starting point: the structure of dialectical argumentation. Any complete case in support of a claim must have the structure we have described. By no means all arguments will go to this length, nor do they need to. But any shorter argument can be identified as to where it fits in this dialectical pattern. It will be an argument for a position. Or a reply to an anticipated objection to an argument. Or the refutation of an anticipated objection to a position. And so on.

You will learn through practice to provide just the amount of argument that is called for, and to direct it at the important points at issue. Keep in mind what we said at the outset — that each argument has its audience. Identify yours and direct your arguments to the dialectical challenges that come from it.

What is missing from this chapter is a taxonomy of the different types of argument, with recipes or hints for producing arguments of each type. We have in mind here a list of such items as the following: arguments in support of recommendations of policies or actions; arguments in support of value judgements; arguments in support of causal claims. And so on. Beyond that, there could be lists of the variety of argument subject-matters within each type. Arguments about values subdivide into moral, aesthetic, prudential, religious, and others. There are arguments for theories in the social sciences and arguments for theories in the physical sciences; and within each grouping, the differences between particular scientific fields will be relevant. Learning all of this requires, first, an understanding of and practice with the types of consideration common to arguments of each general type. (For example, arguments recommending policies usually invoke the distinction between ends or goals, and means of achieving those goals, together with an apparatus for ranking alternative means to a given goal.) Second, one needs to learn something about each specific field about which one wants to argue. This calls for a well-rounded education.

Both these objectives are highly desirable. We believe that the first could be achieved in a course devoted entirely to the construction of arguments. The second requires a sound liberal education, which one really only begins at university or college. The consequence is that we can do little more than try to set you on the road to an ability to formulate arguments, and hope that you expand and deepen this ability as your education proceeds. If you keep in mind the dialectical pattern of argumentation, and try to employ it whenever you construct arguments, you start out on the right foot.

EXERCISES

1. *Directions:* How many positions are expressed in each of the following sentences? If there is just one, restate it to make this clear. If there are more than one, state each one separately.
   (a) The Yukon, which is now a territory, should be made a province.
   (b) Quebec should be allowed to secede from Canada on a ten-year trial basis, with an option to renew.

(c) Alberta should share its oil revenues with the other provinces, but Newfoundland and Nova Scotia should only have to pool theirs with the other Maritime provinces.

(d) If God exists, then evil is an illusion.

(e) While marriage is a desirable institution, it should not require sexual exclusivity.

(f) Mussolini was merely a banal thug, whereas Hitler was evil incarnate.

(g) The end of American imperial hegemony is at hand, however there is no new world power to replace it, unless the Arab oil sheikdoms or Japan should be counted.

(h) The twenty-first century belongs to China, not Japan.

2. *Directions:* Which of the following sentences expresses just a position (or more than one position), and which expresses a part of an argument combined with a statement of a position? Write out separately each position expressed, and mark it as such. Write out separately each premise (or premises) offered as a partial argument for a position expressed, and mark it as such, identifying the position it is supposed to support.

(a) The 1982 professional football players' strike in the United States marked the end of the "Sunday afternoon TV syndrome" in many U.S. (and Canadian) households.

(b) The invasion of the Falkland Islands by Argentina signals a new period of South American expansionism.

(c) No war between the great powers can be justified now that any such war entails nuclear annihilation.

(d) Springsteen has the best lyrics and the best sound: he's simply the best rock and roll musician on the scene today.

(e) Although the Women's Movement has made impressive gains in the past two decades, its goals are very far from being realized.

(f) One would have expected that after Watergate, Nixon's political impact would be finished, yet he still commands considerable respect in many quarters, as the turnout to his rare public appearances attests.

(g) Simply because of their immense populations, the Third World countries will be setting the international political agenda for the 1980s and 1990s.

(h) If you can afford a colour television set, you can afford to donate to local and international charities.

3. *Directions:* For each of the following "issues," identify at least *three* positions that could be taken on it: (a) Noise in the library. (b) Landlord-student relations. (c) The merits of your campus newspaper. (d) Athletic scholarships. (e) Equal pay for equal work. (f) Affirmative action.

(g) Nuclear deterrence. (h) Marriage. (i) House-husbands. (j) The job-training role of colleges and universities.

4. *Directions:* For a select number of the positions you identified for 3, above, formulate two arguments in support of each position and two arguments against each position.

5. *Directions:* Select an issue about which you have strong opinions. Identify a position on that issue with which you strongly disagree. Formulate three strong arguments *in support of* that position. (Avoid straw-manning by producing dumb arguments.)

6. *Directions:* Identify an issue that interests you, but on which you cannot decide what position to take. Set out all the reasonable positions, including all the actually-defended positions, that may be taken on this issue. Make sure these positions are actually incompatible. Formulate as many reasonable arguments *against* each of these positions as you can. State as many objections to each of these arguments as you can.

7. *Directions:* Write an essay which follows the dialectical argumentative pattern on some issue that you consider important and that perplexes you.

CHAPTER NINE

ANALYSING EXTENDED ARGUMENTS

The Method Explained

In the previous chapters, we have been featuring what might be called "snippets"; i.e., short arguments or excerpts from longer ones. Our assumption has been that it is easier to learn to detect fallacies in a restricted setting. The time has come to switch the focus and come to grips with reality. For it is one thing to be able to identify fallacious reasoning in snippets, and quite another thing to practice the art of logical criticism on "the real thing" — those longer pieces of reasoning which confront you in your everyday reading. The purposes of this chapter is to present a method for evaluating extended arguments.

By an **extended argument** we mean the entire passage as it occurs in its natural setting, whether in an editorial, opinion piece, letter to the editor, or speech in Parliament or the House of Representatives. Such passages often contain several different but related arguments rolled into one, as the writer or speaker attempts to "make the case" for his position. The evaluation of such passages present special problems for two reasons. First, they are too long to be gone over with a fine-toothed comb. Hence a useful method of analysis must guide you in the task of extracting the essence of the argument. Second, such passages will often contain more than one logical flaw. Hence a useful method of analysis must also guide you in ranking criticisms in their order of importance.

For ease of reference, we shall refer to the entire passage in which the extended argument occurs as the **text.** The method we shall present will show you how to go about extracting the extended argument from the text, thereby compiling a subtext which then becomes the focal point of your evaluation. In the remainder of this section, we introduce our four step method for the analysis of extended arguments. In the following section, we illustrate how it works by applying it to a couple of examples.

Step 1: Write a Synopsis of the Argument

A preliminary step, it goes without saying, is a careful reading of the original text. Failure to grasp the entire sense of the text skews subsequent analysis and results in the creation of straw men. Having read and digested the text, you should begin by constructing a **synopsis,** by which we do not mean a mere summary or restatement of the text. Rather a synopsis is a logical description of the argument in that text which begins with an identification of the main conclusion (whether this was implicit or explicit in the text) and then proceeds to describe the various strategies used to generate that conclusion.

The key to writing a good synopsis is intelligent use of the paragraph structure of the original text. Most writers use the paragraph structure as their unit of development and attempt to present their case point by point. It is useful to assign a letter to each individual paragraph of the text to facilitate reference to it. With respect to each of the individual paragraphs, you should ask yourself: what role or function does this paragraph play in the argument as a whole?

Some of the typical functions are listed below:
— providing background information
— explaining a crucial term in the argument
— making a comment or observation
— stating the conclusion
— stating (and defending) a premise
— defending a premise against general skepticism
— defending a premise against actual or anticipated objections
— defending the conclusion against actual or anticipated counter-argu-
  ments
— summarizing an alternative position (prior to arguing against it)
— tracing the logical consequences

During the construction of the synopsis, you should also be weeding out material which is extraneous to the argument. Such material includes the following:
— background information
— explanations not part of the fabric of the argument
— digressions and asides
— repetition of points already made
— rhetorical devices and flourishes

To illustrate how to write a synopsis, below we print the entire text of an argument you have already seen excerpts from. The paragraphs are lettered. Read the entire text carefully. Then write your own synopsis, and compare it with ours.

162   **a**   Latest crime statistics from Denmark provide a striking illustration of the beneficial effects of that nation's experiment in pornography, and will provide a powerful argument for those favouring the legalization and open availability of pornography here in Canada.

b   According to the figures, sexual offenses against females in Copenhagen, the heart of the "dirty picture" business, dropped 59% from 1965 to 1970. During the same five years, cases of exhibitionism or indecent exposure dropped 58%; peeping, down 85%; child molestation, down 56%; and verbal indecency incidents decreased 83%. There was no noticeable effect on cases of rape and intercourse with minors.

c   According to one expert, the availability of pornographic material provides the psycho-sexual stimulation for those people who would otherwise take illegal means to seek such stimulation.

d   Whatever weight attaches to the moral or good-taste arguments against pornography, it seems doubtful that they will prevail, in the long run, over the increasingly liberal attitudes in modern society, particularly when the liberal position is buttressed by proof that legalized pornography leads to a decline of sexual crime.

e   In Canada, pornography and the issue of legalizing it are probably still too emotion-laden to be subject to dispassionate debate. As a result, the confusing situation with respect to pornography will probably continue, which is unfortunate.

f   It is unfortunate because the necessarily haphazard way of enforcing pornography legislation cannot help but make the law and the process of its enforcement look ridiculous, thus undermining the respect for law on which every civilized nation depends.

This is our synopsis of the argument. The issue dealt with in this editorial is whether or not pornography should be made legal in Canada. The editorialist's position is nowhere explicitly asserted but is evident in **a** and **e**. So we take the conclusion to be: "There are good reasons for legalizing pornography in Canada now." The argument for this conclusion has three phases. In **a–c**, the editorialist provides warrants for the conclusion by claiming (implicitly) that legalizing pornography would reduce sex crimes in Canada. Paragraph **a** is introductory in function, anticipating the causal claim implicit in **b** and supported by the statistics cited there. Paragraph **c** provides a hypothesis to support the correlation in **b**. The second phase of the argument occurs in **d**, where the editorialist is *anticipating counterarguments* to his conclusion; namely, the argument that opposes legalization on moral grounds, and the argument that opposes it on grounds of "good taste." The arguer tries to undercut these arguments by claiming that they cannot withstand the force of growing liberal attitudes. The last phase of the argument takes place in **d** and **e**, where the attempt is made to show what the consequences of not legalizing pornography will be (namely, undermining respect for law).

The value of a good synopsis is that it highlights the main features of the argument and thus sets up the next step.

Step 2:   Identify Main Premises and Conclusion

In order to do this (especially with longer arguments), you may find it helpful to sketch a tree diagram of the **macrostructure** of the argument. By macrostructure, we mean the main branches of the argument together with the conclusion. We distinguish this from **microstructure,** i,e., the logical structure of internal arguments for individual premises.

In describing macrostructure, there are two basic patterns to be aware of. Sometimes two or more branches of the argument *converge,* join together, to support the conclusion. In this pattern, each of the branches has independent stature so that they can be appraised apart from one another. The other typical pattern is that in which two or more branches are *linked;* that is, they are meant to be taken together and so, when evaluating this pattern of argument, such premises must be considered together. To indicate this pattern in the tree diagram, we suggest that a "+" be shown between branches that are linked.

In drawing the tree diagram of macrostructure, use the letters assigned to the paragraphs in the synopsis. Also, as you will see, you should provide a tag or code to identify the idea connected with that particular branch of the argument. For the tree diagram is intended to give you a visual picture of how the various branches are combined. In more complicated cases, with five or six main branches, and others leading into these, your memory will need some reinforcement.

Here then is our diagram of the macrostructure of the argument for the legalization of pornography:

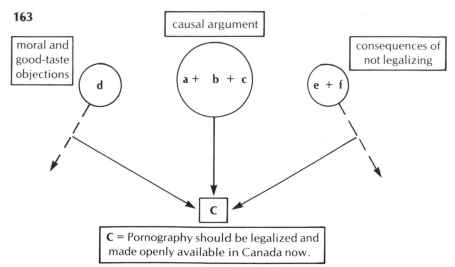

163

To explain briefly our conventions here, note that the arrow runs directly from **a–c** (sex crime decreased) to the main conclusion. With the other two branches, we show an arrow with broken lines leading in a direction away from the conclusion which is then intercepted and routed back toward the main conclusion, to highlight the fact that here the arguer makes use of an indirect strategy. In branch **d**, the arguer is attempting to fend off objections to the conclusion. In **e–f**, the arguer is trying to show that the logical consequences of not legalizing pornography are undesirable, hence reinforcing his position.

Our diagram shows that the argument has three main branches all of which converge upon the conclusion. Hence the structure of the main argument is now clear:

164 P1: Legalizing pornography would decrease sex crimes in Canada. (**a–c**)
P2: The objections to legalizing pornography cannot withstand the force of growing liberal opinion. (**d**)
P3: Failure to legalize pornography has the undesirable consequence of undermining respect for law. (**e–f**)
C: Pornography should be legalized and made openly available in Canada now.

Now that the structure of the main argument is before us, we are ready to begin the process of evaluation. Our procedure will be to look first at the main argument to see whether it is fallacious or not. After that, we must inspect the internal arguments (if any) provided in support of the main argument. But here a question arises: are all of the main premises of equal importance in the argument? Our intuitions and our experience show that the answer is "No." This realization points to the need for one final step, prior to actual evaluation.

Step 3: Put the Main Premises into Hierarchical Order

By **hierarchical order**, we mean a list of the main premises in their order of importance. How will you determine this? In evaluating premises for importance, there are two factors to take into consideration: *emphasis* and *force*. We shall briefly discuss each of these.

Emphasis

How much emphasis has the author placed on this particular branch of argument? The best way to answer this question is to see how much effort and space the arguer devotes to the presentation of the premise. If, for example, in an argument running over some six paragraphs, the arguer spends three paragraphs developing one branch of the argument while spending only one paragraph on, say, the other two, it seems clear that the author places greater emphasis on the first branch. Accordingly, it belongs above the others in the hierarchy. Strong criticism of this branch will have greater impact on the argument than criticism of the others, and this point needs to be remembered when you turn to evaluation.

Force

In making a case, the arguer will often summon all the arguments that she can muster for the position, even though some one or two of them will have perceptibly greater "clout" than others. In constructing the hierarchy, the branches with the greater force belong at the top. For example, one might seek to develop the case for capital punishment by arguing both that it is a deterrent to murder (first branch) and that it is more economical (second branch). Clearly the first branch should be put first in the hierarchy, since by itself it has (if well-argued) considerable thrust, and also because the economic argument is a subsidiary one.

By judicious reflection on the branches of the argument and the factors of emphasis and force, you should be able to rank the main premises in hierarchical order with the most important ones at the top and the less important at the bottom, realizing that, of course, branches may be of equal, or co-ordinate, importance. The purpose of this ordering is clear: when you evaluate the internal arguments, your first move should be to inspect the arguments for the branches at the top of the hierarchy, and work your way down from there.

Our hierarchy for the pornography argument is as follows:

165   P1   (the causal argument)
          P3   (the argument from consequences)
          P2   (the argument against possible objections)

Our hierarchy is not complete without the reasoning in support of our ranking, so the following justification should be added.

P1 (the causal argument) is the most important branch because it receives the greatest emphasis (the editorialist spends three out of the six paragraphs developing it) and because it has the greatest thrust (for if legalizing pornography would decrease sex crimes, then that is a good reason for taking that action, since sex crimes are highly repugnant and any way of reducing them deserves serious consideration). The second place in the hierarchy belongs to P3 (the argument from consequences). Both factors, emphasis and force, suggest this placement. The writer spends approximately two paragraphs in support of this point and it has thrust: the well-being of society requires respect for law, and the author claims that this respect is being threatened by the present laws against pornography. The least important of the three premises is P2 (the argument against possible objections). The editorialist only mentions the objections but does not spell them out in detail nor does he give any systematic attention to them.

With this hierarchy to guide us, we can now approach the task of evaluating the argument in an orderly (rather than haphazard or "hit-and-miss") fashion. First we look at the main argument to see whether or not it is satisfactory. Then we look at the internal arguments in the order in which their premises occur in the hierarchy.

Step 4: Evaluate the Argument

In evaluating arguments, you will be looking for any instances of fallacious reasoning. The aim of the first seven chapters of the text was to prepare you to detect fallacious reasoning, and even more important to equip you to defend your judgements. However, in inspecting extended arguments for fallacious reasoning, there are two ground rules or principles that need to be adhered to in order to keep your criticisms effectively focused and logical. They are (1) The Principle of Discrimination and (2) The Principle of Logical Neutrality. We need to discuss each of them.

The Principle of Discrimination

The basic idea can be put roughly as follows: in criticizing an argument, you should strive to get to the heart of the matter. A critic who gets sidetracked and spends his efforts criticizing peripheral flaws while major ones go unnoticed does not display the quality of discrimination. It would be comparable to a movie critic who spent most of his review berating the performance of a minor actor while failing to note weak performances by the principal performers. In requiring you to get to the heart of the matter, the Principle of Discrimination simultaneously proscribes the two most common faults in criticism of arguments: nit-picking, and latching on to the first complaint that comes into your mind. Neither of these all too common tendencies makes for effective logical criticism.

If there is a fallacy in the main argument, then this criticism will normally take precedence over others. It should come first in your write-up. But most often the problems will occur in the interior parts of the argument, and here the hierarchy constructed at Step 3 comes to the fore. Look first at the internal argument which supports the premise highest in the hierarchy. Any fallacies that occur in that argument have the potential for forming a major critique of the whole argument.

A major criticism of an argument has the following properties. First, the criticism focuses on a premise (or argument for the premise) which is high up in the hierarchy and therefore crucial for the success of the argument. Second, the fallacy that (one will argue) occurs in that premise (or argument for it) is a serious logical error.

A fact which we hope is evident but which we have not dwelt upon at length is that not all warranted charges of fallacy are equally devastating to an argument. It is difficult to make this point in the abstract, but if you wish to refresh your memory, reread our discussion in Chapter 2 of the point that not all fallacy charges are equally serious. With this point in mind, and realizing that consideration of hypotheticals leaves much to be desired, we nevertheless present the following two attempts to illustrate what we are driving at. Suppose that the hierarchy of the argument we are dealing with is as follows:

166   P4
       P2
       P3
       P1

Case A: Suppose now that we can justify a charge of *questionable cause* against the argument for P4, and also a case of *improper appeal to authority* (type 5) against the argument for P3. Which of these criticisms does the Principle of Discrimination tell us to give emphasis to in our write-up? Clearly, to the first, since the premise involved is more important and the fallacy involved (*questionable cause*) is more serious. A critic who featured the charge of *improper appeal* would evidence lack of discrimination. *Case B:* Suppose the same ranking of premises, and suppose now that we can justify a charge of *straw man* against the argument for P3 and also a charge of *hasty conclusion* against the argument for P2. P2 is more important than P3, but the charge against it somewhat less serious. Which criticism leads? Our answer is that these seem to be of roughly equal importance, though individual circumstances might result in one or the other being the best choice.

The Principle of Discrimination is basic for the practice of cogent logical criticism. Our treatment has been brief. But then the principle does not allow of algorithmic application, and nothing can substitute for sound judgement developed out of much practice.

The Principle of Logical Neutrality

The basic idea behind this principle is this: don't attempt to disguise substantive criticism as logical criticism. Our formulation of this principle implies that there is a precise boundary between substantive criticisms and logical ones. Alas, the boundary is not easily drawn. But there are cases where the difference is clear. For instance, to reject an argument because one of the premises is problematic is to make a *logical* criticism of that argument; to reject the argument because one of the premises is false is to make a *substantive* criticism. Both are perfectly proper criticisms to make. The point we wish to make is that they are different *types* of criticism.

Let's work with the example alluded to above. The claim that a given premise is problematic is a claim about the logical *status* of that statement in a specified *context* (i.e., within the argument into which it has been incorporated). To call that premise *problematic,* then, is to point out that in this context it fails to function adequately as a premise because it ought to have been defended but wasn't. That very same statement could occur in some other argument without being problematic, however. In saying, on the other hand, that a premise is *false,* we are making a statement about its relationship to the world which is independent of its occurrence in this or that argument. If the premise is false, it will presumably be false in any argument.

To take an example from current debate: perhaps one might attack the position of those who favour abortion on demand by claiming, "Those who support abortion on demand are guilty of bad argumentation, because they assume that the fetus is not a person, but that is false." Such criticism is substantive criticism. On the other hand, to claim "Those who support abortion on demand are guilty of bad argumentation, because they assume that

FIGURE: FLOW-CHART OF METHOD FOR ANALYSING ARGUMENTS

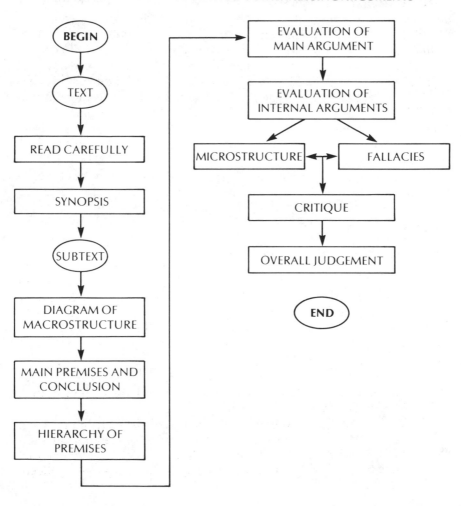

the fetus is not a person, but that is a *dubious assumption,*" is to begin a logical criticism.

The point of the Principle of Logical Neutrality is to require that one be clear on the nature of the criticism one offers and that one not be allowed to pass off substantive criticism under the guise of logical criticism.

After you have checked the main argument and the internal arguments and located any instances of fallacious reasoning, the task that remains is that of writing up your criticisms showing proper discrimination. The evaluation should conclude with an *overall judgement* of the argument which adequately reflects both its strengths and weaknesses.

We have appended a flow-chart which highlights the phases of analysis as we have discussed them in this part of the chapter.

The Method Applied

In this section, we shall apply the four-step method to two extended arguments, one of them opposed to capital punishment in Canada, the other in favour.

You have already seen an excerpt from the first argument in the first section of Chapter 3. The entire argument is a long one, but not atypical of the sort of passage one regularly sees and with which one needs to be able to reckon.

Here is the original text, the paragraphs having been lettered to facilitate later reference.

167   a Sir: The federal report by University of Montreal criminologist Dr. Ezzat Abdel Fattah (*Star,* Dec. 16) appears to represent an excellent public service. The statistics gathered seem to suggest that the death penalty fails to deter murder.

b Such findings are consistent with those in other countries, such as the United States. Statistics compiled in that country have provided less than no support for the capital-punishment advocates. If anything, data there suggest that capital punishment increases the murder rate (even discounting those murders the state committed allegedly to deter murder). For instance, the more southern states of the U.S.A. where capital punishment was still enforced were found cursed with the highest murder rates.

c Such statistics as indicated above do not conclusively prove anything, based as they are on mere correlational (rather than experimentally-controlled) data.

d Nevertheless, experimentally-controlled data in this area are non-existent; so we are stuck with these mere correlations. But such facts do definitely seem to throw cold water on any argument that legal murder (i.e., capital punishment) acts as a deterrent to illegal murder.

e Yet the above is not the only kind of evidence that capital punishment fails to prevent illegal murder. For instance, some countries have publicly executed pickpockets.·And while some pickpockets were being hung, others circulated among the observers, picking pockets.

f Criminologists inform us that most murders are hot blooded, and between relatives, acquaintances and close friends. It is psychologically obvious that hot-blooded murders are impulsive, rashly performed by a person so overwhelmed by emotion that he has lost control (rather than by a cold-blooded calculator of the advantages and penalties involved).

g As famous Attorney Belli observed in one of his newspaper columns, of all the killers he has spoken with, none ever told him that just prior to committing the homicide he had stopped at the library to check on the penalty.

h Imagine yourself a prisoner in the federal penitentiary in Arkansas of which criminologist Murton was warden. If you were a random prisoner there, then since only about a dozen of the several thousand convicts were on death row, chances would be a small fraction of one per cent that you would have been sentenced for execution.

i In that circumstance how would you feel toward the men who, unlike yourself, were on death row? Chances are you would feel a profound sympathy for your fellow convicts and a profound hatred for a society that could do such a thing. At least that is what Warden Murton found.

j And the reason is an axiom among social scientists: "The greater the love of the in-group, the greater the hatred of the out-group."

k When you herd men into prisons, you tend to solidify them against a common enemy — the guards and others not in prison. If in addition you place a portion on death row, you so embitter against society that vast majority eventually to be released that you increase the probability that when they get out they will commit hostile acts (including murder).

l Sometimes after an execution the victim is found innocent after all. Until science has found a way of restoring such dead to life, it is difficult to see how anyone with a concept of justice should wish legal executions of such innocent men on his conscience.

m Who gets executed for murder is in fact probably much more closely associated with racial, sexual and economic prejudice than with who actually commits murder.

n In the United States the number of poor Negro men who have been executed for murder is legion; the number of rich, white, women victims of capital punishment can be counted on the fingers of one hand. (And it would be erroneous to conclude that the latter group did not commit a large share.)

o The vast majority of Canadian policemen appear to favour capital punishment, especially when one of their colleagues is murdered in the line of duty. These policemen are entitled to their opinion.

p However, the public should not take their views on this subject seriously and the mass communication media (with special reference to *The Windsor Star*) should not continue to give so much space to their views.

q The reason is that it is difficult to conceive of a group more incompetent on the subject of capital punishment than police organizations. Two basic reasons for their incompetence in this area exist: 1) Policemen are too emotionally involved in the issue to think about it with the detachment needed for sound judgement. 2) The interpretation of the statistical and other evidence as to whether capital punishment acts as a deterrent is far beyond the modest intellectual achievements of the typical policemen and their organizations.

r Obviously, however, there are also other reasons many people favor capital punishment besides suffering under the apparent delusion that it acts as a deterrent.

s Some people, perhaps convinced their own lives are failures, have become bloodthirsty and they have a sadistic need for capital punishment. Having grown up in a so-called Christian culture, they may rationalize this need — convincing themselves that capital punishment acts as a deterrent.

t Such individuals, regardless how overwhelming the evidence becomes against capital punishment as a deterrent, will remain unconvinced.

Step 1:   The Synopsis

We begin by identifying the conclusion, which is not difficult in this instance. Though much of the argument is given over to LaFave's attempt to argue that capital punishment is not a deterrent, the reasoning in **r–s** makes sense only if we suppose LaFave to be against capital punishment, period. As the overall conclusion, then, we identify the following: *capital punishment should not be allowed in Canada*. (We have relativized the argument to the Canadian scene, since LaFave was writing in Canada to a Canadian audience. Given the fact that he takes evidence from the United States, it is possible that he really intends his conclusion to cover the U.S. as well.)

The bulk of this passage, **a–k**, deals with the question of deterrence. Here LaFave develops two lines of argument. In **a–d** he argues against the idea that capital punishment is a deterrent, using statistical grounds. In **e–k** he offers us what is in effect a psychological argument for the same point. In **l–n** the author attempts to show that a system of capital punishment will have undesirable consequences: in **l** he argues that innocent persons may be put to death; in **m–n** he argues that capital punishment is inequitably applied in practice. In **o–q** (the part we have seen before), LaFave attempts to defend his position by anticipating the objection that the police favour capital punishment. He tries to show that this is not a strong objection. In **r–t** LaFave seems to be trying to take the ground out from beneath alternative arguments which would favour capital punishment.

Step 2: Identification of the Main Premises

Our tree diagram of the macrostructure of this argument may be seen in the accompanying diagram.

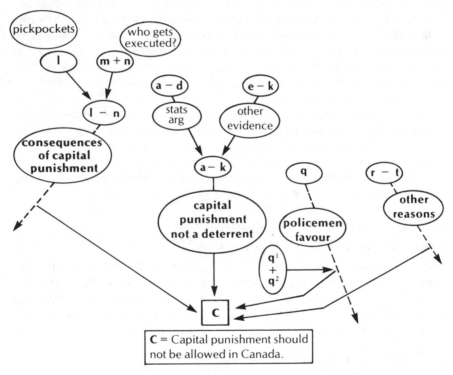

From this diagram, we can easily read off the main premises:

169 P1: Capital punishment is not a deterrent to murder. (**a–k**)
P2: A system of capital punishment has undesirable consequences. (**l–n**)
P3: The fact that policemen are in favour of capital punishment is not a good reason for having capital punishment. (**o–q**)
P4: Other reasons given for capital punishment are not good ones. (**r–t**)

Notice that we have indicated where in the original text of the argument we have drawn the main premises from.

Step 3: Hierarchy of Premises

Clearly P1 belongs at the top of the hierarchy. LaFave devotes well over half of his argument to attempting to establish this premise, so it is given a strong emphasis. Moreover, the issue of deterrence tends to dominate the debate, so that if LaFave makes a strong case for his claim that capital punishment is not a deterrent, then his argument will have clout.

If we look to the criterion of force rather than emphasis, we will place P4 next in the hierarchy. For in this part of the argument, LaFave proposes to show that other reasons given for capital punishment also fail. Taken in concert with P1, P4 will combine to make a strong case. The next slot in the hierarchy belongs, we think, to P2. If there are good reasons for a particular policy, then its having undesirable consequences may just be an effect we will have to live with. If, as LaFave has alleged, there aren't good reasons, then the presence of undesirable consequences is a good, if subsidiary, reason for not adopting the particular policy. The last slot in the hierarchy goes here to P3. True, LaFave does give this branch of argument more than the cursory treatment given to P4. However, the force of this premise is debatable. Even if it is true, as LaFave alleges, that we should not take the views of policemen with any great degree of seriousness, still accepting this doesn't advance us markedly toward the conclusion. As we see it, then, the hierarchy of premises is: P1/P4/P2/P3. We shall inspect the internal arguments in this order.

Step 4: Evaluation of the argument

Evaluation of the Main Argument

The main premises all pass the relevance test, so that the only question which remains (since all of them are defended) is whether they are sufficient or not. And we have already answered that question in constructing the hierarchy of the premises: if P1, P4, P2, and P3 prove acceptable, then LaFave will have given a strong argument for his position.

Evaluation of the Internal Arguments

We shall begin by inspecting the argument given for the first premise in the hierarchy, P1. Here there are two supporting arguments. The first one, **a–d**, is based on statistical grounds. We think that this argument is well turned out, properly qualified (LaFave grants that statistical arguments aren't conclusive in **c** but points out in **d** that we cannot have experimentally controlled data).

The second argument, **e–k**, is not as easy to characterize but is broadly speaking an empirical one with three branches: in **e** LaFave claims that in cases where capital punishment was used against pickpockets, it failed as a deterrent (implying that, *a fortiori,* it will fail to deter murderers); in **f–g** he argues that capital punishment doesn't deter the most common form of murder — hot-blooded murders; and in **h–k** LaFave tries to turn the argument around, arguing that capital punishment in fact acts as an incentive to murder.

The argument in **e** is undocumented and undeveloped, so we will be charitable and treat it as a bit of flavouring and spice rather than a serious attempt to argue.

The argument in **f–g** is another matter. Here LaFave seems to be presenting a serious argument based on psychological reasoning. Let us then examine the reasoning closely. The basic assertions here are these:

170   (1) Most murders are commited in hot blood (so we are informed by criminologists); (**f**)
   (2) Murders committed in hot blood are rash, impulsive, uncontrolled; (**f**)
   (3) Such murders are not committed by individuals who stop to weigh the advantages and penalties. (**f–g**)

The implicit conclusion to this line of reasoning must be that capital punishment would not be a deterrent in most cases. However, to reach this conclusion, LaFave must be making an assumption: capital punishment can serve as a deterrent only if people consider the consequences of their actions prior to acting. Here we think LaFave has made a *dubious assumption.* One could argue that the threat of death serves to influence behaviour by encouraging people to develop habits of action which comply with the law. The development of such habits would override momentary irrational impulses so that people would not have to stop and think. Since such a teleology strikes us as plausible and is not ruled out, and since the assumption mentioned above is necessary for LaFave's conclusion to follow, we would offer the charge of *dubious assumption* as a fairly major criticism of the argument.

Next in line is the argument in **h–j**. Here LaFave argues that if we have a system of capital punishment, then we may expect that prisoners who are released from prisons in which there are murderers on death row will be motivated to commit hostile acts (including murder) when they are released. The problem with this argument is that it turns on an empirical point: whether released prisoners (from certain institutions) do exhibit the tendency to commit hostile acts, including murder. The only compelling way to shore up this point is by providing the evidence, and since LaFave is clearly familiar with the body of evidence (**a–b** makes this clear), he should have called attention to it here. As it stands, this argument is based on inadequate evidence and hence is guilty of *hasty conclusion.*

The next branch of argument to be considered is P4. Here LaFave purports to argue that other reasons (beside the deterrence argument) for favouring capital punishment are not good ones. The argument suffers from two flaws: *ambiguity* and *ad hominem.* We can draw a bead on the breakdown here if we note, first, that LaFave does not follow through on his advertisement. That is, what we expect him to do is confront the other arguments cited in support of capital punishment, such as the argument from retributive justice. Instead, LaFave "psychoanalyses" those who oppose his view. Instead, that is, of showing that and where their arguments break down, he diagnoses them as "bloodthirsty" and "sadistic." But surely there are arguments that can be appraised without reference to the psychological states and conditions of those who venture them. Thus, LaFave commits *ad hominem* by attacking persons rather than arguments. This leads to the second point. LaFave has shifted the meaning of "reason" here. In **r**, we suppose him to mean "reason" in the sense of "logical reasons" for favouring capital punishment. Instead, in **s** and **t**, he goes on to speculate about "psychological reasons" why someone might favour capital punishment. The argument exploits this ambiguity, commits *ad hominem* in so doing, and thus fails to convince.

The next branch to be considered is P2. Two criticisms emerge when we consider that argument. First, we note that LaFave's premises refer us to raw numbers, whereas the implicit conclusion must be taken as referring to ratios or percentages. It may be true that the number of poor black men executed vastly exceeds the number of rich white women. But that may be explained simply by the fact that the number of poor black men who commit murder (and thereby become "eligible" for capital punishment) vastly exceeds the number of rich white women who commit murder. Absolute numbers are insufficient; we need percentages to support the claim of inequity. Hence LaFave's argument is guilty of *hasty conclusion*. (If, as seems likely, the additional evidence is readily provided, this charge of fallacy is not terribly damaging and would not have a prominent place in our write-up.) Second, LaFave's data are taken from the United States, whereas his conclusion (if it is to yield evidence for the main conclusion) must be taken to apply to Canada. The assumption necessary here — that if capital punishment were unfairly applied in the United States, it would also be unfairly applied in Canada — strikes us as dubious. Though it would be naive to think that racism does not exist in Canada, it has never been shown to exist on the scale or in the intensity found in the United States.

Finally, we come to the argument for P3. On the surface, it looks as though LaFave commits *ad hominem* here by attacking policemen rather than their position. However, in this dialectical context, the issue is credibility — and that is what LaFave seems to question. He cites two grounds: first, policemen are too emotionally involved. Second, policemen lack the competence to interpret the statistical evidence. But as to the first, it remains to be shown that police are so deeply involved that their capacities to think have been impaired. As to the second, a great many policemen belong to unions or associations which may well have in their employ persons capable of handling statistical evidence. LaFave has given us two instances of *problematic premise* here.

We have completed our inspection of the entire argument and must now put our criticisms into an order reflecting our judgement of their relative importance, concluding with our overall judgement on the argument.

171   Though not without its strong points, particularly the argument in **a-d**, LaFave has not presented a strong argument for his position. The main argument is solid, but there are logical defects in each of the four branches of argument supporting the four premises. In particular, the argument for P1 (the claim that capital punishment is not a deterrent) suffers from both *dubious assumption* and *hasty conclusion*. These charges strike at the core of his argument and represent the strongest criticisms of his position. The next strongest criticism is the charge of *ad hominem* and *ambiguity* in connection with P4 — LaFave's attempt to dismantle other arguments for capital punishment. If his argument is going to be successful, he must address himself to substantive versions of these ancillary types of argument for capital punishment. The argument for P2 has two flaws, one of which may be easily repaired but the other (the assumption about the comparability of the U.S. and Canada) is not as readily remedied. The criticisms of his argument for P3 (against the policemen) are the least damaging, but this particular argument appears to be the least effective of the lot. All in all, then, LaFave's argument needs fairly extensive repair before it could be considered compelling.

Having just subjected one possible case against capital punishment to criticism, and with the spirit of logical neutrality and balance to uphold, we now examine an argument for capital punishment.

172   **a** The debate on capital punishment shares with discussions of other life and death decisions (those involved in abortion, for example, and those involved in euthanasia) the emotional tensions that surround extreme and irreversible acts. To carry out the death penalty, to undergo an abortion, and to instruct the doctor to unplug the life-support system are all acts which do not permit any further relationships with the victim. Capital punishment differs from abortion and euthanasia, however, in standing as a punishment. Neither the unborn fetus nor the terminally ill patient are, normally, seen as having somehow committed a crime. Indeed, opponents of abortion and opponents of euthanasia commonly argue that these procedures are unjustifiable, because their victims are innocent. They have not, in any sense, deserved punishment. People who argue in favour of abortion and/or euthanasia are sometimes invited to put themselves in the position of the victims.

b Opponents of capital punishment also invite those who argue in favour of it to put themselves in the position of the condemned man (it is usual to leave women out of consideration, and in fact far fewer women than men have been executed in the U.S.). This tactic, however, steers us past the point. For what is at issue is the guilt of the condemned man, and the emotional repugnance we might feel at being asked to sit on death row ignores the fact that we are not guilty.

c Similarly off-base is the widespread argument that capital punishment imposes a terrible risk upon innocent persons. It has been argued that the possibility that one innocent person might be falsely condemned is enough to make capital punishment illegitimate. For how can society compensate the victim for its error?

d But the issue is not whether capital punishment may or may not be imposed without error. It is, rather, whether any person justly convicted of a capital crime should or should not be executed.

e Since the death penalty cannot be regarded as a form of chastisement or rehabilitation, the heart of the debate may be located in the issue of its value as a deterrent. I shall set aside as irrelevant the question of retribution, since torture would seem to be superior to execution as a means of paying back the offended. Torture, it might be noted, is the obvious target of the Constitution's objections to "cruel and unusual punishment."

f As for the deterrent value of the death penalty, one must have recourse to statistical data. The issue is not whether some people may be deterred from capital crimes through the threat of execution, for everybody knows that some people are not deterred. The issue is whether *you* and *I* are deterred.

g Here a comparison is needed. We need to consider the number of capital crimes, such as murder, that are committed annually, on a per capita basis, in a country that is in many respects similar to the United States but has a different approach to the issue of capital punishment. Here a good choice is England.

h The population of England is about 42,000,000, or roughly one-fifth that of the U.S. During the decade from 1968-77, England averaged about 36 murders per year while the U.S. figure was about 5,000. In other words, the rate of murder in England during this decade was less than one twenty-fifth that of the U.S.

i Both countries had, during this period, a system of law including capital punishment for murder. But in the U.S. no condemned person was in fact executed over the ten-year span being considered — except Gary Gilmore, who refused to appeal his conviction and in fact demanded that he be executed according to law. In England, by contrast, convicted murderers move speedily towards execution.

j One might consider here the contrast between English and American laws on guns. The advocates of strict gun-control in the U.S. are fond of connecting the relatively low rate of murder in England with England's very strict enforcement of laws respecting the registration and bearing of firearms. They argue that this enforcement protects the public.

k But if this argument holds water, then surely it must follow that strict enforcement of laws respecting capital crimes should also yield results. One recalls how quickly hijackings ceased when sky marshals were known to be ready to shoot skyjackers.

l What we have now is a system that makes no sense. Knowing that they will, in practice, be condemned to life imprisonment, criminals convicted of capital crimes are ready to kill in order to stay out of prison. Those who are finally caught are forced to suffer the torture of hopeless incarceration. And meanwhile, the public receives no protection.

m This is, indeed, "cruel and unusual punishment."

Step 1: Synopsis

Although the author nowhere explicitly states the conclusion, we infer from **e**, **k** and **l** that she favours capital punishment. Paragraph **a** serves to provide lift-off for the argument, the writer comparing capital punishment with other life and death issues (euthanasia and abortion) and then distinguishing it from them. This paragraph is largely extraneous to the author's argument. In **b** the writer identifies a possible objection to her conclusion (put yourself in the position of the condemned) and then tries to defuse the objection (we are not guilty of murder). In **c** the writer anticipates another possible mode of objection to her conclusion (there is a risk that an innocent person will be executed). This objection is countered in **d**: the author claims that this objection is beside the point. In **e** the writer sets forth the claim which is fundamental for her strategy: that the crucial issue in the debate is deterrence. In **f–i** the writer presents facts which, she believes, show that capital punishment is a deterrent. In **j–k** an analogical claim is used to show that capital punishment is a deterrent. In **l–m** the writer tries to show that the absence of capital punishment has unacceptable consequences (the public is not protected and individuals are subjected to cruel and unusual punishment), thereby arguing indirectly for a change in the present situation.

Step 2: Identification of Main Premises

Our synopsis reveals four main branches of argument, as depicted in the diagram of macrostructure below.

173

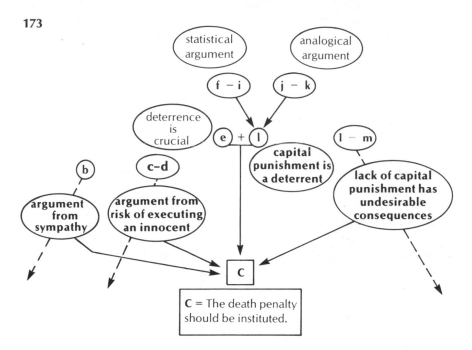

From this diagram we can read off the main premises:

174

P1: The argument against capital punishment based on sympathy for the criminal is ineffective. (**b**)

P2: The argument against capital punishment based on the claim that an innocent person might be executed is irrelevant. (**c–d**)

P3: The crucial issue is whether or not capital punishment is a deterrent. (**e**)

P4: Capital punishment is a deterrent. (**f–i + j–k**)

P5: The lack of capital punishment creates risks for citizens and causes cruel and unusual punishment. (**l–m**)

Step 3: Hierarchy of Premises

It is evident that, for the author's purposes, P3 is the most important premise. Were it rejected, the argument goes down the tubes. Second place in the hierarchy goes to P4, which itself is supported by two different arguments: the statistical argument and the analogical one. The author's emphasis on this line of argument is clear from the amount of space given to it. The next most important branch is that developed in P5, for if the lack of capital punishment did have these consequences, then (since they are clearly unacceptable) that would lend added strength to the call for restoring capital punishment. Finally, and of co-ordinate (though little) importance are P1 and P2. The author's treatment of these is sparse, and even if those arguments against capital punishment fail, the conclusion doesn't follow as there may be other (and stronger) arguments against it. Hence our hierarchy is: P3/P4/P5/P1 & P2.

Step 4: Evaluation of the Argument

Evaluation of the Main Argument

The premises are all relevant to the conclusion and taken together they would, if acceptable, provide enough evidence for the conclusion. Hence we turn attention to the internal arguments for these premises, beginning at the top.

Evaluation of Internal Arguments

The argument for P3 is not developed in great detail, as the author has chosen to deal almost peremptorily with the other reason often brought forth to justify capital punishment: retributive justice (clearly the author is correct to set aside rehabilitation). The author's argument is an odd one, and we would ponder it at length if it were necessary. But since so much of the recent debate has centred on the issue of deterrence, it seems a better use of time and energy to look carefully at the argument for P4, to which we turn next.

For P4 the author presents two arguments. The first is drawn from statistical data and involves a comparison of respective murder rates during the period 1968-77 between the United States (where there was no capital punishment) and England (where it is alleged that "convicted murderers move speedily towards execution"). Alas, our author has her facts quite wrong, for no one has been executed in England since 1965, when capital punishment was made illegal by an Act of Parliament. This is a substantive rather than a logical criticism of the argument. However, it puts the argument in serious straits, for it is not one that the author can readily repair. The comparison with England will have to be dropped. And if the writer wishes to offer a cogent statistical argument, she will have to offer a much more complete (not to say accurate) set of statistics compiled from both countries that do, and countries that do not, have capital punishment on the books.

There are several other infelicities in the argument, but it would be carrying coals to Newcastle to carry on at this point, since a grievous blow has been dealt by the facts. Had the first criticism not been so lethal, we should have gone on inspecting the rest of the argument, since it is always possible that the criticisms can be rebutted and that our sense of discrimination has failed us — the result being that a more important criticism is placed further down the ladder than it should be. And, we should mention, the whole purpose of criticism is not to shred the argument, but to offer enlightened criticism and thereby enrich the dialectical process of the exchange. But in this case, we have entered a substantive criticism of first magnitude which just about guts the argument. Though this will happen from time to time, our general advice is that one should carry out the process of evaluation to its conclusion.

EXERCISES

Directions

Use the four-step method to evaluate the following extended arguments. The first two are shorter and more straightforward than the last two. You will see that number 3 contains two extended arguments taking opposite positions on the issue of censorship. You will need to decide which of the two makes the stronger case. For number 4 you have already seen the argument to which it is responding: the LaFave letter on capital punishment found on pages 217-219.

1. *Background:* This is a letter to the Regina *Leader Post,* October 1974:

    Why pick on dogs? What about other nuisances on city property? The suggestion made by the parks boards that owners who allow their dogs to relieve themselves in the park pay a fine is ridiculous.

    Have they forgotten that the dog is an animal and as such cannot ask its master to "go to the washroom"? What is the owner to do? The owner pays a license fee for the privilege of keeping a dog. He also observes the law that forbids him to let his dog run loose.

    In taking his dog for a walk on a leash, he is within the law. The fact that the dog might have to perform a natural function is automatically included under the law, because of the dog's status as an animal.

2. *Background:* A letter to *The Vancouver Sun* about pesticides, October 1974:

    It seems to me that people are going too far when they claim that it is not safe to eat apples and pears because pesticide sprays have been used.

    What they do not seem to know is that sprays against fruit pests, the codling moth and pear psylla, for instance, have been used in the Okanagan for 50 years at least. If sprays are dangerous, this surely would have shown up by now in Okanagan medical records. I was born in the Okanagan and lived there for 30 years but I, my daughter and granddaughter seem quite healthy and I see no evidence of genetic damage.

If sprays had not been used during all those years the insects would have taken over and there would now be no apples and pears, or else wormy ones. The entomologists are trying to find alternate ways of controlling insect pests but entomologists are hard to come by.

I should like to suggest that an orchardist using spray is no more dangerous to the human race than the automobile which is not only air polluting but uses a vital resource which is fast disappearing.

3. *Background:* The following pair of articles on the topic of censorship appeared on the Op-ed page of *The Windsor Star* on February 23, 1982. (1) Do an analysis of each argument, focusing on the strongest possible criticism of each and providing an overall evaluation. (2) All things taken into consideration, which of the two makes the better logical case for his position? Defend your claim.

Censorship: On one side support . . . (John Coleman)

Censorship is a delicate, emotional issue. It promotes constant debate which leads to no clear cut answers.

As chairman of the Ontario Censors (*sic*) Board, Mary Brown has been embroiled in some nasty fooforahs over what will appear in public film theatres in this province.

She's often branded a Neanderthal by the art community, civil libertarians and film buffs. They criticize her powers as a movie "mind policeman."

I met Mary Brown this week and she is not an ogre. She is rational, reasonable and carrying out a difficult job with a new approach most movie-goers are still unaware of.

"The role of the board has been distorted — the timing may be right to take another look at it since we are not in the middle of an emotional issue," says the tall, blonde, middle-aged mother of six.

The board, in general terms, has a mandate to ban or suggest cuts where scenes seriously contravene community standards. Sexual violence and child exploitation are the two prime targets.

Last year, of 1,795 films screened, only sixty-four were cut and only five banned.

I don't agree with everything Brown does, but I came away from the board's small, brick building in Leaside believing it serves a necessary function.

Along with five other reporters, I saw what only a handful of cabinet ministers and policy-makers get to see — fourteen minutes of scraps from the cutting room floor of the censors (*sic*) board.

Brown admitted she was reluctant to screen it, not only for impact, but because of the age-old arguments of taking clips out of context. The screening was not a media setup perpetrated by Brown. It came from a long-standing invitation by former Consumer and Commercial Relations Minister Gordon Walker.

The question I've been asked over and over again is simple enough: What did you see? The general feeling is that most of the board's work is removing titilating (*sic*) sex. Wrong.

About three of the fourteen minutes were scenes of sexual penetration or oral sex. All outlawed on the screen by the Criminal Code of Canada. Don't blame Mary Brown for chopping this stuff.

Another few minutes involved excessive, prolonged violence like the bludgeoning and kicking of a chained man spitting blood between crying and moaning. A Nazi soldier's throat was slowly carved open and the camera centred on gurgling blood. There was a side shot of an ancient Roman urinating.

That aside, what I found disturbing and even distressing was the depiction of sexual violence. Nearly all of it exploiting women.

A bloodied woman was scalded in boiling water. Two women were whipped into bleeding masses and left on meat hooks.

There were scenes of women, bloodied and chained being raped. In another clip a woman's fingers were chopped with a knife, limbs severed with a chainsaw. Intestines were dragged out of her twitching body by a gloating male.

Not prudish or squeamish, I find this type of depiction and degradation unnecessary in films made for no other purpose than entertainment and profit.

If there is anything redeeming in this type of stuff, it's hard to find.

All these films, censored, were shown in Ontario.

I find it difficult to rationally argue for censorship, yet my instincts tell me it is necessary.

As an art form, film is not necessarily a thinking man's or woman's game. It's pretty base stuff — most arts appeal to developed instincts and taste. Films are different.

The Production Code of the Motion Picture Association of America put it this way: "This art (film) appeals at once to mature, immature, developed, undeveloped . . ."

Mary Brown talks about "the fallout of 42nd Street," and the low life that abounds there, spurred by film pornography, drugs and prostitution.

"I can't say movies affect behavior — that is paternalistic," said Brown. "Does the community as a whole have the right to tell the fifteen per cent of regular theatre goers what it has a right to see? It does.

"Pornography on Yonge Street has an impact on me whether I go to the movies or not."

Some argue that in a free society we should have the right to choose what we see. But give film distributors a free rein and where do the limits of responsibility stop? I'm not sure. Nor am I naive enough to risk it.

Censorship critics point to Manitoba where films are only classified. What they don't point out is that most theatre owners only handle films checked through the Ontario Censors Board. Also, many other provinces screen movies which have passed through the Ontario Censors Board.

You can either conclude that Ontario is an arbiter of taste for Canada, or other provinces trust its judgment.

Some of the censors board's fiercest protests have come over films like the prize-winning film The Tin Drum and respected filmmaker Louis Malle's Pretty Baby — both concerned with a combination of children and sex. Here the lines of acceptability begin to blur and public debate is warranted.

Under Brown's chairmanship the board has become more public. It is more accountable, has a rotating part-time board and beginning this month only bans films as opposed to its previous cutting and snipping procedures.

The board is listening and it should continue to listen to the public.

The days of 1934 when the Ontario censors cut "my wife is going to have a baby," from a film are long gone.

I'm not comfortable supporting the concept of the Ontario Censors Board, nor at this point am I comfortable without it.

. . . *and on the other side contempt.* (John Laycock)

Ontario's movie censors, I see, have dusted off their old propaganda trick of spoiling newspapermen's lunches.

Every few years or so the censors splice together a reel of horrible snippets from the movies they have cut. Ready to upchuck at the grotesque spectacles they have viewed, the commentators are then softened to the censors' arguments defending their jobs.

The *Star's* John Coleman acknowledges that this procedure forces out-of-context judgments: Even the Bible can be chopped down to repulsive sex and violence, so this familiar line of thinking maintains. He credits chief censor Mary Brown with recognizing the objection too.

Yet she shows her horror-of-horrors anyhow. And he believes it anyhow.

Yes, the out-of-context objection is an old argument. It is also a valid argument. That's why censors have to fight back with emotional shock tactics (and no matter who, technically, issues the invitation to these screenings, it is the censor who is responsible for the show).

Regular movie-goers don't need a special screening of super-illicit cuts to know how vile movies can be; what reaches our theatres can be plenty rough enough. Sometimes I turn away from the screen in disgust. I *am* squeamish.

Yet opposing censorship is not the same as defending slime on the screen. I constantly attack movies demeaning humanity (of either gender; sexual violence demeans men too). But censors don't want me — or you — making up our minds like that. They want to do it for us.

Mary Brown, and apparently John Coleman, support a system that takes the freedom of choice away from the public. Censors replace individual opinion with their own judgment — like movie critics, except there is no alternative.

I'm quite happy to have you go to the show and enjoy something I loathed. No censor can join me in saying, "Make up your own mind." Instead, in Ontario, the movie censor says, "I will make up your mind for you."

Windsor residents sneak off to Detroit and find out what they are missing. Are we more corrupt than Toronto? Are the other Canadian provinces? Mary Brown may convince her guests that the other censors trust her board to save their souls; those censors' public statements of bewilderment at Ontario decisions seem to have not penetrated her blue curtain.

Mary Brown presents herself as spokesman for the "majority" of the community. She is, of course, not elected to that post by the community. She is responsible only to the provincial government, like plenty of other appointed officials — but none of them with the power to regulate thought and information, as opposed to highway safety or drinking hours. The movie censor is unique in meddling with morals without direct public approval.

The censor is also redundant. No legislated censor boards exist anywhere in the United States today, according to Variety, the showbiz newspaper. Obscenity north of the border can be dealt with by the Criminal Code. The courts are a system the community can scrutinize, according to public laws and precedents, with means to measure community standards and opportunities for appeal. The legal system's handling of obscenity is not exactly perfect — it's more a quagmire, actually. But it is a fairer and more democratic process than the arbitrary and secret procedures of Ontario's film censors, setting their own rules with no requirement to listen to anyone. And when Mary Brown falls back on arguments that she is cutting footage that is legally obscene, she is taking the law into her own hands with no appeal and therefore no authority.

The court of public opinion is a better forum than a hidden chamber where censors arrogantly assume they can accurately measure and satisfy the full range and colorful variety of opinion in this province. Critics, beset by their readers' disagreements, know better. Brown's social-science attempts to make the board more "representative" of the province would flunk first-year sociology.

Public debate, pressure on the boxoffice, complaints to theatre and movie owners, letter-writing, positive action — that's the way democratic societies work. Ontario does work that way too, except at the movies. "Art" has nothing to do with it.

Books are regulated only by the law and the marketplace. The same is true of plays and paintings, of records and radio and signs painted on your forehead. Film exhibitors are no more, or less, the corruptors of society than the rest of these communicators. Mary Brown can't touch any of the rest. Neither can anyone else without due process of law — even though all these media do cause offence to parts of the community. The censor can't regulate films on television, not even ones that have been banned from theatres — Pretty Baby and Beau-Pere could undoubtedly be broadcast uncut without fear of prosecution, maybe even Tin Drum before she chopped it. Station switchboards might light up with complaint; that's what free expression of opinion is all about. The "majority" Brown so likes to talk about regulating what "fifteen per cent" see in picture houses simply have not found prior censorship necessary in any other means of communication. Her authority lingers only out of habit and scare tactics.

John Coleman did not like what he saw at Mary Brown's horror show — who can blame him? — and he wants to avoid the discomfort again. But freedom doesn't work that way. Taking responsibility for yourself can be uncomfortable, distasteful, even dangerous. It certainly can be inefficient. Democracy often is. But freedom of choice requires taking risks, not running away from them. Censorship is the easy way out, particularly when it resorts to a horror show that makes reporters gag when they should be asking hard questions.

For instance: If Mary Brown were licensing newspapers, would these conflicting opinions appear on this page? Answer: Of course not, because Coleman and I have left the final choice to our readers. Mary Brown keeps the choices to herself.

4. This letter to *The Windsor Star* is a response to Prof. LaFave's letter analysed in this chapter:

The logic of the professor's argument escapes me completely and being a "man of modest intellectual achievements, a typical policeman" I defer to his superior intelligence.

The first portion of Professor LaFave's letter indicates his knowledge of the United States and its customs; his lack of knowledge of Canadian policemen is apparent in the latter part of his letter and is exceeded only by his colossal vanity. After permitting the policemen the luxury of having an opinion, he then instructs the public and the news media to ignore these opinions — The Lord giveth and the Lord taketh away.

Admittedly risking the ire of Professor LaFave, I nevertheless would like to correct several of his mistaken assumptions regarding policemen (with whom it is glaringly evident that he has had no social contact) and their views toward capital punishment. No rational person expects any punishment to halt murder — particularly the "hot blooded" type "between relatives, acquaintances and close friends." However, any experienced policeman knows that capital punishment is a definite deterrent to murder committed during the course of another offence — robbery, rape, etc.

How do I know this? From more than 20 years of association with criminals who have little, if any, knowledge of psychology but who realize that once capital punishment has been utilized, they have no hope of a life sentence, which today means a parole after seven to 10 years, including weekend passes to fill the interim.

The murders that concern most policemen are the murders committed for profit or to eliminate witnesses, committed by cold blooded professional criminals and these are the murders . . . that are increasing and will continue to increase until, Heaven forbid, our country can then be statistically compared to the U.S.A.

I can't offer a remedy for this situation but possibly the professor, with his educational background, can. In fact he may have in his letter but if he did, it was hidden in his verbiage. Like most psychologists he is familiar with the human mind as portrayed in his textbooks but he fails to realize that there are, in every community, persons to whom the life of another means absolutely nothing, to whom several years in prison also means nothing and whose only interest is in furthering their own ends.

The value of capital punishment as a deterrent may be arguable but there is no argument that today's "life sentences" is any deterrent. Our main concern is the safety of the public in our country and we ask only that punishment of some deterrent value be incorporated into our laws.

While Professor LaFave could not "conceive of a group more incompetent on the subject of capital punishment than police organizations," I've had no difficulty at all and suggest an organization composed of psychology professors of Lawrence LaFave calibre.

CHAPTER TEN

DEALING WITH NEWS MEDIA

Introduction

Much of the information we use when we assess the persuasive appeals constantly directed at us comes from the information media: TV, radio, newspapers, magazines. Yet the media shape the message. In order to interpret this information intelligently, you ought to have a general understanding of how information is picked up by and filtered through the different news sources, as well as up-to-date knowledge of the practices and policies of the particular outlets from which you get your information: your local newspaper(s), radio and TV stations, national CBC and CTV news and current affairs programs, *Maclean's*, and probably several American sources. It is important, for logical self-defense, to be knowledgeable and intelligently critical about the information media, so we offer this chapter to raise consciousness and stimulate your own further research.

With this purpose in mind, we provide two items here. The first is a checklist of questions that everyone ought to be in the habit of asking when reading the newspaper or listening to or watching the news. The second is a list of projects intended to lead you closer to the understanding we just spoke of.

News Checklist

In the list that follows, we present a cluster of questions under each heading, and after the questions, a brief explanation of why they should be asked. You should be able to answer these questions after a careful reading or viewing of any news report. Unless you can, you have a good chance of digesting misinformation. Hence, your needs as a media consumer — your need for an accurate and complete picture of ongoing events — won't be met. There is then the danger that you'll base your assessment of persuasive rhetoric on this false understanding of events.

All Media

Billing

(a) Does the headline (or title) accurately and fully indicate the contents of the story or article?
(b) Do picture captions suggest interpretations of photographs with other plausible interpretations?

Rationale

(a) Headlines can give a slant to a story not warranted by the text. By referring to only one of several parts or aspects of the story, they can give it undue prominence.
(b) Photo captions can give a totally inaccurate interpretation of the event pictured.

Completeness

(a) Is the account full, clear, and coherent? Are there inconsistencies, puzzling assertions, questions left unanswered?
(b) Are there technical (or pseudo-technical) terms or statistical data that you don't fully understand?
(c) Are the details too skimpy to form a clear picture of the event?

Rationale

(a) News reports are usually gathered and written in a hurry to make deadlines. Coherence and completeness are casualties of the rush. Events may still be unfolding when the reporter must write the story. Parts of the report may be second hand; sources may give conflicting accounts.
(b) Reporters, like the rest of us, are sometimes smitten by meaningless jargon; stories may omit technical explanations as too cumbersome; newswriters may assume more knowledge in their audience than it possesses, or may not themselves understand what they are reporting.
(c) Readers and viewers tend to kid themselves about how much they really learn from news reports. Do you have a complete picture of the events? If so, could you describe and explain them to someone else?

Sources

(a) Where did the story come from? Is it a report of a press release? A rewrite of a public relations handout? A news conference? A leak? A "background"

interview with an official who refuses to be identified? Is the story the result of the reporter's observations, research, interviews?
(b) Does it come from a wire service (CP, AP, UPI, Reuters, AFP)? From a news service (Southam, FP, Financial Times; some American news service)?
(c) How could the writer whose story you are reading, listening to, or watching, have obtained the information he or she is presenting?

Rationale

(a) Every large corporation, union, government department, institution (e.g., university) has a public relations officer who writes "news" releases publicizing the outfit and putting its interests in the most favourable light. Often these releases get into the media unverified, or only slightly rewritten. News conferences can be stagemanaged to overdramatize, divert attention, obfuscate. Leaks and backgrounders can be self-serving.
(b) Wire services tend to avoid controversy and overrepresent "establishment" news sources; foreign wire services (all but CP, and UPI in Canada) plus CP reports of foreign events from elsewhere than London, Paris, or New York (where CP has its own bureaus, and doesn't depend on AP stories), write for their own national points of view — American, British, French — not with Canadian interests and outlooks in mind.
(c) Some events are not accessible and reports can be based on rumour, stereotypes, or political prejudice. Reports from some locations (e.g. wars) may be censored. Study the habits of accuracy and the personal biases of local reporters and columnists on whom you frequently rely for information. Some reporters cover a "beat" (e.g., city hall, labour, education) for years and acquire great knowledge of its inner workings and politics, but some also establish a cozy working relationship that may result in self-censorship or biased reporting.

Background

(a) What is the historical context into which the story fits? Is it about an event that connects with other recent or less recent events? Is it a development of earlier events? Is it a response or reaction to them? How did it come about?
(b) Why is it being reported? Why is it being reported *now* ?
(c) Is it an "update" report on an ongoing event, or a fuller account of events earlier reported in less detail?

Rationale

(a) Most, if not all, events make sense only when understood against the past background from which they have emerged. (The "past" may be as recent as the previous day, or go back over a period of years.)
(b) The "reporting" may itself be part of the event — what *makes* it news; hence, what occasions the report may help explain the significance of the events reported.

(c) Often news reports presuppose that readers or viewers are familiar with prior accounts or earlier developments.

Balance

(a) Does the story report the views of *all* the individuals or groups who have an interest in a dispute?

(b) Does the story present events or issues from one perspective when others are available? Can you identify that perspective? What other perspectives are there? How might those same events be reported from those other perspectives? Does the report try to get you to draw a conclusion or share a judgement? Is its angle justified?

Rationale

(a) Each adversary in a dispute tends to picture his or her side in the right and the other in the wrong. A fair judgement requires that all claims be considered.

(b) Tom Wicker, an American columnist, has noted that the practice of objectivity is an act favouring the status quo.[1] Every report has *some* angle, if only the angle that no interpretation, no background, no judgement should be given (thus contributing to the image of a world of unrelated, "neutral" events, on which we bring our "personal" and "subjective" judgements to bear). Most language is evaluative, judgemental, by virtue of the words used (and those not used). You can either unconsciously accept the reporter's outlook, or identify it and thereby gain the option of rejecting it.

Connections

(a) Will the events reported affect you directly? Might they touch you indirectly? What should you do as a result of the information? Watch for further developments? Change your mind about a previous opinion? Behave differently in some respect in the future?

(b) Do the events connect with other, similar, events and form a pattern? What is their significance? What do they mean? What do they portend?

Rationale

(a) Forewarned is forearmed. You can put the information you receive from the media to good use if you're thinking while you ingest it.

(b) This is perhaps the most significant question on the list. The mosaic of information from the media to some extent creates or reinforces an overall picture of the world. It reflects a theory, or interpretation, or understanding, about the nature of society — its function and purpose, its possibilities

---

[1] As reported in Robert Cirino, *Power to Persuade: Mass Media and the News* (Toronto and New York: Bantam, 1974), p. 202.

and its confines. (This is not done intentionally; it's not controlled: we aren't suggesting manipulation.) Either you accept that theory by default, or you develop and bring your own theory into play, using it to place and connect and exhibit the significance of events reported in the media.

Importance

(a) How important is the event reported compared to other stories elsewhere in the news the same day? Does it merit its prominence (front page, big headline; top of the news — or second-last page, small headline, short account, etc.)? What is its importance relative to other recent and current events?
(b) Was the event staged or created exclusively for the media?

Rationale

(a) *Some* stories have to be on the front page or at the top of the news; some have to go on the second-last page; some stories that are written or filmed are just not printed or shown; most events aren't even reported. Editors make these decisions, but you don't have to agree with them. Also, there have to be stories on the front page even when there are no "front page" stories. You, the reader or viewer, are the only one to judge the relative importance of day-to-day events.
(b) Many events — some press conferences, even street violence — are pseudo-events in the sense that they are put on *just* for media coverage.

TV News

In television news, obviously the big difference is the visual ingredient. Film not only seems to bring you closer to events; it also is an enormously more powerful medium than words for creating an impression about the events reported. Remember, however, that TV newsfilm is always edited. Film footage is chopped up and then pieced together by an editor who must make judgements about what to show, what to leave out, what shots to juxtapose, what order to present events in, where to interpose still photos, how to pace the story, how much time to allot to it. Each filmed news item is a work of journalistic art; that means it's part *creation*. (We're not saying the film is faked.)

Narration

Does the voiceover suggest an interpretation that the film does not by itself bear out?

Rationale

Same as for photo captions: narration can convince you to "see" what is not there in the film.

Film

(a) Does the film use props? Is it posed? Is the film actually shot from the events reported, or is it old film from the station's or network's library?
(b) Does the film emphasize certain aspects of the events (e.g., action: violence), giving them undue prominence?
(c) Is the story on the news only because of its visual interest?
(d) What bias or perspective did the editing of the story produce? What impression did you get about the events you were viewing? On reflection, is that impression warranted?

Rationale

(a) Given the power of visual impressions, it's mandatory to know whether the image you're left with really captures the event reported.
(b) Film of a single fight at a demonstration can be used to give the impression the whole demonstration was violent (even when the announcer's or reporter's voiceover states otherwise).
(c) Other things being equal, of two equally important stories the one with interesting film will get into the news and the one without film will be cut. A corollary of this TV truism is that TV news stories tend to come from urban centres where camera crews are stationed.
(d) See the general comments under the heading "TV News," above. We might add here that editing can not only influence your interpretation of the meaning of what you see and your value judgements about it, but it can also actually affect your impression of the facts you witnessed.

This checklist and the accompanying rationales for the items on it suffer at least two defects: they are abstract and they are opinionated. We must leave it to you to apply questions to concrete examples — to a particular day's newspaper or news broadcast or, better still, to a series of both. See what particular questions our necessarily abstract ones generate. Also, check whether our outlook towards the information media bears up under examination.

These questions are not intended as veiled criticisms of the media, nor as recommendations for changes in its policies or practices. Neither are we saying they should not change in various ways; on that issue, we pass. Our perspective is that of the news and information consumer, not that of the journalist. The goal is short term: the intelligent use of the media as they now operate.

Projects

The questions on our checklist came from a certain limited acquaintance with how the media function and from a point of view that is skeptical of the capacity of the mass media to provide a totally adequate diet of information. The limitations and bias of the checklist are not serious failings in a device designed to pique your curiosity rather than sell you a bill of goods. However, asking yourself those questions is at best only half enough. To be able to use the media intelligently, you have to investigate two general topics: (1) how the various media actually operate, day in and day out; (2) the ideological role of the media.

Finding Out How the Media Operate

(a) The first thing to do is to read everything you can get your hands on about the media. Much more information about American media is available than about Canadian media, and the situations in the two countries are very different. Laws governing the media differ — e.g., advertising in them, coverage of the courts — and in the broadcast media there is nothing remotely like the CBC in the U.S. Hence, much that is written about the media for U.S. readers is irrelevant to us in Canada. Here are four good paperback books about the Canadian media we've come across.

Donald R. Gordon, *Language, Logic and the Mass Media* (Toronto: Holt, Rinehart and Winston of Canada, 1966). An informative basic account of the workings of Canadian newspapers, radio and TV news.

Benjamin Singer (ed.), *Communications in Canadian Society*, 2nd rev. ed. (Toronto: Copp Clark, 1975). A collection of articles and excerpts from books, mostly about the information media. Has a good bibliography.

Dick MacDonald (ed.), *The Media Game* (Montreal: Content Publishing, 1972). A collection of articles about Canadian news media from the journalists' magazine, *Content.* Much information and many interesting criticisms of the media by journalists.

C. Stuart Adam (ed.), *Journalism, Communication and the Law* (Scarborough: Prentice-Hall of Canada, 1976). A collection of excellent informative and critical articles written for the book by practising and academic journalists. Excellent bibliography, especially for Canadian material.

Note that the last three of these books are written mainly for journalists or students of journalism. Only Gordon explicitly adopts the consumer's viewpoint.

(b) Once you know how the media operate in general in Canada, you should try to find out about the outlets that you come into contact with personally: local newspaper(s), radio and TV stations. Invite the editor or managing editor of the paper, and the station manager or news manager of the radio and TV stations, to talk to your group. (Usually they're delighted to come.) He or she will probably prefer to give at most a short talk, then answer your questions, so prepare them in advance. (You should ask questions about the ideological role of the medium at this time too. See below.) In addition, you might visit the newspaper, radio, and TV newsrooms. Talk to reporters, editors, newswriters. (You might have to assign small groups to different tasks.) See if you can follow a reporter or a camera crew around for a few days. All of this will produce fascinating insights into the whole news operation — though it will also tend to distract you from the basic question for the defensive consumer: in what ways does all this affect the information I get as I sit reading the paper or watching TV?

(c) A third way to learn about the media is to systematically study newspapers and newscasts over an extended period of time: at the very least a week. Compare stories within each medium. Get an out-of-town newspaper or two during the same period. Watch different channels and listen to different radio stations. Also, compare different media. Study TV, radio, and newspaper treatments of the same story. Such observation of the media in action is useful for reality-testing the descriptions of the ideal you might get from articles — cf. (a) above — or even informal talks and question-and-answer sessions — cf. (b) above. We have observed that many (not all) newspeople tend to be unreflective about their working assumptions.

Discovering the Ideological Role of the Media

By the "ideological role" of the media we don't mean only or primarily the political views influencing the information packaging by the media. We are referring more generally to the overall world view the media propagate, usually unintentionally. Here are three of many possible avenues of discovery.

(a) Investigate the "working categories" of the media. These are the conceptual groupings into which they sort the realities they report, and consequently into which the information we consumers receive about those realities is parcelled. We'll list a few such categories as examples; your own research will uncover others.

Newspapers try to keep a strict separation between *factual* information, which goes into the news columns, and *opinions* about that information, which goes into editorials or news analysis or opinion columns. Is such a distinction between fact and opinion supportable? What are the defining features of each? What is the effect of working in terms of this division of reality upon the picture of the world the newspaper conveys?

An obvious working category is the concept of "news." What is or should count as news? What are the defining characteristics of events that are news or newsworthy? What definitions of news are operative? (Do they differ from medium to medium? E.g., does film make a difference so far as what is "news" for TV goes?) What assumptions or other factors might affect editors' judgements about what is newsworthy? What is the effect of the news media's operating with this category called "news" on the picture of the world received by the consumer?

The newspaper divides its information according to an explicit conventional set of categories: news, editorial material, features, entertainment, business, sports, family, to list the main ones. Do the events in the world actually sort themselves out in this way? What effect does this organization have on the image of reality we consumers receive by reading the paper each day?

(b) A second way to become aware of the media's ideological impact is to look for their own conception of their role and the standards they try to meet in filling it. For example, many editors, producers, and reporters see themselves as having a responsibility to "mirror" society. Your research should quickly uncover expressions of or reactions to this belief. What are the practical consequences of the idea that the function of the news is to mirror events in the world? What is the cash value so far as influencing the content and form of information the media carry? Is it really possible for the media to "mirror" society in any intelligible way? If not, as some have argued — if this mirror metaphor is a myth — then what is the effect of journalists' working in terms of this myth on the information they produce?

A value taken very seriously by media people in both rhetoric and practice is "objectivity." The idea is that the media should not doctor the information they convey or serve as apologists for any political point of view. But what is a workable definition or set of conditions for objectivity in the media? Can the media be "objective" in any realistic sense? If not, how does their belief that they should try (and that they usually succeed) affect the information received by the consumer?

Or again, what should a reporter's role be? We've heard it argued that a reporter should be: (i) an impartial *reporter;* (ii) an *adversary* of those in positions of power, a protector of the common people's interests; (iii) an *advocate* of a publicly acknowledged point of view. Which view prevails? Are there differences between the media here? Are there differences between individual reporters whose work you read, hear or see? And, as always, what is the effect on the message?

(c) The third factor that might affect the picture of the world emanating from the media consists of what we call — without begging any questions — "hard determinants." We are thinking here of things such as financial resources, technological restrictions and other effects of technology, concentration of media ownership, the economic interests of media owners, the education and training of reporters and editors, to mention a few factors. Each of these, and others this list might suggest, should be studied for its effect on the overall outlook shaping the information processed by the media. We urge you to look for concrete connections here, not generalizations before the facts. It's easy to say, for example, that because the owners of private media outlets are business people, the news is therefore likely to be slanted to favour the business point of view. But is that true? How, in detail, do the owners have any influence on the information or editorial slant of their media? Indeed, do they have any influence at all? What influence specifically? You'll have to pose questions like these if you hope to learn anything about the influence of these "hard determinants" on the flow of information.

We have tried to produce both suggestions for research and examples of the sorts of questions to ask in order to learn about the media. Many more such questions than the ones we've listed here need to be answered. If our checklist and project ideas stimulate you to investigate, but, more importantly, to think about the significance while you seek information, then they will have served the purpose of making you a more reflective consumer of media information.

Suggestions for Further Reading

Altheide, David and Snow, Robert P. *Media Logic.* Beverly Hills; Sage Publications, 1979.

Cirino, Robert. *Power to Persuade: Mass Media and the News.* New York: Bantam, 1974.

Diamond, Edwin. *Good News, Bad News.* Cambridge: MIT Press, 1980.

Doig, Ivan and Doig, Carol. *News: A Consumer's Guide.* Englewood Cliffs, N.J.: Prentice-Hall, Inc., 1972.

Epstein, Edward Jay. *Between Fact and Fiction: The Problem of Journalism.* New York: Vintage Books, 1975.

— *News From Nowhere.* New York: Random House, 1973.

Gans, Herbert J. *Deciding What's News.* New York: Vintage Books, 1979.

McGinniss, Joe. *The Selling of the President 1968.* Pocket Book Edition. Richmond Hill, Ontario: Simon & Schuster of Canada, 1970.

Mendelsohn, Harold and Crespi, Irving. *Polls, Television, and the New Politics.* Scranton: The Chandler Publishing Company, 1970.

Siebert, Fred S. and Peterson, Theodore and Schramm, Wilbur. *Four Theories of the Press.* Urbana: University of Illinois Press, 1974.

Singer, Benjamin D., ed. *Communications in Canadian Society.* Toronto: Copp Clark Publishing, 1972.

Trueman, Peter. *Smoke and Mirrors: The Inside Story of Television News in Canada.* Toronto: McClelland and Stewart, 1980.

CHAPTER ELEVEN

ADVERTISING: GAMES YOU CAN PLAY

The Logic of Advertising

If you're like most people, you probably find it hard to keep your cool when the topic of advertising comes up. Ads are annoying, repetitious, offensive, degrading, deceptive, and sometimes patently false. That's a generalization, to be sure, and by now you know the dangers of such statements.

Not all ads have the odious traits just cited. Think, for a moment, of that record you just bought on sale. How did you find out about the sale? Advertising, of course. Where did you first learn about the products and services you're satisfied with? Again, advertising. In an economy like ours, with new products entering the marketplace almost daily and old ones being improved, advertising often performs the much-needed task of informing the consumer of the available products and services so that he or she can make a rational choice.

It would be extremely naive to think, however, that the sole purpose of advertising is to provide information and rational persuasion. If that were the case, we could comb them for fallacies, just as we would any argument. It's true that many ads have a superficial resemblance to arguments, so they encourage us to approach them in this way. Think of ads which use the line, "Here are the reasons this product is the best." But this line is usually nothing more than a façade or window dressing, for, although advertising is an attempt to persuade, the type of persuasion generally used is not rational. Instead, advertising attempts to persuade us by appealing to our emotions (our hopes, fears, dreams), to the vulnerable spots in our egos (our desire for status and recognition), by applying pressure to the tender areas of our psyches.

This assault on consciousness is accomplished by what is known in the trade as "creative strategy," or what we will more accurately call, a **gimmick.** A gimmick is an attention-getting device with a persuasive hook, designed to attract the consumer's attention and create a favourable climate for the product. The gimmick may be a straight-out emotional appeal; it may be an unstated implication or suggestion; or it may involve getting you to make an unwarranted assumption.

In sum, advertising has a logic of its own. Thus, learning how to evaluate ads from the standard logical point of view becomes a gratuitous exercise. We propose instead to say something about the logic of advertising, about the various gimmicks and ploys it uses. We'll be reviewing some of them and giving examples; we also have some pointers on what to look out for. Armed with these clues, you will be in a better position to defend yourself against these gimmicks; or at least you'll know what's coming.

But watch out for the boomerang effect. That is, in order to heighten your consciousness about the gimmicks used in ads, you must pay close attention to them. Yet that is exactly what advertisers want. So, in a sense, you'll be playing right into their hands. But the alternatives are even less attractive. You can attempt to ignore advertising, which is virtually impossible; or you can pretend that you are ignoring it, not really susceptible to its influence, which is most unlikely. Under the assumption that advertising is here to stay, we advise you make the best of the situation, learn the games they play, and what some of their tactics are so that, if nothing else, you can have some fun trying to detect the gimmicks being used.

Advertising is a fascinating subject and many books have been written about it. We'll simply mention the four that we have found particularly helpful:

Carl Wrighter, *I Can Sell You Anything* (New York: Ballantine Books, 1972). This is perhaps the single most valuable (and entertaining) source-book for learning the tricks of the trade, particularly about television advertising. It is replete with examples. Unfortunately, Wrighter discusses ads from U.S. network television of some ten years vintage. So you may not have seen them or may not remember them.

Jerry Goodis, *Have I Ever Lied to You Before?* (Toronto: McClelland and Stewart, 1972). Goodis has some worthwhile things to say about advertising in this country, and about advertising generally:

175   Let me just say it again: the difference between good advertising and bad advertising is simply (1) ingenuity, (2) taste, (3) truth, (4) humanity. And the all-purpose, magic-formula secret ingredient is a little love for the consumer. And just a modicum of respect for his or her intelligence. (p. 133)

Sam Sinclair Baker, *The Permissible Lie* (Cleveland and New York: World Publishing Company, 1968). Baker's book is somewhat outdated and also focuses on the U.S. scene. But it has many useful nuggets of information and history.

Ellen Roseman, *Consumer, Beware!* rev. ed. (Don Mills: New Press, 1974). An invaluable source for anyone who wants to develop an aggressive, consumer-oriented approach toward advertising. It tells of the legal avenues open to anyone who wants to combat deceptive, misleading, or false advertising.

Advertising Claims: How to Defuse Them

At the heart of all advertising lies *the claim*. Whether supplemented by visuals or made more palatable by a catchy tune, the claim is the anchor for all gimmicks in each ad. The claim's function is to capture your attention and to present you with the product's (or service's) *reason for being*. It tells you what the product is going to do for you and why you should buy it rather than some other brand. Consequently, the claim should also furnish you with your *reason to believe*, which is why you so often hear or see the phrase "Here's why" in ads.[1] It signals the advertiser's attempt to put across the product's reason for being, and your reason for believing. Effective commercials — those which increase the product's sales and share of the market, or at least create a favourable selling climate — are based on the all-important claim. TV commercials, for instance, typically use a claim as a springboard for a story line or demonstration. For these reasons, settling on the right claim is usually the most strenuous part of building an advertising campaign. An example of a claim is one currently in use for Coca-Cola: "Coke is it!" Stop and ask yourself: what does this mean? What is the "it" that Coke is?

An obvious point: a great deal of thought is given to the creation and the formulation of every advertising claim. We make that point because when you are confronted with it in print or on TV, the advertising claim appears to be casually formulated, almost nonchalant. This is especially the case with a medium like TV, where verisimilitude suggests spontaneity. However, there is nothing capricious, haphazard, casual, or nonchalant about any advertising claim. It has been ruthlessly scrutinized before it ever reaches your eyes or ears. If you are willing to analyse advertising claims, you'll begin to notice some interesting things.

As we said, most advertising claims employ a gimmick. To spot it, you must know what to look for and what to listen for. You must know how to question the advertising copy. You have to be able to figure out exactly what

---

[1] The terms "reason for being" and "reason to believe" are Wrighter's. Cf. *I Can Sell You Anything*, p. 44.

has been said and why. Just as important, you have to be ready to figure out what has *not* been said, and why it hasn't. You must also learn to watch for nuance, implication, suggestion — all species of utterance which purposely fall short of forthright assertion.

In the next few paragraphs, we'll give you some pointers about what to watch for.

Learn to Distinguish between Fact and Opinion

When advertisers make factual claims, they must be able to support them if challenged. If they assert that, for example, their automobile "has the smoothest ride of any," then they must be able to support that claim. If, on the other hand, they put that same statement in the form of an opinion by saying, "We think you'll find that our car has the smoothest ride of any," they're home free. They have simply given you their opinion. Or perhaps they will solicit someone else's opinion (a celebrity's) and pay that person for it; or take an ordinary-looking person and let him or her state the opinion. Remember this point: factual claims must be supportable and are challengeable; they can be held in court to be misleading, deceptive, or false, and those responsible can be fined if convicted. On the other hand, there are very few restrictions on the expression of opinion, which is why you should ask: who is offering this opinion and why?

Here's an example:

176   Carrington. It's special. And in our opinion, like no other whisky in the world.

Here we find a claim labelled opinion in black and white. But what about the claim, "It's special"? Is that fact? Opinion? What? It is, of course, *vague.* What does "special" mean? Do you know? More important, do you know what it means in this context? This brings us to our next point.

Read Ads with a Dictionary Handy

Words in ads have a way of not quite meaning what you think they mean. "Special," for example, has several meanings: "1. distinctive, peculiar, unique; 2. unusual, uncommon, exceptional, extraordinary . . ." Which of these is meant in the Carrington ad? Better have a careful look at the copy which leads up to the claim in question:

177   Carrington is distilled in small batches, aged and mellowed in seasoned oak casks; it's light in look and smooth in taste.

Possibly the basis for the claim that Carrington is special lies in the fact that it is batch-distilled. Since most whisky manufacturers these days use a process known as continuous distillation, that would make Carrington "special," i.e. uncommon. If you are cynical another possibility might suggest itself: the graphics accompanying the copy show that Carrington comes in a bottle which has an unusual, unique shape. So Carrington could claim to be "special" because of that. However, neither of these facts provides a reason to believe that the whisky in that peculiar bottle or that is made in small batches is any better than any other whisky.

Generally, then, we think it is educational to practise reading ads with a dictionary close at hand: advertisers have mastered the art of exploiting the difference between what words actually mean and what you are likely to think they mean. Think, for instance, of the word "strength," as in the claim, "That's why there's Javex Bleach for the Unbleachables. Javex *strength*. Javex *power*. To get out the dirt and stains detergent alone can't." You hear the word "strength" here, and it suggests a product that is muscular — more muscular than its competition. But look it up. "Strength" means "the power or capability of generating a reaction or an effect." "Wisk puts its *strength* where the dirt is." How does it read when we make this substitution: "Wisk puts its 'capacity to generate an effect' where the dirt is."? There'd be no problem substantiating that claim, would there? Wisk contains chemicals. When those chemicals are immersed in water, they will generate an effect. But what kind of effect?

Here's another word to watch for: "quality." "At Zenith, the quality goes in before the name goes on." "Quality" can mean "superiority," but could Zenith substantiate that their products are superior? Perhaps. But there is another sense of the word: "the essential nature or character of a thing." So the question is: does Zenith's claim mean anything more than: "At Zenith, we put the essence of the television (i.e., picture tube, chassis, circuits, etc.) into our product before we put our name on it"? While putting in all the essential components is no doubt a sound practice, it does not furnish the buyer with any reason to believe.

Watch for Implications and Suggestions

One rule of thumb to follow in unpacking factual and quasi-factual claims is this: if advertisers can make a strong statement about the product, they will. If, therefore, an ad makes only an indirect statement (an implication, a suggestion, or a hedge), it is probably because the advertisers want you to think what they cannot come right out and declare. Suppose, for example, there was hard proof that Flash is the best toothpaste on the market. The ad will come right out and state that. If, however, Flash is one of many equally good toothpastes, the advertisers cannot make that strong statement. Instead, they must be content to suggest or imply. They will word the claim in such a way as to encourage you to (mistakenly) draw the inference they want. They might then say, "Nothing works better than Flash in fighting cavities." All this claim does is rule out the possibility that another product is better than Flash, while leaving open the possibility that many others are just as good. A less than forthright claim, then, one that implies, suggests, or tempts you to make the statement, is something to be leery of.

Watch for Pre-emptive Claims

There is a reason that advertisers have to resort to gimmicks. To understand their problem, consider the words of a legendary figure in the annals of advertising, Rosser Reeves:

178   Our problem is — a client comes into my office and throws two newly-minted half-dollars on my desk and says, "Mine is the one on the left. You prove it's better."[2]

The point of Reeves' remark is this: most brands are similar. The differences between them are marginal and/or subjective. The problem advertisers must confront is how to make their product appear to be better than the others, how to place it in a favourable light and implant the name of the product in the consumer's mind.

That is the problem. For one solution, we turn to the words of yet another legendary figure, Claude Hopkins:

179   Another early adman, Claude Hopkins, had no trouble proving that Schlitz beer was better than all others. He visited the factory, watched the beer being made, and came up with the slogan, "Washed with live steam." When told that this was standard procedure in the beer industry, Hopkins wasn't worried. "The vital fact was not what the industry did, but what the individual brewers said they did, and the steam bath had never been advertised," he explained.[3]

Hopkins introduced a basic strategy which advertisers have been copying ever since: take a basic ingredient or a standard feature common to all products of a given type and price, and construct the advertisement around it. Of course, you have to be the first to use this strategy, but if you are the dividends are many. First, the claim will be the truth. Of course, it will not be the whole truth. In the case of Schlitz, the whole truth would have been: "Washed in live steam, as is every other beer." Second, in the context of advertising, the pre-emptive strategy ratifies an assumption which the consumer finds it natural to make; i.e., the natural assumption that the feature around which the claim is built is unique to that product. Thus, it would be only natural for consumers to have assumed that Schlitz was the only beer

---

[2] As recounted by Martin Mayer, *Madison Avenue U.S.A.* (New York: Harper and Brothers, 1958), p. 53.

[3] As recounted by Ellen Roseman, *Consumer, Beware!*, p. 127.

washed in live steam. Why? Because it seems preposterous to sound the trumpets for a feature or ingredient which is common to all products, and thus does not serve to differentiate. Who could get excited by an ad for a television set which said simply: "Our set has a picture tube"? Unless advertisers explicitly claim uniqueness for some feature or ingredient of their product, then, don't *assume* it; that is, don't do the work for them.

To get around the fact that the difference between most products of a given type are only marginal and subjective, advertisers have developed a number of other strategies. Here are some things to watch for.

Watch for the Word "Different"

Beware of the use of "different" and its implications. One product may be different from all others and yet not be any better. The crucial question to ask is: is the difference marginal or functional? And remember that when advertisers use the word "different," it's because they want you to *think* "better."

Watch for Comparisons

Comparisons are usually tricky. The question to ask yourself is: what is being compared to what and why? The strongest possible comparison would be: "My product is better in every way than anyone else's." But you will probably never see such a strongly worded comparison, because then the advertiser and manufacturer would have to back that claim up with proof, if they were challenged, and few products have such superiority.

A recent whisky ad runs, "Introducing Town & Country. A better whisky." That's a perfectly vague and innocuous comparison, isn't it? Better than what? The ad doesn't say. Better than no whisky at all? Better in what way? Again, it doesn't say. The ad continues, "Town & Country spent longer in the barrel than most Canadian whiskies." Does the fact that it was in the barrel longer than most mean that it is better than most? Not necessarily. Whisky improves with age, but only up to a point. Just what point that is, is a matter of considerable debate. It also depends on the process of distilling and on taste. And don't forget the price factor, too. Wiser's Deluxe uses this claim, "Four years older than Canada's two best known whiskies. But priced the same." Does that mean that Wiser's is better simply because it is older? Not necessarily. Again, with whisky as with anything we eat or drink, the subjective factor of taste is an important consideration.

In any comparison, cost is an important but often unmentioned factor. One pain reliever may have "twice as much of the pain reliever doctors recommend," (i.e., acetylsalicylic acid), but it may cost twice as much, too. It may get into the bloodstream faster, but by how much? And how much of a difference will that really make in relieving a headache?

With any comparison, it is important always to establish what is being compared to what and why.

Watch for Semantic Claims

These claims are not really so much about the product as they are about the product's name or label. This is often a variation on the *Pre-emptive Claim.* For example, Colgate is currently using the following claim: "Only Colgate has MFP." MFP is their mysterious-sounding abbreviation for a fluoride ingredient. Is Colgate the only toothpaste with fluoride? No. Then how can it be claimed that "Only Colgate has MFP"? Because they are the only ones who *call* fluoride "MFP" and they own the trademark on the letters! That is the reason for the claim of uniqueness here; that's why they can get away with saying that "Only Colgate has MFP." But in effect this is not a claim about the product. It is a claim about *their name* for one of its ingredients. It is a *Semantic Claim.*

Gasoline ads frequently employ the "Mystery Ingredient" version of the Semantic Claim, for they often construct their ads around an additive with a set of initials: "HTA," "TCP," etc. The classic example of this is a Shell TV ad of several years back. The ad compared the mpg (km/l) of a car using Shell without Platformate to the mpg of that same car with Platformate. The ads never said exactly what Platformate was, content simply to describe it as a "mileage ingredient" (an ingredient for increasing distance per tankful of gasoline). The implication of the ad was that other gasolines were like Shell without Platformate, so Shell had some terrific new discovery. In fact, Platformate turned out to have been simply Shell's name for an ingredient contained in almost every premium brand of gasoline. A comparison here was based on nothing more than a Semantic Claim.

Another way of working the Semantic Claim involves use of "the." Several years ago, Uniroyal gave the label "The Rain Tire" to one of its products. This label is very suggestive. The implication is that the tire was designed specifically for maximum performance on wet roads. An added implication is that if it does so well on wet roads, it will be even better on dry ones. All of this has been suggested and implied by the title, "The Rain Tire." None of it has been *stated.* No real claim has been made.

So don't be hooked by names, titles, labels and mysterious ingredients.

Watch for "Weasel" Words

These words *help* the advertiser say something which sounds much stronger than the facts will allow. First on the list of weasels is "help(s)." "To help" means "to aid or assist." So "Crest helps prevent cavities" means simply "Crest aids or assists in preventing cavities." That claim is undoubtedly true. The problem is that we've become so accustomed to hearing this great *qualifier* that we hardly hear it at all; we tend rather to hear what comes after it. So if we take their claim to mean that Crest prevents cavities, well, that's not strictly speaking what they said, is it? No toothpaste can positively prevent cavities. Yet every parent devoutly wishes that keeping children cavity-free could be as easy as buying that tube of toothpaste.

A recent ad for 2nd Debut Liquid Make-up claims, "Built in Moisturiser Helps Keep Skin From Drying . . . " Right, because nothing will keep skin from drying. Later in that same ad, we read:

180 "That's because 2nd Debut Liquid Make-up contains CEF . . . Cellular Expansion Factor. CEF *compels* the dry skin to again drink in fresh, pure moisture . . . *helps* plump up the skin from underneath, makes it soft with the precious dewy look of youth." (Emphasis ours.)

Note the use of "helps" again; and we cannot help but wonder just what CEF is, nor can we help but wonder how it can *compel* the skin to drink.

Second by a nose to "help" is the weasel "like." "Like" is what is known as a transfer word, and here is the way Wrighter explains it:

181 "Like" is a qualifier, and is used in much the same way as "help." But "like" is also a comparative, with a very specific purpose; we use "like" to get you to stop thinking about the product per se, and to get you thinking about something that is bigger or better or different than the product we're selling.[4]

Here's an example of the transfer effect, an ad for Black & White Scotch from the November 1974 edition of *Maclean's:*

182 Discovering Black & White Scotch is like:
  1. Finding out the penny stock you bought and forgot about is worth five bucks a share.
  2. The blind date you dreaded turns out to be a long-stemmed beauty called Rose . . .
  3. The gorgeous creature who just moved in across the hall loves Mozart and her favourite drink is Black & White too. Girl's got taste.

Just how discovering Black & White is similar to any of these items is unclear. But the transfer effect is surely noticeable. (Could the similarity be that all of these are instances of "discovering" something — and the similarity begins and ends there?)

The classic case involving this weasel was a campaign for Ajax Liquid Cleaner some years ago which centred around the claim that "Ajax cleans like a white tornado." On the surface, this claim violates the transfer effect because there is nothing particularly pleasant about tornados: they're devastating killers in a great many cases. But ordinarily they're grey or black, or appear to be. Ajax, however, is a *white* tornado and lives in a bottle. So it's

---

[4] Wrighter, *I Can Sell You Anything,* p. 26.

as though they had tamed Nature, brought Nature's raw power under control, and put it in the bottle. None of this is stated, of course.

Television advertising is a realm unto itself, and much too complicated to be dealt with fully in the short space available here. What TV ads have going for them is the visual effect, the impression of reality, immediacy. There are basically two types of television ad: (1) the demonstration and (2) the dramatization. We'll make just brief comments on each in turn.

Demonstrations

In a demonstration, we supposedly see the product in use and some benefit of the product is shown. The thing to ask here is: exactly what is being demonstrated? To this end, you may find it useful to turn off the sound and simply watch, so that what you see cannot be influenced by the voiceover. Several years ago, STP used an ad which showed very clearly that the human hand cannot hold onto the tip of a screwdriver which had been immersed in STP. That is all that was demonstrated. While it was being *shown*, here is part of what the viewer was *told:* "STP reduces friction in your engine." The "demonstration" did not lend any substance to the claim. After all, skin and metal are very different. Unless you keep the "show" (demonstration) separate from the "tell" (voiceover), the two may blend together effortlessly in your mind, creating an impression that the claim has actually been demonstrated.

A classic in this genre is one of Bounty towels ("The Quicker Picker-Upper") that featured the following demonstration. Two glasses with equal amounts of liquid are shown. A sheet of Bounty is immersed in one glass, a sheet of "another leading paper towel" into the other. Then the two glasses are turned upside down. We see that the Bounty towel has apparently absorbed all of the liquid, because nothing drips out; but some liquid comes out of the other glass, so the other hasn't absorbed everything. What has been demonstrated? Here's Wrighter's commentary:

183 If you believe the pictures, then they have just proved that Bounty towels absorb more liquid than the other paper towel. But what did they actually say? "Bounty. The quicker picker-upper." They say that Bounty picks up *faster* than the other. They have shown you one thing but they have said something else. Don't misinterpret what I'm saying. Bounty knows exactly what it's doing. They are presenting you with a new idea in paper towels: speed in absorption. But it's very hard to prove that two inanimate objects move at different speeds, so the demo they use is the closest they could come to it. They use the words to get you to see what they want you to see.[5]

---

[5] Wrighter, *I Can Sell You Anything*, p. 81.

Notice again how the ad was designed so that the "show" and the "tell" would coalesce. That Bounty towels absorb liquid more rapidly than "another leading paper towel" is not necessarily enough to make them better. Perhaps they absorb *less* liquid, but do so more quickly.

In viewing TV commercials in which a demonstration of the product in use is featured, be sure that you understand exactly what is being demonstrated. And don't allow the words (the "tell") to influence what you're seeing (the "show").

Dramatizations

Dramatizations are just that: little pieces of drama with a cast of characters, actors and actresses, a script, a director, a budget, a shooting schedule. Of course, they're made to look as spontaneous and lifelike as possible. Advertisers use them when they have a product that cannot easily be shown in action. For example, advertisers for detergents and bleaches find this approach a natural because it's hard to get a close-up picture of the enzymes and additives "eating stains" in your clothes while they're tumbling around inside a washer. So they set up a situation which calls for their product, cut to a close-up of the box or package, then back to the situation to show the resolution. It's the "Before" and "After" routine.

Typical of such TV commercials was one aired several years ago for Alberto VO-5 Shampoo. In outline, it began by showing a woman (she's an actress, remember) before she had washed her hair. Then we see her sudsing away, with lots of lather. Then, presto! Her hair looks fantastic after that one shampoo with Alberto VO-5. The *impression* created by this sequence is that the shampoo was responsible for her beautiful-looking hair. No doubt she did shampoo with the product. But that doesn't mean that washing with VO-5 is the only thing that happened between the "Before" and the "After." Never mind that the actress or model chosen has lovely hair to begin with, she has probably also had her hair professionally set, dried, and combed. But none of this is alluded to. This visual impression was reinforced by the claim, "She's got hair she can wash and wear." Taken one way, this claim was totally meaningless. Could someone wash their hair and not wear it? Taken a different way, this claim was probably meant to connect up with the wash-and-wear revolution in fabrics. Most consumers consider these fabrics a real godsend because they eliminate the need for ironing clothes. The fabric is ready to wear after washing. The implication of "wash-and-wear hair," then, is that you'll be able to bypass some steps. This could not be stated, of course. If you wash your hair, with Alberto VO-5 or any other shampoo, you'll still have to dry it and brush it and comb it and perhaps put hair spray on it. But we never see this process. For, in such commercials, just as in plays, more of the action takes place off stage. The problem is that we have no way of knowing what has happened offstage. Even if we did, the immediacy of TV tends to lure us into forgetfulness of the off-stage activity.

Dramatizations are particularly effective in hammering away at our emotional foibles. The advertiser can zero in on some weakness in our self-images, such as our fears of being offensive (ads for dandruff removers, mouthwashes, and deodorants) or of being behind the times ("You mean you haven't heard about new, softer, more absorbent Toilet-tish?") How ecstatic must have been the advertiser who stumbled across the word "halitosis" in the dictionary! And think of the ad for Wisk: "Ring around the collar." We see the embarrassed wife, suffering what seems to be the ultimate ignominy — public revelation of her inadequacy at the washing machine! "What will people think? They'll think I don't take good care of my husband, that I don't really love him." Comes the answer to this severe trauma: "Wisk!" In such commercials, persuasion is accomplished, but not by dispensing reasons for a conclusion. Instead, the advertiser attacks your fears and desires and hopes you'll look to that product for help.

As you watch these dramas unfold, remember what we said at the beginning. The people are actors working from a script, and the entire production is under the advertiser's control. While it is carefully designed to look spontaneous and lifelike, you won't see anything they don't want you to see. You won't see the people they interview with hidden cameras who do not praise the product to the hilt. That footage winds up on the cutting room floor.

It seems appropriate to conclude this chapter, and the book as well, with a few reflections on a most profound comment about advertising. The owner of Revlon is reported to have once said, "I don't sell cosmetics; I sell dreams." Think about this statement in connection with these lines from Graham Nash's song, "Teach Your Children"; "And feed them on your dreams/the one they pick's/the one you'll know by."

We've been a bit harsh on advertisers. They often sell us fantasies wrapped in fancy semantic clothes and designed to catch us where we dream. But those dreams that make it all possible are, after all, *our* dreams. So, whether we turn our attention to arguments, editorials, and political rhetoric, or to the news media, or to advertising, we are perhaps too willing to settle for shoddy goods. We don't say this to exonerate the media and advertising, but rather to add a bit of perspective, and to locate some of the responsibility for this situation where it really belongs — on all of our shoulders.

The index of success we have in mind for this book, therefore, is not really whether it has taught you how to spot fallacies of logic, misleading headlines, or advertising gimmicks, for, being able to pick them out, while certainly not unimportant, is just a means to an end. If, on the other hand, this text has caused you to become more aware of your own level of acceptance in these vital areas, has sparked you to become less willing to accept bad arguments, poor news reports, deceptive advertising, then it has achieved everything that we can reasonably have expected.

INDEX

Fallacies treated in this text are indicated by bold type.
Numerals in bold type indicate thematic treatment of a particular fallacy, or definition of a concept.

DATE DUE